FROM LABOUR LAW TO SOCIAL COMPETITION LAW?

FROM LABOUR LAW TO SOCIAL COMPETITION LAW?

Editors
Marc Rigaux
Jan Buelens
Amanda Latinne

Authors
Jan Buelens
Wolfgang Däubler
René de Quenaudon
Filip Dorssemont
Teun Jaspers
Barbara Kresal
Fleur Laronze
Amanda Latinne
Esteban Martinez
Giovanni Orlandini
Kelly Reyniers
Marc Rigaux
Willemijn Roozendaal
Jens M. Schubert

intersentia
Cambridge – Antwerp – Portland

Intersentia Publishing Ltd.
Trinity House | Cambridge Business Park | Cowley Road
Cambridge | CB4 0WZ | United Kingdom
tel.: +44 1223 393 753 | email: mail@intersentia.co.uk

Distribution for the UK:
NBN International
Airport Business Centre, 10 Thornbury Road
Plymouth, PL6 7PP
United Kingdom
Tel: +44 1752 202 301 | Fax: +44 1752 202 331
Email: orders@nbninternational.com

Distribution for the USA and Canada:
International Specialized Book Services
920 NE 58th Ave Suite 300
Portland, OR 97213
USA
Tel.: +1 800 944 6190 (toll free)
Email: info@isbs.com

Distribution for Austria:
Neuer Wissenschaftlicher Verlag
Argentinierstraße 42/6
1040 Wien
Austria
Tel.: +43 1 535 61 03 24
Email: office@nwv.at

Distribution for other countries:
Intersentia Publishing nv
Groenstraat 31
2640 Mortsel
Belgium
Tel.: +32 3 680 15 50
Email: mail@intersentia.be

PUBLICATIONS ON LABOUR LAW

From Labour to from Social Competition Law?
Marc Rigaux, Jan Buelens and Amanda Latinne (eds.)

ISBN 978-1-78068-221-1
D/2014/7849/57
NUR 825

GPRC
Guaranteed
Peer Reviewed
Content

British Library Cataloguing in Publication Data. A catalogue record for this book is available from the British Library.

CONTENTS

LABOUR LAW OR SOCIAL COMPETITION LAW? THE RIGHT TO DIGNITY OF WORKING PEOPLE QUESTIONED (ONCE AGAIN)

Observations on the future of labour law

Marc RIGAUX*

PROLOGUE

It may seem dangerous to express oneself on the future of labour law. There is no doubt that anyone attempting to predict the probable developments by presenting hypotheses regarding these developments runs the risk of making errors. Especially the impossibility to guarantee the relevancy of the chosen parameters and a correct evaluation of the nature of their relations could lead to erroneous predictions. The same applies when one has the ambition to pronounce oneself on the future of institutions, structures or procedures laid down in and protected by law. The objective of our initiative is threefold. First of all, we want to call attention to a number of phenomena and processes both within and outside the law that affect the protective mechanisms and essential functions of labour law. Secondly, we want to point out their main causes and principal consequences. Finally we will suggest some remedies to try to preserve the essential task of labour law. We plan to achieve these objectives by developing the following four themes: the existential relation between labour law, the labour market and social competition; the historical tie between labour law and human dignity; the relationship between labour law, market law and (social) competition law; and finally the risk of a renewed contestation of the dignity of working people.

---

* University of Antwerp, Belgium.

I. LABOUR LAW, LABOUR MARKET AND SOCIAL COMPETITION

A. A DIFFERENT APPROACH OF LABOUR LAW

An approach inspired by the sociology of law. We perceive (labour) law as a set of rules emanating from society. Law and legal practice are not value-free. On the contrary, they are the result of values. As for labour law, this covers a tension field between the social competition linked to the free labour market and the citizenship which is the product of the political order of the state. Labour law deals with the labour relations that constitute power relations. The study of labour legislation starts from the production relations typical of the capitalist market economy. The sociological approach also means that the usefulness and efficiency of a rule is also measured with regard to its real application and not only with regard to its legal applicability.

Approach from a comprehensive legal perspective. Law is considered to form a homogeneous entity within which legal rules of a different nature and of a different origin interact. Thus the rules of public law interact with those of private law and vice versa; or more precisely put, the traditional partitions between national, European and international law systems have ceased to exist. The concept of the so-called legal homogeneity reinforces the law's ability to cover and solve the most diverse social problems. There are practically no "legal loopholes" any longer. But this comprehensive approach also has some disadvantages. The interaction this approach advocates is a direct threat to the specificity of the legal branches. The interaction between the superior standards of European economic law and the rules of national labour law threatens to jeopardise the protective task of the latter. However, it goes without saying that this comprehensive approach attaches great importance to the fundamental (social) rights.

Integral and integrated approach. Because of the comprehensive legal approach it has become difficult to sustain the autonomy of labour law. In fact, labour law is part of the wider legal field of market law and the legal provisions regarding occupational activities. Including labour legislation in those broader entities does not only provide a better understanding of the legal mechanisms, but above all it opens the door to more coherent explications of certain current developments. Most of all, the integral and integrated approach stimulates the study of labour law regulations in proportion to the entire economic reality in which they function.

B. MARGINAL CORRECTION OF THE LABOUR MARKET

As we specified and explained in previous publications, labour law only provides a marginal correction of the free labour market. Without ever having the ambition to modify the functioning of the market thoroughly, labour law does attempt to eliminate and diminish the most antisocial consequences. In fact, labour essentially aims at protecting the workers against the excesses of the social competition generated by a free (an overly free) labour market. As we have written on repeated occasions, the actions of the labour law authors basically relate to three areas: taking and advocating accompanying measures for the functioning of the labour market; attempting to neutralise the economic inequality between employees and employers by encouraging standardisation of pay and working conditions; and finally, turning the employee into a (potential) citizen within the enterprise. Without underestimating the importance of the correction provided by labour law we do want to state that it is nevertheless necessary to be aware of its limitations. First of all, it is important to observe that the legal measures only relate to a fraction of the workers, more specifically the wage earners; self-employed workers are in principle excluded from the application of labour law. Secondly, one should not ignore that at world level only a minority enjoys high-quality and consistent employment protection. This observation is not insignificant in an age in which the labour market aims at being a global market and in which social competition is definitely becoming globalised. And finally, let us recall that labour law does not but contribute a marginal correction to the labour market, without actually modifying any of the very bases and principles of this market's existence and functioning.

C. PRELIMINARY CONDITIONS FOR CORRECTION

Social adjustment of the labour market was made possible because three primary conditions had been met. There was a political structure, in this case a state, capable of imposing restrictions upon the economic actors as regards the functioning of the labour market. There was a social counterforce which urged the political institutions to take measures to protect the workers. And finally, there was a kind of citizenship that made it possible to translate these social acquirements into individual rights for wage earners. At present these preliminary conditions are far from being fulfilled at the transnational level, a situation which explains the absence of adequate social adjustment of the long-standing Europeanised and globalised labour market and social competition.

D. THE LIBERALISATION OF THE (LABOUR) MARKET AND THE LACK OF ADEQUATE SOCIAL CORRECTION AT THE TRANSNATIONAL LEVEL

For several decades now we have been witnessing a growing tendency towards the liberalisation of the markets, both worldwide and at the European level. The almost complete disappearance of the planned economies at the end of the twentieth century has allowed the capitalist economy to impose itself as a unique reference model. As a result of the globalisation of the markets these have freed themselves from the political tutelage of the nations. The global economic order (or disorder) now seems to be governed by nothing but the markets (or the stock markets). In vain, politicians try to define the leading principles of the economic world order. Needless to say that in these circumstances a social correction of the globalised labour market is sorely lacking. At EU level one cannot but observe that the social correction which are beginning to take shape is an adjustment whose future is rather uncertain. In fact, the national systems of social correction, on which the European correction is based, have started to compete and erode. The absence of an adequate counterforce at the transnational level after the collapse of the communist systems, seems to us the major cause for the fact that the need for a social correction of the market economy is questioned once again. Therefore it seems clear that the liberalisation of the markets is an existential threat for labour law.

II. THE HISTORICAL LINK BETWEEN LABOUR LAW AND HUMAN DIGNITY

A. THE PRIMARY FUNCTION OF LABOUR LAW

The genesis of labour law shows a direct link between the establishment of labour legislation and the manifest need to improve the living and working conditions of the 19th-century workers. So with a view to fighting human exploitation, the social legislator started by dealing with the deplorable working conditions of the most vulnerable to subsequently tackle the destiny of the other workers. The need of an intervention by the social legislator only confirmed the incapacity of the free labour market – whose functioning was (and is) based on the freedom and equality in law – to preserve the dignity of working people. Indeed, the market relations emphasised (and emphasise) the economic inequality between employment seekers and employment providers, between employees and employers even more. Actually, the economy treated and still treats work and the worker as a commodity. Because of the dissociation, generated by civil law, between the work and the person producing the work, the fact that behind the commodity there was a human being was overlooked. The development of labour law coincides with the worker's recapture of his capacity as a human being and citizen. Hence the organic and undeniable link between labour law and the preservation of the worker's dignity. So through the promise of consistent protection, the preservation of the wage earner's dignity did not take long to become the primary function of labour law.

B. THE PRINCIPAL FUNDAMENTAL RIGHT OF HUMAN DIGNITY

The right to lead a life in accordance with human dignity is without any doubt the principal fundamental right. Of all the fundamental rights this is the most fundamental one. Its realisation implies the realisation of all the other fundamental rights, independent of their nature. So the right to human dignity also includes civil and political rights as well as social and economic rights. The right to human dignity is guaranteed by a large number of international, European and national sources. Roughly speaking, labour law can be considered as the concretisation of the right to human dignity in the area of labour relations. In fact, its concretisation preceded the proclamation of this fundamental right. Quite a number of concrete measures had already been taken at the legislative level before the right to human dignity was proclaimed as a human right. Although the fundamental right of the dignity of working people extends to different types of workers and different legal positions, labour legislation basically focuses on wage earners working under an employment contract. Still, the fight against social fraud proves that social exploitation especially affects the various categories of non-wage earning workers. Hence the question whether it would not be a good idea to partially extend the scope of the legislation regarding labour protection to certain groups of self-employed workers. They too have a right to dignity at work. It turns out that the freedom of work in itself does not suffice to guarantee them the respect in their capacity as human beings, nor to arm them efficiently against abusive practices of their principals. For quite a number of self-employed workers economic inequality and dependency prevail over liberty and equality in law.

C. THE (WAGE EARNING) WORKER: FROM COMMODITY TO CITIZEN

During the first part of the industrial revolution the labour relations were governed by market law. The freedom of enterprise and work were the foundations. Contract law, governed by the freedom and equality in law, ensured the application. There was no distinction between the worker and his or her labour capacity and potential. The price of the work as a commodity corresponded with the worker's economic value. Just like his work, the worker was perceived as a thing… And a thing may well constitute the object of rights, but hardly the subject. As a result of the emergence of labour law paid work was partially withdrawn from market law. The establishment of a fully developed labour law system allowed the worker to obtain, gradually, the status of citizen within the enterprise. Even in the enterprise the worker remains a full citizen, bearer of his or her fundamental rights. Moreover, he or she also acquires political rights within the enterprise, more specifically with regard to the election of representatives within the consultative bodies.

III. LABOUR LAW, MARKET LAW AND SOCIAL COMPETITION LAW

A. THE FOUNDATION OF LIBERAL SOCIETY

1. *The concept of liberal society*

A society can be defined as a collection of people who have organised themselves to live in community in order to satisfy more efficiently their needs, and for that purpose have divided the tasks according to the specialisation principle. In fact, a society constitutes above all a structured collection of systems for the satisfaction of needs. Quite a number of systems are based on networks that operate according to fixed procedures. Each system has its own management mechanism. At the level of the society a comprehensive management mechanism defines and determines the manner in which the relationship between the specific systems is developed. Liberal societies have adopted parliamentary democracy as their comprehensive management mechanism. Society is organised within a nation-state. In principle the individuals (citizens), considered to be free and equal in law, choose freely which systems for satisfaction of needs they want to adhere to and under which conditions. The market is the regulating mechanism par excellence of these systems and their management mechanisms. In fact, liberal society builds itself based on individual freedom. The individual, considered to be autonomous, decides freely and fully aware on his/her individual, social, political and economic destiny. His/her actions are based on freedom and equality in law. Citizens are deemed to be equal from the moment they have the same rights. Equality in law is measured in terms of possession of rights and not in terms of the possibility to assert them. The refusal to define freedom and equality on the basis of the individual's real economic situation has an advantage as well as a disadvantage. The advantage of the presumption of freedom and equality lies in the dynamism it generates. Since one is not obliged to examine and verify the economic reality, the action is direct. Even if because of their economic condition the free market imposes unfavourable conditions upon the economically weak, the latter remain nevertheless responsible for their choices and actions. They bear the legal and moral responsibility as individuals. They cannot but accept these conditions. Although the liberal approach facilitates the dynamism of (economic) action, it also contains a big social disadvantage. It is a direct road towards exploitation and exclusion. Faults which in the long term will jeopardise the advantage of the action dynamism.

2. *The market as a regulatory mechanism for the satisfaction of social needs*

Here we are dealing with the fundamental question of the nature of the relationship between those who are capable of satisfying the needs and those who have the needs. Can the latter freely decide whether or not to join a system and to accept its conditions, or is it imposed upon them? Depending on the nature of the need to be satisfied, society leaves the person in need free or not free to choose the system which he or she can join. In the market economy it is in principle the market that produces the choice of system. The persons in need are considered to be able to choose freely (in law) whether or not they want to join a system. They are also given the freedom to choose the persons that will satisfy their needs on the basis of price-quality ratio. However, the fact is that when the satisfaction of needs is withdrawn from the market, it is not only possible to impose a certain system but also to appoint the person or instance that is to satisfy this need. By not considering the economic condition of the person in need liberal society ignores the fact that certain people do not have the necessary financial means to have access to the systems.

3. *Arrangements to manage and control systems aimed at the satisfaction of needs*

The issue of the arrangements for control and management contains a formal aspect and a material one. The formal aspect refers to the legal form and position of the systems. The material aspect relates to the manners in which they are functioning. Determining the possible legal forms involves a certain number of parameters, such as the relation of the system with the commercial circuit, the possibility that joining the system is free of charge, the free or obligatory nature of the participation. The material aspect refers to the manners of functioning. Is the system partially or fully subject to market laws or does it abide by its own rules of functioning? Under the impulse of the EU more and more systems are getting subject to market laws. Intended to serve as an operational arrangement the market is not supposed to determine the needs to be satisfied. That is society's responsibility. However, actual practice shows that society has been replaced by the market and that the market decides in society's place which social needs should be satisfied. And this causes problems because the market makes its choices on the basis of cost-effectiveness and not on the basis of the needs of the population and society. This observation concerns the employment system in general as well as the employment of the workers. In both cases it is the labour market which defines the political course.

4. *Freedom and equality in law or freedom and equality in name only?*

As already observed, liberal society is based upon the citizens' individual freedom and equality in law. However, does this mean that this freedom and equality are real and do not just exist in name? The answer to this question is not simple. No doubt it is true that by not considering the economic situation of the citizens the liberal legislator clears the path for a situation where the formal freedom and equality do not necessarily correspond with the material reality. Yet, this does not detract from the fact that in order to realise genuine freedom and equality one has to start by giving citizens the same rights. But there does not end the task of legislators wishing to realise genuine freedom and equality. They also have to establish arrangements capable of verifying the citizens' economic situation and, if need be, of making corrections. In other words, to achieve real freedom formal and material equality between the citizens is required. So far the legislators have kept from applying corrections on a general scale. They have settled for limited and specific corrections aimed at remedying concrete situations. The social corrections of the free labour market are a good example of this. By means of the fundamental social rights the need to proceed to occasional corrections of the formal freedom and equality has been elevated to the level of constitutional principle.

B. WORK AS AN OBJECT OF MARKET LAW AND COMPETITION LAW

1. *The foundations*

It goes without saying that the citizen's freedom to be master of his/her own fate constitutes the ultimate foundation of liberal society. Citizens are supposed to be able to decide freely with regard to their personal, economic, social and political circumstances. The right to choose their economic and social activities freely finds its confirmation in the freedom of enterprise and freedom of work. So in principle, citizens choose freely (in law) whether or not they want to sell their labour potential as wage earners or self-employed workers, or whether they want to run a business and use the work of others.

In both cases the main objective is to ensure an income. The income of those who sell their labour takes the form of wages or fees. The income of those who run a business is the profit they make with their commercial activities. In both cases the citizen enters into competition with other citizens pursuing the same goal. Since liberal society by definition does not plan the way in which the social needs are satisfied, the market almost naturally imposes itself as a regulatory mechanism. So liberal society takes the market economy as the scheme for the control and management of the systems for satisfaction of the social and economic needs. This means that in liberal society parliamentary democracy and the market economy are closely linked. Both have their origin in the citizen's right to be master of his/her political, social and economic destiny. The right to perform professional activities is part of market law and competition law. At present these rights are solidly anchored in positive law by European and international provisions, situated at one of the highest levels in the hierarchy of legal standards. And finally let us not forget to emphasise the importance of the contract in the liberal law approach. The contract is the instrument par excellence to develop market activities. The individual freedom of contract, based on the individual's autonomy of will is without any doubt the leading principle of this approach.

2. *Labour law and the limitations of the freedom of the market and competition*

Even though the freedom to develop freely chosen economic activities is the corner stone of market law, the truth requires us to state that this freedom is far from absolute. With a view to preserving the freedom of the market and competition the legislature has been obliged to intervene and regulate. To ensure the quality of products and services the legislator felt it necessary to regulate certain occupational activities. The very same legislator has not hesitated to limit market freedom in order to protect the environment. So both the free market and free competition have been marginally corrected with a view to satisfying social needs that were ignored and neglected by the market. This concerns only marginal corrections because they still confirm the freedom of the market and free competition. Actually, quite often they push the market to take a different direction and to develop products and services which in a lot of cases are linked to other professional activities. These corrections are mainly the product of the interventions by the national and European legislators and intended for the national and European markets. At present the internationalised markets have "freed" themselves from the political tutelage. They view the corrections as obstacles to their freedom and would like to get rid of them. So the market determines itself and heads for disaster because it is "freed" from the politics trying to protect it from its own excesses.

In principle the labour market and social competition are governed by the same fundamental freedoms. Providers and customers of labour potential consider their relations to be based on liberty and equality in law. The freely concluded contract (in law) is the instrument confirming their cooperation. Of all the forms in which work can be sold and bought on the market, only the work people carry out as wage earners is the object of consistent and elaborate regulations. Without tampering with the principles of the free market and free social competition labour legislation adjusts these in order to correct the most inacceptable effects of the economic inequality between the parties of the employment contract. The main body of labour market adjustments made by the legislature is to be found at the national (European) level and addresses the national labour market. As the labour market has definitely been internationalised and Europeanised, social corrections have been put to the test with regard to the competition. The national labour law systems have been sucked up by a negative spiral of social competition. They are perceived as barriers to the proper functioning of the now transnational free labour market. As we have demonstrated above, the establishment of national labour law allowed the worker to achieve citizenship within the enterprise. The erosion of the social corrections threatens labour law in its very existence. The wage earner is gradually becoming a commodity once again. His/her destiny is increasingly determined by market law and social competition law. His/her right to dignity at work seems to be questioned once more.

3. *The liberalisation of the labour market: an existential threat*

As we have already stated, society is internationalising. It is breaking up with the nation-state to such a degree that its systems for the satisfaction of needs are becoming transnational and seem no longer able to rely on national political structures for their survival. This also applies to the systems of supply of labour force. As a result of the ITT revolution, the developments in communication and transport, the breakthrough of free trade workers can be called upon wherever they can be found and made to work under the conditions locally applicable. This has led to a (new) concept of the labour market. The physical proximity of workers seems to become less and less a condition to take part in the same labour market or to participate in social competition. The current legal concepts of the labour market seem to be outrun, to a large extent, by the economic and social reality.

The liberalisation of the labour market is supported by various sources of law at international, European and national levels. All of these have in common that they oppose the social corrections that were installed by the labour law authors in the past, or at least to make them more difficult on the labour market. At the global level legal constructions imposing free exchange favour, directly and indirectly the globalisation of the markets. Even if they do not directly attack the restrictions of the free competition at the local or national level, they do put pressure on those local and national systems by making them compete. At the level of the European Union especially the market freedoms and accompanying regulations and directives have contributed to the liberation of the markets. The case law of the European Court has only reinforced the scope of these texts. Finally, at the national level the liberalisation of the (internal) market has mainly been caused by the regulations regarding the flexibility of the labour relations and working conditions.

4. *The liberalisation of the labour market: an existential threat to labour law*

The liberalisation of the market definitely forms an existential threat to labour law. The market ideology which praises the autonomy of the individual seems to have done its work. Indeed, the advocates of the liberalisation typify the restrictions regarding social competition as obstacles for the proper functioning of the (labour) market. They appear to have forgotten the reasons for which the social legislator once introduced these. They seem to be convinced that social exploitation and exclusion are things of the past and that by good management of their labour potential the individual workers are quite capable of avoiding the traps of social exploitation and exclusion. They seem to want to ignore the economic and social reality as shown by the statistics of the European Union and the International Labour Organization. At the legal level the elimination and erasure of the social corrections generate a genuine restoration of the individual autonomy of will. This is a situation that corresponds with the logic of the market structure to which labour law was an exception. Market law, which is based on freedom and equality in law, is gradually reoccupying the entire field of the wage earners' labour relations. Moreover, the philosophy of the individual's autonomy, the pillar of the market ideology, fits in perfectly with that of the individual's autonomy of will. Economic inequality, in so far as its existence and significance are not denied all together, is perceived as an historic accident. And whatever the case, the economically weak bear the moral responsibility for this because it can only mean that they failed to manage their labour potential properly. But let's not err. The market ideology can impose itself thanks to the favourable market relations (power relations). Only an adequate counterforce is capable of turning this situation round. Failing this, labour law will continue to be threatened.

IV. THE RIGHT TO DIGNITY OF WORKING PEOPLE QUESTIONED (ONCE AGAIN)

A. SOCIAL CORRECTION JEOPARDISED AT THE INTERNATIONAL LEVEL

The preponderance of the national states has been highly reduced by the globalisation of the financial, economic and social relations. The national states have lost control over the markets, as it were. To a certain degree they themselves have become a commodity whose value is determined by the market. The financial soundness ratings attributed to the states by the stock exchange which determines their position (value) on the financial markets is a perfect example of this. The absence of an adequate political power at the transnational level gives the markets the opportunity to impose their power relations on the national states. The markets' liberation from all institutional barriers is a well-known consequence. So the social corrections of the free social competition as developed by the national legislators are easily perceived as obstacles to the free functioning of the labour market. Needless to say that in these circumstances social corrections of the labour market are missing at the transnational and international levels. At the transnational level corrections fail to appear and at the national level they are threatened. In fact, under the pressure of the markets the national legislators often find that they are encouraged to free the labour market from these corrections which are considered to be obstacles to a proper market functioning. The incitement to liberate the market has a twofold nature. There is the formal encouragement emanating from transnational bodies. Others remain informal and are the result of the unfavourable competitive position of the work force of a given state.

B. COMPETITION BETWEEN THE NATIONAL SYSTEMS OF SOCIAL ADJUSTMENT

The internationalisation of the markets (especially of the labour market) has had the effect that the various national systems of social adjustment have been made to compete. For the national European states this competition takes two forms. Within the European Union the competition is made to take place within the institutional framework of the economic and commercial unification. It is accompanied by social and political measures. Nevertheless it continues to be very real and generates a negative spiral of social competition. At the international level there is practically no institutional framework at all. Here we are dealing with a factual competition which also leads to a negative spiral of social competition.

C. IN SEARCH OF AN ADEQUATE TRANSNATIONAL SOCIAL COUNTERFORCE

If European society wants to preserve its social values and wishes to continue to give a place to the protection of the dignity of working people, it will have to create conditions to this effect. Therefore the European legislators should take the necessary measures to control the social competition at the level of the European labour market. Two elements seem to us necessary to achieve this objective. First of all, it would be advisable for the European legislators to ensure the legitimacy in European law of the content of the national systems of social adjustment and to acknowledge their legal equivalence vis-à-vis the market freedoms. Subsequently, it would be advisable to consider a joint management of the European labour market and the social competition it generates. And finally, it would be advisable to set up an institutional set of instruments which would allow the development and growth of social dialogue at the three usual levels. But let's not fool ourselves. Legal intervention from Europe will not come about without the assistance and support of an adequate social counterforce.

DROIT DU TRAVAIL OU DROIT DE LA CONCURRENCE SOCIALE ?

De droit à la dignité du travailleur est-il (à nouveau) remis en question ?

René de Quenaudon*

A quoi sert le droit du travail ? Quelles sont ses finalités, ses fonctions ? Ce n'est pas le droit du travail qui va répondre à cette question car ce que nous appelons ainsi est une convention académique pour désigner un ensemble de règles régissant le travail salarié. Alors faut-il interroger chacune de ces règles et faire une moyenne des réponses trouvées pour savoir quelles sont les fonctions du droit du travail ? Là encore, ce n'est pas possible car la règle de droit ne répond pas à ce genre de question. La règle de droit du travail dit ce qui est, ordonne ou interdit, comme toute règle de droit. Souvent, elle ne le dit pas clairement et il faut solliciter un tiers, le juge, pour avoir une réponse. En tout cas, la règle de droit n'indique pas sa finalité ; celle-ci est à découvrir ou plutôt à imaginer. C'est là une question de représentation que l'on se fait du droit du travail par rapport à la société ou de la société par rapport au droit du travail. La représentation est donc soit particulariste (1) soit holistique (2).

1. La représentation particulariste. Cette représentation est plurielle. En voici deux illustrations.

1.1. La thèse d'un droit de réaction et de progrès. Cette représentation part d'un constat historique, à savoir que le droit du travail est un droit spécial, qui s'est constitué progressivement, à partir de la seconde moitié du XIXe siècle, au moyen de lois venant déroger au droit commun, c'est-à-dire au droit civil, droit marqué du sceau de l'individualisme. En somme, le droit du travail est un droit de réaction, réaction contre l'exploitation du travailleur livré au bon vouloir de son patron en raison de l'inégalité économique et sociale dans laquelle il se trouve. Réaction aussi contre l'entreprise autocratique, celle de « l'employeur

* Université de Strasbourg, France.

seul juge »[1]. En somme, selon cette représentation, l'histoire du droit du travail « témoignerait d'une orientation constante dans le sens du progrès social »[2], d'un droit « unilatéral », essentiellement bénéfique pour les salariés. Ce à quoi il est encore ajouté que cette image est celle que partage, en France, la doctrine dominante[3]. En réalité, cette doctrine d'un droit du travail progressiste est elle-même divisée. Il y a ceux qui pensent que le droit du travail, ainsi représenté, est le résultat d'un progrès des idées et la preuve d'une société capable à se transformer ; il y a aussi ceux qui voient dans le droit du travail un ensemble de conquêtes sociales arrachées par la classe ouvrière à la bourgeoisie. La force de cette thèse est qu'elle est en phase avec une représentation historique encore assez largement partagée, semble-t-il, dans les milieux académiques et dans l'opinion publique. Sa faiblesse est qu'il est malaisé, en dépit des apparences, de définir le progrès, y compris le progrès social. C'est une notion contingente, qui varie au gré des indicateurs que choisit l'observateur.

1.2. La thèse d'un droit, fruit d'un complot. Selon les opinions, le droit du travail serait une ruse du Capital ou une ruse du marché[4]. Pour une raison de place dans ce court article, nous nous en tiendrons à exposer brièvement la première opinion. Elle se réfère à la doctrine marxiste de l'histoire[5]. Celle-ci postule qu'une « conception scientifique du Droit du travail »[6] est possible. Par opposition à un tel droit, le droit du travail dans une économie de marché est qualifié de « droit capitaliste du travail »[7]. Ce droit est perçu comme ayant une « structure dialectique. On veut dire par là qu'à un moment donné, ce droit exprime simultanément le régime d'exploitation de l'homme par l'homme et les moyens d'en limiter la rigueur[8]. Il est à la fois un « corps de règles qui régit l'exploitation du travail humain en régime capitaliste » et les « instruments légaux de lutte de la classe ouvrière et les avantages conquis à l'aide de ces instruments »[9]. En somme, sa fonction est de servir de ruse au Capital[10]. En introduisant un peu de liberté, d'égalité et de fraternité dans le social et l'entreprise en particulier, il permet au capitalisme de pérenniser un ordre social contestable. La force de

---

1 Formule tirée du célèbre arrêt *Etablissements Brinon* : Cass. soc. 31 mai 1956 : Dalloz 1958 p.21, note G. Lyon-Caen.

2 J. Pélissier, A. Jeammaud, A. Supiot, *Droit du travail*, Dalloz, 23e éd. 2006, n° 31. Comp. la 25e éd. (2011), rédigée sous la plume des professeurs J. Pélissier, G. Auzero et E. Dockès, ouvrage dans lequel le chapitre « Le droit du travail dans la société » et son paragraphe « Protection des travailleurs ou service du capitalisme » ont disparu.

3 J. Pélissier, A. Jeammaud, A. Supiot, *ibid.*

4 V. J. Pélissier, A. Supiot et A. Jeammaud, *op. cit.*, n° 33, p. 42 s. et note 3.

5 V. *ibid.*, n° 32, p. 40.

6 G. Lyon-Caen, *Les fondements historiques et rationnels du Droit du travail*, publié au *Dr. ouvr.* 1951, p. 1 et repris au *Dr. ouvr.* 2004, p. 52 s.

7 V. F. Collin, R. Dhoquois, P. H. Goutierre, A. Jeammaud, G. Lyon-Caen et A. Roudil, *Le droit capitaliste du travail*, Presses Universitaires de Grenoble, coll. Critique du droit, n° 5, 1980.

8 G. Lyon-Caen, art. cit.

9 *Ibid.*

10 Rappr. V. J. Pélissier, A. Supiot et A. Jeammaud, *op. cit.*, n° 33, p. 42.

cette représentation tient à son antithèse, c'est-à-dire à la possibilité de proposer un modèle de substitution, un droit du travail socialiste. Un tel droit a une traduction dans la réalité mais celle-ci relève plus du passé (l'Union soviétique et les démocraties populaires d'Europe de l'Est[11]) que du présent Sont-ils nombreux ceux qui, en Europe, voudraient remplacer leur droit « capitaliste » du travail par un droit « socialiste » du travail à l'instar de celui qui existe, en théorie et en pratique, en République populaire démocratique de Corée ou dans la République de Cuba ? Quoi qu'il en soit, une autre représentation du droit du travail est en train de se dessiner.

2. La représentation holistique. Partons de la thèse, forcément discutable, que le droit est une médiation[12] entre des valeurs que se donne une société et le raisonnable qui encadre leur mise en œuvre. Parmi les valeurs, les finalités du droit, il y a bien entendu le juste – qui se traduit en droit du travail par la protection du salarié –, mais aussi l'ordre, la sécurité, la paix auxquels viennent s'ajouter, pour le droit français, de multiples héritages (la Révolution française de 1789, l'Etat social avec le préambule de la Constitution de 1946 et, désormais, l'Etat sociétal avec la Charte de l'environnement de 2005). Quant au raisonnable, plus encore qu'aux exigences de la rationalité, c'est ce qui est réalisable, équitable, proportionné[13]. L'Etat sociétal, c'est celui qui met en œuvre le projet politique que l'on appelle le développement durable, c'est-à-dire « un développement qui répond aux besoins du présent sans compromettre la capacité des générations futures à répondre aux leur »[14]. Cette notion a des conséquences juridiques, y compris en droit du travail, dont on ne commence qu'à saisir l'importance. Là encore, les contraintes éditoriales nous obligent à nous en tenir à quelques exemples.

2.1. Droit du travail et gouvernance. Dans le contexte du développement durable, la gouvernance est un processus de décision collectif n'imposant pas systématiquement une situation d'autorité. La « bonne gouvernance » se caractérise notamment par la participation, la transparence, la responsabilité, l'efficacité et l'équité. Elle veille à ce que les priorités politiques, sociales et économiques soient fondées sur un large consensus au niveau de la société ». La fonction du droit du travail est donc de faire en sorte que la gouvernance prenne en compte les aspirations non seulement de ceux qui détiennent traditionnellement le pouvoir mais aussi de leurs parties prenantes. A cet

---

11 V.M. Laszlo Nagy, « La dérégulation en droit du travail dans les pays socialistes », *Revue internationale de droit comparé*, vol. 42 n° 1, janvier-mars 1990, pp. 27-35, spéc. p. 29.

12 V.F. Terré, *Introduction générale au droit*, Dalloz, coll. Précis, 9e éd. 2012, n° 49 s., pour qui le droit est une médiation entre le juste et le sage- *Adde* J. Freund, *Politique et impolitique*, Sirey, 1987, p. 285 s.

13 Rappr. G. Cornu, *Vocabulaire juridique*, PUF, 6e éd. 2004, V° Raisonnable.

14 UN, *Report of the World Commission on Environment and Development: Our Common Future*, 1987.

égard, au niveau de l'Etat, on peut se référer au rôle actuel[15] des partenaires sociaux et de l'évolution qu'il devrait connaître dans les prochains temps[16]. Au niveau de l'entreprise, la promotion actuelle de l'économie sociale et solidaire, notamment à travers le statut des sociétés coopératives de production (SCOP)[17], fournit une illustration de rencontre entre la dimension sociale et la dimension économique de l'entreprise puisque chaque salarié prend part aux décisions qui engagent l'entreprise et ceci sur la base du principe un homme une voix. En ce qui concerne la prospective juridique, le rapport Gallois[18]propose « d'introduire dans les conseils d'administration ou de surveillance des entreprises de plus de 5000 salariés au moins quatre représentants des salariés, sans dépasser le tiers des membres, avec voix délibérative, y compris dans les comités des conseils ».

2.2. Droit du travail et économie. Les liens entre le droit et l'économie ont été relevés il y a fort longtemps, que ce soit, par exemple, par A. Smith, D. Hume, K. Marx ou, plus récemment, par les partisans de l'analyse économique du droit[19]. L'équilibre à trouver est celui d'un emploi durable dans une entreprise durable, respectueuse de l'environnement en général et de la santé de ses salariés en particulier. Cela suppose des règles de droit effectivement appliquées et sociétalement efficaces. La négociation entre les partenaires sociaux est appelée à jouer ici un rôle central[20].

2.3. Droit du travail et environnement. Le social et l'environnement ont au moins deux points communs : ils sont politiquement des questions – la « question sociale » est nées au XIXe siècle, l'environnementale un siècle plus tard – et ces questions donnent lieu à une régulation de protection et de promotion du travailleur dans le cas du social, de protection et de mise en valeur de l'environnement dans le cas de l'environnemental. Ceci étant, on les présente souvent comme deux questions qui se télescopent : le travail tuerait l'environnement – songeons à toutes les activités polluantes et destructrices de la nature – et l'environnement ferait disparaître le

---

15 V. art. L 1 du Code du travail.

16 *Le Monde* du 14 juin 2011, François Hollande : « Il faut avoir confiance en la démocratie sociale ».- *Liaisons Sociales*, n° 16228 du 22/11/2012 : L'actualité économique et sociale en bref.

17 V. *Blog Le Monde* du 24 novembre 2012, par Antonin Sabot SCOP Fontanille : « On reprend possession de notre usine ».

18 Louis Gallois, Pacte pour la compétitivité de l'industrie française, Rapport au 1er ministre, 5 novembre 2012, p. 21. V. égal. le projet d'accord national interprofessionnel du 11 janvier 2013 pour un nouveau modèle économique et social au service de la compétitivité des entreprises et de la sécurisation de l'emploi et des parcours professionnels des salariés publié par *Les Echos* du 12 janvier 2013.

19 Comp. B. Deffains, Le défi de l'analyse économique du droit : le point de vue de l'économiste, *Petites affiches*, 19 mai 2005 n° 99, p. 6.- G. Canivet, L'analyse économique du droit par la chambre sociale de la Cour de cassation, *Dr. soc.* 2005, 951.- T. Sachs, *La raison économique en droit du travail, Contribution à l'étude des rapports entre le droit et l'économie*, th. Paris Ouest Nanterre La Défense, 24 octobre 2009, dir. G. Borenfreund.- J. Icard, *Analyse économique et Droit du travail*, Université Panthéon-Sorbonne, Paris 1, 8 déc. 2011, dir. B. Loiseau.

20 V. le projet d'ANI du 11 janvier 2013, préc.

travail – songeons à la fermeture de la centrale nucléaire de Fessenheim où il y a d'un côté les écologistes et de l'autres, main dans la main, les syndicats et Electricité de France[21]. Toutefois, à côté de ces cas d'affrontements, il y a aussi des rencontres pacifiques car il est tout à la fois de l'intérêt de l'entrepreneur et de l'intérêt des salariés que le travail se déroule dans un environnement sain. Le droit traduit, sans doute insuffisamment mais déjà un peu, cette rencontre, qu'il s'agisse des relations collectives[22] ou dans les relations individuelles[23] de travail[24].

3. Conclusion. Le projet politique que l'on appelle le développement durable n'est pas une solution miracle en vue de dépasser les contradictions nées de la confrontation entre notre aspiration collective à posséder toujours plus de biens et les ressources limitées que la planète nous procure. C'est plutôt un ensemble de procédures qui, au sein d'une organisation, a pour objet d'éclairer le décideur afin qu'il fasse le choix de la solution la plus soutenable parmi celles qui s'offrent à lui. Comme toute décision, il est rare qu'elle contente tout le monde, que ce soit au sein d'une organisation publique ou privée. Ainsi que l'écrit une ancienne dirigeante de la CFDT, « la recherche d'un « équilibre coopératif » entre les multiples pressions que subissent les dirigeants au nom de la prise en compte de la dimension économique, environnementale et sociale du développement durable est une chimère. Chacun est légitime dans son registre, fondé à tenir son discours, à préconiser ses solutions. Mais les intérêts des uns et des autres ne sont pas identiques, les horizons auxquels ils se réfèrent sont différents. La seule bonne volonté des acteurs ne peut les rendre convergents. C'est dans l'organisation de leur confrontation, que l'arbitrage puise sa légitimité »[25]. Le rôle de la règle de droit est de mettre en place ces procédures et d'en assurer le respect.

---

21 V. *Le Monde* du 14 décembre 2012 : Fessenheim accueille son « fossoyeur » par une grève.

22 V., par exemple, art. R. 4612-6 du Code du travail – Ordonnance n° 2009-229 du 26 février 2009 prise pour l'application de l'article 12 de la loi n° 2008-757 du 1er août 2008 relative à la responsabilité environnementale et à diverses dispositions d'adaptation au droit communautaire dans le domaine de l'environnement.

23 V. article L 4131-3 du Code du travail qui peut être compris comme englobant le risque environnemental (« défectuosité [...] dans les systèmes de protection »).

24 Plus largement, v. A. Bugada, « L'influence du droit de l'environnement sur le droit du travail », *Semaine sociale Lamy*, 2005, n° 1232, supplément du 17 octobre 2005.- A. Mazeaud, « Environnement et travail » in *Mélanges en l'honneur de Michel Prieur*, Dalloz, 2007, p. 561-579.- Marie-Pierre Blin-Franchomme et Isabelle Desbarats : *JurisClasseur Environnement et Développement durable*, Fasc. 2330 : environnement et droit du travail, 8 mai 2008.- F. Héas, « La protection de l'environnement en droit du travail », *Revue de droit du travail* 2009, p. 565.

25 N. Notat, *L'entreprise responsable, une* urgence, éditions dialogues, 2012, p. 71-72.

INSTRUMENTS OF LABOUR LAW

It is high time to start wondering whether labour law has not changed into social competition law, meaning that the right to dignity of working people is questioned (once again)

Jens M. Schubert*

I. INTRODUCTION

The role, the function and the understanding of labour law is permanently under dispute. This discussion exposes very clearly how a state, a market, a legal or a political system interprets the legal and social standing of employees/workers. The primary question in this context is whether labour law should protect the employees and ensure that they are treated in a dignified way under decent labour conditions (as was the main concept in the past). Or do we have to accept that labour law is part of an overall competition in which employees and labour conditions are objects of the market?[1]

This contribution examines which instruments of labour law exist. These instruments give an impression of the status of labour law and possible changes in the recent past. The author's point of view is based on German and European labour law, but some statements are valid for at least Central and Northern Europe as well.

* Ver.di, Vereinte Dienstleistungsgewerkschaft, Germany.

1 See Marc Rigaux, Labour law or social competition law? Labour law: an element of market law and the law regarding professional activities?, in this publication, p. 1 et seq.

II. INSTRUMENT – AN AMBIVALENT TERM

When talking about instruments it becomes apparent that this term does not have a single meaning or a single content. Very often labour law provides instruments to enable and secure dignified work or decent working conditions, which is sometimes criticised as too romantic. This surely includes instruments for better workers' participation in the enterprise. At the same time there are opinions which point out that we need better instruments to create jobs even if that means that we have to talk about precarious jobs. The creation of jobs can be used as a justification to lower labour law standards ("the protection of employees is too high so the employers are deterred from creating new employment relations"). In macroeconomic terms, social law or labour law rules are already relevant as an economic factor (economically speaking: location factor) in each Member State and in their relations with each other. Even the fundamental freedoms are instruments that have an effect on social or labour law as seen in the cases Viking, Laval and Rüffert.[2] Moreover, sometimes it seems that competition is a goal in itself (in contrast to Article 3 par. 3 TEU).

Additionally, a new dynamic comes into the discussion as a result of measures which are meant to attenuate the consequences of the economic and financial crisis. Regulation No. 1176/2011 (as part of the so-called six pack)[3] relating the prevention and correction of macroeconomic imbalances contains, for instance, hidden possibilities for the European Commission to influence the national labour market. Whereas Article 1 par. 3 and in Article 6 par. 3 of the regulation respect social dialogue, recital 20 clearly mentions the wage policy. The so-called European Semester brings pressure on Member States to change their wage policy. In its recommendation for the state of Belgium the European Commission said that Belgium should:

> "réformer, en consultant les partenaires sociaux et en respectant les pratiques nationales, le système de négociation collective et d'indexation des salaires, afin que la croissance des salaires traduise mieux l'évolution de la productivité du travail et de la compétitivité."[4]

---

[2] ECJ, 11/12/2007, C-438/05 (*Viking*); ECJ, 18/12/2007, C-341/05 (*Laval*); ECJ, 3/4/2008, C-346/06 (*Rüffert*). Concerning these cases see Ulrike Wendeling-Schröder, "Fundamental freedoms of the EC Treaty versus the fundamental right to take collective action" and Jens M. Schubert, "The 'second round' in the relationship between fundamental freedoms and fundamental social rights", both contributions in *Fundamental social rights in Europe: Challenges and opportunities* (eds. Ales/Jaspers/Lorber/Sachs-Durand/Wendeling-Schröder), Intersentia 2009; Teun Jaspers, "The right to collective action in European law", in Cr*oss-Border Collective Actions in Europe: A legal challenge* (eds. Dorssemont/Jaspers/van Hoek), Intersentia 2007, p. 23 et seq.; about the reception of *Viking, Laval* and *Rüffert* in different countries, see Andreas Bücker/Wiebke Warneck (eds.), *Reconciling fundamental social rights and economic freedoms after Viking, Laval and Rüffert*, Nomos 2011.

[3] OJ EU L. 306/25, 23/11/2011.

[4] SEC(2011), 802 final, p. 6.

Such a recommendation combined with binding regulations are instruments to influence labour law and shift the costs of the financial crisis (partly) onto the workers.

This is perhaps quite an abstract approach, but we need another preliminary remark before we start describing various instruments: we have to think about different perspectives.

III. PERSPECTIVES

Of course we can discuss labour law instruments from an employee's point of view. The amount of the salary, working hours, how many free days you get, is there a works council, is it possible for me to bring my ideas into the job, etcetera, are all relevant questions for workers. At the same time, it makes sense not to forget the employer's point of view. (Generally), they prefer instruments that enable good working results, flexible working time or lower competences for works councils.

But this approach is too narrow. We have to acknowledge that both the individual states and the EU have their own point of view on this matter: the states sometimes wish to protect their labour market, whereas the EU has a concept of harmonisation in mind.

All these different perspectives regularly lead to differently used instruments with diverse effects. Depending on the acting body the strength of an instrument can vary.

IV. THE CLOUD

Labour law instruments can be bundled in a "cloud" that shows the complexity of the topic. On the one hand there are the well-known three powers (the legislative, judiciary and executive branch) with their power to influence the framework of labour. On the other hand we can find concrete instruments of individual and collective labour law plus further law instruments. This cloud does not say anything about how to evaluate these instruments or who can benefit from them.

Illustration 1

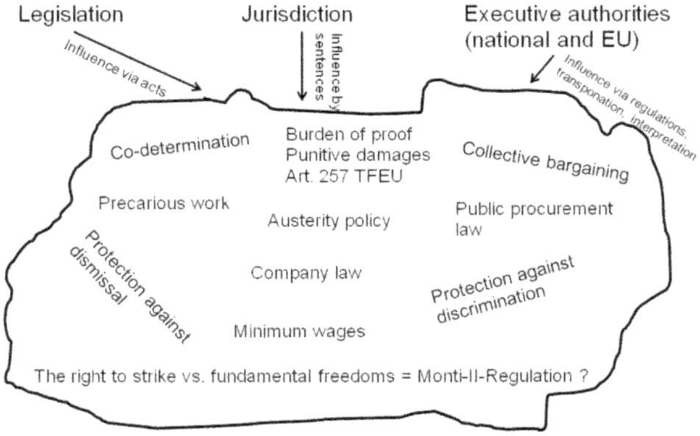

The picture shows the range of instruments but, as in a cloud, it is difficult to see all interactions. Indeed, it would be a mistake to search for labour law instruments only in labour or employment law. Instruments such as the burden of proof or an effective tort law can have an influence on labour law, like the austerity policy (with restrictions to the labour market as a whole) or a too "generous" company law in Europe can too (the overly generous nature of company law is manifested in two ways: the interpretation of the freedom of establishment by the ECJ[5] and the existence of specific European company types[6]). Precarious work is a phenomenon which can be manifested in the form of instruments like fixed-term employment contracts, temporary work or part-time work. Interference with these instruments has massive consequences for the single employee and the labour market as a whole. Precarious work is an instrument to influence social competition between precarious workers and workers in a standard employment relationship.[7] Furthermore, it plays an important role within the competition of states as mentioned above.

The Rüffert case underlines that even public procurement law can affect labour law conditions in a negative way.[8] More broadly, if it is possible to undermine the right to strike by using the fundamental freedoms in a clever way, these doubtlessly important freedoms can be perverted as an instrument against

---

5 Decisions like *Centros* (ECJ 9.3.1999, C-212/97); *Überseering* (ECJ 5/11/2002, C-208/00), *Inspire Art* (ECJ, 30/9/2003, C-167/01) are relevant here. These decisions deal with the move to another Member State. This has to be distinguished from the removal from a Member State: *Cartesio* (ECJ 16/12/2008, C-210/06) and *Vale* (ECJ 12/7/2012, C-378/10).

6 European Company (SE), European Cooperative Society (SCE) or the European Private Company (SPE), that is discussed, with its huge consequences for co-determination on the company level.

7 John Pearson, in *Standard work: an anachronism?* (eds. Jan Buelens/John Pearson), p. 3 et seq.; Raimund Waltermann, Expertise B, 68. Deutscher Juristentag, "Abschied vom Normal-arbeitsverhältnis?"; Jens M. Schubert, "Das Normalarbeitsverhältnis in der arbeits- und sozialrechtlichen Wirklichkeit", *NJW* 2010, 2613 et seq.

8 ECJ, 3/4/2008, C-346/06 (*Rüffert*).

employees' and trade unions' interests[9] – despite European principles or rights, anchored in articles like Article 28 of the EU Charter of Fundamental Rights or Article 3 TEU or Article 9 TFEU.

V. INDIVIDUAL LABOUR LAW INSTRUMENTS

The most important individual labour law instrument is the employment contract. The law relating to the employment contract belongs more or less to civil law. In Germany, for instance, workers are consumers[10] with the consequence that the law concerning consumer protection is more or less applicable to the employment contract. Moreover, contract law is rather widely restricted in order to secure a certain level of protection for workers (special rules for illness, holiday, exemption from attachment of wages etc.). In some other European countries the employment contract is not deeply regulated or the working relationship falls fully under liberal contract law (e.g. Great Britain).

In order to understand the instrument of a labour contract and its effect, it is therefore necessary to ask whether national legislation demands fair and balanced labour conditions which restrict contract law. This restriction of the freedom of contract is justified because of the typical structure of an employment relationship (dependency of the worker) and because of constitutional reasons too.[11] A labour contract is simply not comparable to an act of sale. Then again, national law has to be examined for loopholes with which those fair conditions can be undermined. In the Kücük case a lady worked at a German Civil Court (!) and the employer (the state) used 13 fixed-term labour contracts in a row, which simply circumvents the rules of protection against dismissal. Unfortunately, the ECJ rarely corrects this problem in its case law.[12]

Further individual labour law instruments include:

- Legal standards regarding workers' salary: some countries have opted for a system to install minimum wages by law (e.g. France) or collective agreements with erga omnes effect (e.g. the Netherlands). A minimum wage is (depending on the amount) an effective instrument for preventing social dumping. The difficulties regarding the introduction of a nationwide minimum wage in a bipartite tariff system is perhaps a typically German problem (the new grand coalition has planned to introduce a minimum wage of € 8,50/hour in 2015

9 Concerning the proposal to regulate the relationship between fundamental freedoms and fundamental social rights (Monti II Regulation) see Jens M. Schubert, Hugo Sinzheimer Institut – Schriftenreihe Vol. 6 "Der Vorschlag der EU-Kommission für eine Monti-II-Verordnung".

10 German Federal Labour Court, 25/5/2005, 5 AZR 572/04.

11 See Article 27, 30, 31 EU Charter of fundamental rights; in Germany, the Federal Labour Court has ruled that labour is not only a means of earning money, it is also a means of participating in society and it forms part of workers' dignity, 27/2/1985, GS 1/84.

12 ECJ, 26/1/2012, C-586/10; Federal Labour Court of Germany 18/7/2012, 7 AZR 443/09.

respectively 2017). On a European level, Article 153 par. 5 TFEU is an obstacle for the EU to regulate matters of wage setting. The Rüffert decision and the mentioned new austerity policy, however, show that there is a huge influence on the genesis of wage systems, even on collective agreements or the trade unions' freedom to manoeuvre.

- The protection against dismissal (very often a topic of political debates, which mostly aim at reducing the protection).
- The protection against discrimination. This pillar is quite a solid one.[13]
- Several forms of precarious work.

VI. COLLECTIVE LABOUR LAW INSTRUMENTS

Collective labour law instruments are more often focused upon, they are political instruments, too. There are three elementary and indispensable instruments. Amendments or modifications to these are a huge interference to a sensitive system and to a system which ensures that workers can participate and get dignified working conditions. We are talking about:

Collective bargaining: the only instrument that is able to balance interests and support workers on a "higher" level; the conditions obtained through collective bargaining are better than the conditions that could be obtained through negotiation on the contractual level. Collective bargaining has to be free of state influence or EU measures. Austerity policy is a huge danger here.[14] Collective bargaining is secured by EU Law (Article 12, 28 EU Charter of fundamental rights, Article 152, 153 par. 5 TFEU), the European Convention of Human Rights (Article 11), the ESC (revised, Article 6), ILO Conventions 87, 98 and many national constitutions (in Germany: Article 9 par. 3 basic law).[15] Collective bargaining and collective agreements, the whole social dialogue is part of democracy. Consequently, collective agreements can be part of the process of public procurement. In Germany, as a result of the reception of Rüffert some federal states have introduced new acts in which the relevant collective agreement is of decisive importance, underpinned by state wage regulations.[16]

---

13 See e.g. Article 21, 23 of the EU Charter of fundamental rights; directive 2006/54/EC; ILO Convention 111 and in Germany, the Allgemeines Gleichbehandlungsgesetz.

14 See the expertise by the former judge of the German Federal Constitutional Court Brun-Otto Bryde, *Soziales Recht 2012*, p. 2 ("Europäisches Grundrecht der Tarifautonomie und europäisches Sozialstaatsprinzip als Schranken europäischer Wirtschaftsregulierung").

15 A description of the German collective labour law systems is given by Ulrike Wendeling-Schröder/Jens M. Schubert, *The Essence of Social Dialogue in (South East) Europe* (eds. Marc Rigaux and Jan Rombouts), Intersentia 2006.

16 Further information Andreas Bücker/Matti Hauer/Torsten Walter, in Andreas Bücker/Wiebke Warneck (eds.), *Reconciling fundamental social rights and economic freedoms after Viking, Laval and Rüffert*, Nomos 2011, p. 73 et seq.

Directly linked to collective bargaining is *the right to strike*: this right is not only a fundamental right or a general principle, it is also a human right (Article 11 ECHR).[17] Current discussions in the U.S. and in Germany about the restriction of this right (especially in services for the public) must be countered.[18] One attempt to balance fundamental social rights and economic freedoms after *Viking* and *Laval* can be found in the proposal of Mario Monti for a new regulation. The proposal has, however, been withdrawn. Several Member States had criticised the proposal, since it would violate the principle of subsidiarity. The proposal showed that the "right to strike" instrument is affected by the case law of the EJC (which is a plus) but unfortunately, it gives priority to the fundamental freedoms. The proposal violated Article 28 of the EU Charter of fundamental rights and the principles mentioned in Article 3 par 3 TEU and Article 9 TFEU.[19]

Thirdly, the *co-determination* at the company/enterprise level (works council on a lower level (firm)) has to be mentioned. The rules laid down in directive 2002/14/EC describe a minimum. It is still possible to avoid co-determination by changing the head office of a company or by outsourcing. These possibilities should be limited. In detail:

Co-determination[20] can be an instrument of participation and control if the legal framework provides more than information rights. It is necessary to understand co-determination as an instrument for *duly* information about relevant economic actions and aims of the company, for the right to make proposals and to control management. The instruments provided for by Directive 2001/86/EC are steps in the right direction, but two instruments are missing: the right to veto in cases of high significance for the workers and an express right of omission (via injunction, too) if the company's management does not inform the control body.

Works councils (in countries where these exist) are elements of participation on the company (firm) level. In Germany, works councils supervise the observance of labour law like data protection or health and safety and are involved in decisions concerning dismissal and restructuring. Their powers go far beyond merely information and consultation.[21] In this context, the German system could become a model for other States.

---

17 ECHR 12/11/2008, No. 34503/97 (*Demir and Baykara*); ECHR 21/4/2009, No. 68959/01 (*Enerji Yapi-Yol Sen*).

18 See Jens M. Schubert, "Public Sector Collective Bargaining and the Distortion of Democracy – Do Public Sector Unions Have 'Too Much' Power?, German Perspective", in *Comparative Labor Law & Policy Journal*, Winter 2013, 443 et seq. with further evidence.

19 Schubert, Hugo Sinzheimer Institut – Schriftenreihe Vol. 6 "Der Vorschlag der EU-Kommission für eine Monti-II-Verordnung" with further evidence.

20 There are different types of co-determination in Europe: the English board (monistic) system and the continental dual system with a supervisory board.

21 §§ 87, 99, 102, 111 of the Works Council Act, 2001.

VII. OTHER INSTRUMENTS

A. INSTRUMENTS IN PROCEDURAL LAW

Article 19 of Directive 2006/54/EC illustrates how important it is to get fair rules concerning the burden of proof. Without such rules an instrument is pointless run at idle.

One instrument (admittedly, not the one with the highest priority) could consist of setting up specific chambers for labour law at the ECJ. Article 257 TFEU offers this possibility.

Concerning the right to strike, the accession of the EU to the ECHR (Article 6 par. 1 TEU) will have huge consequences. The case law of the ECHR could have a strong influence on the ECJ, even more so than Article 52 par. 3 of the EU Charter of fundamental rights nowadays.[22]

B. ECONOMIC INSTRUMENTS

All instruments resulting from the new austerity policy can have an indirect effect on labour law, especially on wage policy but on social protection too (e.g. pensions, labour market policy measures). Furthermore, the economic fundamental freedoms have already shown their influence on labour law.

C. TORT LAW

The aim to protect against discrimination, for instance, would be unreachable if the law would provide only low sanctions for actions of discrimination. One instrument consists of punitive damages which are allowed in Article 18 of Directive 2006/54/EC[23] and which have the power to deter from discriminatory behaviour. This is in accordance with the unwritten fundamental EU principles of equivalence and effectiveness which demand that the legislation of the Member states ensures the enforcement of European rights and that national law does not undermine these rights.[24]

---

22 With regard to this accession, see Walter Obwexer, "Der Beitritt der EU zur EMRK: Rechtsgrundlagen, Rechtsfragen und Rechtsfolgen", *EuR* 2012, 115 et seq.

23 The English law distinguishes between compensation, exemplary damages and punitive damages, see Jens M. Schubert, "Punitive damages, das englische Recht als Vorbild für das deutsche Zivilrecht?", *Juristische Rundschau Heft* 4/2008.

24 EJC 29/10/2009, C-63/08, margin number 43.

VIII. CLASSIFICATION

After listing and describing the different instruments it is necessary to classify them. This classification is done on the basis of their target:

Illustration 2

Instruments to strengthen dignity at work (*in favour of working people*)	**Neutral instruments that focus on social competition** (*at the expense of working people*)
Protection against dismissal (by national law, Art. 30 EU Charter)	Precarious work
Protection against discrimination (by directives, Art. 157 TFEU, Art. 23 EU Charter)	Fundamental social rights narrowed by fundamental freedoms (Viking, Laval)
Collective bargaining (if free and without boundaries)	Limitations in public procurement law (Rüffert)
Co-determination (if combined with effective rights)	Austerity policy (influences on wage policy)
Burden of proof (e.g. Art. 19 Directive 2006/54/EC)	Company law (as a means to undermine/avoid labour law)
Punitive damages	Flexicurity but without enough security (green book 2006)
Specific chambers of labour law at the ECJ (Art. 257 TFEU)	

IX. EVALUATION AND FINAL THOUGHTS

"Something is rotten in the state of Denmark" (Shakespeare, *Hamlet*, Act 1, scene 4, 90, said by Marcellus). – The main topic of this book shows that there is something rotten in labour law. With regard to the instruments, the result is distressing too. Positive instruments are too weak or too narrow. Labour law is too inflexible to react to attacks by neo-liberal ideas. Negative instruments are constantly invented anew and labour law is one step behind company law. Economic freedoms are higher ranked by case law than fundamental social rights.

However, there is no basic contradiction between competition and the dignity of workers if one follows what is written in Article 3 par. 3 TEU correctly:

> "The Union shall establish an internal market. It shall work for the sustainable development of Europe based on balanced economic growth and price stability, a highly competitive *social market economy, aiming at* full employment and *social progress*, and a high level of protection and improvement of the quality of the environment. It shall promote scientific and technological advance."

Competition is not an objective in itself, competition has to have the aim of social progress.

To criticise is one thing, however. We need alternative instruments and there are:

(1) Social progress clause within primary EU law;[25]
(2) Higher degree of participation on firm and enterprise level (more than information);
(3) No state influence in social dialogue, even in times of financial crisis;
(4) With regard to dignity, we need more programs of qualification within employment;
(5) Better balance between work and private life.

BIBLIOGRAPHY

Bryde, Brun-Otto, "Europäisches Grundrecht der Tarifautonomie und europäisches Sozialstaatsprinzip als Schranken euriopäischer Wirtschaftsregulierung", in *Soziales Recht* 2012, p. 2 et seq.

Bücker, Andreas/Warneck, Wiebke (eds.), *Reconciling fundamental social rights and economic freedoms after Viking, Laval and Rüffert*, Nomos 2011.

Buelens, Jan/Pearson, John (eds.), *Standard work: an Anachronism?*, Intersentia 2012.

Jaspers, Teun, "The right to collective action in European law", in: *Cross-Border Collective Actions in Europe: A legal challenge* (eds. Dorssemont/Jaspers/van Hoek), Intersentia 2007.

Obwexer, Walter, "Der Beitritt der EU zur EMRK: Rechtsgrundlagen, Rechtsfragen und Rechtsfolgen", *Europarecht* (EuR), 2012, 115 et. seq.

Rigaux, Marc, "Labour law or social competition law? Labour law: an element of market law and the law regarding professional activities?", in this publication.

Schubert, Jens M., "The 'second round' in the relationship between fundamental freedoms and fundamental social rights", in *Fundamental social rights in Europe: Challenges and opportunities* (eds. Ales/Jaspers/Lorber/Sachs-Durand/Wendeling-Schröder), Intersentia 2009.

Schubert, Jens M., "Das Normalarbeitsverhältnis in der arbeits- und sozialrechtlichen Wirklichkeit", *Neue Juristische Wochenschrift* (NJW) 2010, 2613 et seq.

Schubert, Jens M., *Hugo Sinzheimer Institut – Schriftenreihe* Vol. 6, "Der Vorschlag der EU-Kommission für eine Monti-II-Verordnung". 2012.

Schubert, Jens M., "Public Sector Collective Bargaining and the Distortion of Democracy – Do Public Sector Unions Have 'Too Much' Power?, German Perspective", in *Comparative Labor Law & Policy Journal*, Jan. 2013.

Schubert, Jens M., "Punitive damages, das englische Recht als Vorbild für das deutsche Zivilrecht?", *Juristische Rundschau* (JR), Vol. 4/2008.

[25] ETUC proposal, see www.etuc.org/IMG/pdf_social_progress_protocolEN.pdf.

Waltermann, Raimund, Expertise B, 68. Deutscher Juristentag, "Abschied vom Normal-arbeitsverhältnis?"

Wendeling-Schröder, Ulrike, "Fundamental freedoms of the EC Treaty versus the fundamental right to take collective action", in *Fundamental social rights in Europe: Challenges and opportunities* (eds. Ales/Jaspers/Lorber/Sachs-Durand/Wendeling-Schröder), Intersentia 2009.

Wendeling-Schröder, Ulrike/Schubert, Jens M., *The Essence of Social Dialogue in (South East) Europe* (eds. Marc Rigaux and Jan Rombouts), Intersentia 2006.

LES CHANGEMENTS JURIDIQUES SUR LE MARCHÉ DU TRAVAIL EXTERNE ET INTERNE

Jan BUELENS*

Parler des changements sur le marché du travail n'est pas une chose anodine. Les changements sont si profonds et ils ont tellement bouleversé le monde du travail, qu'ils imposent un choix dans leur description et leur analyse. Dans ce texte, je prends comme point de départ le changement du mode de production. Ce changement a donné lieu à des répercussions importantes tant au niveau de la flexibilité interne qu'externe. Ensuite, je me concentrerai sur la flexibilité externe avant de terminer par un plaidoyer en faveur d'un droit du travail collectif qui y soit adapté.

I. LE CHANGEMENT DU MODE DE PRODUCTION

Les changements du marché du travail externe sont fortement liés aux changements du mode de production. Le *fordisme* a été remplacé par le *toyotisme*. Le concept central de nouveau système de production est la *lean production*, ou production allégée. Tout le processus de production est calculé au plus serré. On ne produit plus de grandes réserves comme au temps du fordisme, mais on se limite à la production sur demande. Pour atteindre l'idéal de la *lean production*, on a introduit la méthode du *just-in-time*, qui à son tour donne lieu à la création de relations de sous-traitance.[1]

Ainsi, l'entreprise intégrée a été peu à peu reléguée au second plan tandis que le phénomène connu, dans la littérature (juridique), sous le nom d'entreprise en

---

* Université d'Anvers, Belgique.

[1] Voir à ce sujet J. Buelens, *Collectief overleg in (onder)aannemingsverhoudingen*, Bruges, die Keure, 2012, première partie, chapitre 1.
Il faut se rendre compte que le modèle fordiste n'était pas non plus le paradis. Pour cela, il suffit de lire l'autobiographie de Ford et notamment les passages sur les syndicats. En réalité, ce modèle était également un reflet des rapports de force existants et devrait être approché de façon dialectique.
Même si la *lean production* ne se présente pas partout sous cette forme, l'image est forte et sera utilisée dans la suite de ce texte comme un passe-partout, comme *pars pro toto*.

réseau, a connu un succès rapide.[2] L'entreprise en réseau ne produit plus la gamme complète des pièces détachées et n'intègre plus toutes les fonctions. L'entreprise en réseau est une « *entreprise allégée* » reliée à d'autres entreprises au moyen de nombreuses relations contractuelles.[3]

La cause sous-jacente à ces transformations est à rechercher dans la crise économique du début des années 1970. La recherche du profit[4] s'opère par une pression constante sur les conditions de travail.[5] C'est un lieu commun que d'affirmer que cette crise a mené à la libéralisation du marché du travail et à une prolifération de formes de flexibilité dans l'organisation du travail.[6]

Dans ce qui suit, nous allons nous intéresser à l'impact de ce changement du mode de production sur la flexibilité interne (II) et surtout sur la flexibilité externe (III).

II. QUELQUES EXEMPLES DES CHANGEMENTS DE FLEXIBILITÉ INTERNE

Selon le concept du travail standardisé, le travailleur bénéficie d'une série de droits ou garanties, dont entre autres un poste fixe, un horaire fixe, un contrat à durée indéterminée.[7]

Pour imposer la flexibilité interne, le cadre juridique a changé parallèlement aux changements observés dans les pratiques d'entreprises.

En parcourant les trois aspects mentionnés du concept du travail standardisé, les constats suivants peuvent être dressés :

---

2 E. Peskine, *Réseaux d'entreprises et droit du travail*, Paris, Lavoisier, 2008, 4-5; A. Sobczak, *Réseaux de sociétés et codes de conduite: un nouveau modèle de régulation des relations de travail pour les entreprises européennes*, Paris, Lavoisier, 2002, 3; H. Bocksteins, « De netwerkonderneming en het sectoraal sociaal overleg », *RDS* 1998, 517-541; M. Rigaux, « De netwerkonderneming en de toepassing van de CAO-wet: een verkennende schets » dans M. Rigaux et W. van Eeckhoutte, (éds.), *Actuele Problemen van het Arbeidsrecht 5*, Gand, Mys & Breesch, 1997, 470-507; K. Umnuß, *Organisation der Betriebsverfassung und Unternehmerautonomie. Grundlegen für die Reform des organisatorischen Teils der Betriebsverfassung*, Baden-Baden, Nomos, 1993, 210.

3 Cette transformation explique aussi en partie la désindustrialisation apparente: de nombreux emplois industriels ont été convertis en services aux entreprises, un secteur en plein essor.

4 R. Pardolesi en M. Granieri, « Industrial Sub-Contracting: an Introduction to the Legal Issues » in C. Mastellano, *Handbook on Cross-Border Industrial Sub-Contracting*, La Haye, Kluwer Law International, 2001, 17.

5 A. Thébaud-Mony, *Travailler peut nuire gravement à votre santé*, Paris, La Découverte, 2007, 11-12.

6 M. Rigaux, « Le droit du travail, la concurrence sociale et les restructurations: quelques observations d'ordre théorique, destinées à proposer une hypothèse de travail » dans C. Sachs-Durand (éd.), *La place des salariés dans les restructurations en Europe communautaire, contexte économique, droit européen et droit comparé*, Strasbourg, Presses universitaires de Strasbourg, 2004, 88-89.

7 J. Buelens et J. Pearson, *Standard Work: an Anachronism?*, Anvers, Intersentia, 235 p.

- Tout d'abord, le changement de flexibilité interne donne lieu à l'absence de fonctions fixes. Dans la littérature, le toyotisme est caractérisé par la transition de « *la destruction du métier* »[8] vers « *la destruction du poste de travail* ».[9] Mais le droit du travail constitue une digue contre ce changement. Cependant, c'est la jurisprudence qui doit déterminer si le changement des conditions de travail est tellement significatif qu'il est interdit. Et du coup, ceci représente son point faible. Pendant la vague de libéralisation, on a observé un glissement dans l'évaluation des tribunaux vers une plus grande acceptation des changements.[10] De plus, la voie juridique présente un inconvénient majeur, dans la mesure où l'interdiction du changement conduit souvent à ce que le travailleur en question perde son travail. Ce constat nous fait relativiser cette voie juridique.
- Deuxièmement, le changement du mode de flexibilité interne a conduit aux horaires flexibles: il est banal de rappeler que, dès le début des années 1980, la flexibilisation du temps de travail a été une des grandes demandes du banc patronal. Le concept même de *lean production* est tout simplement inconciliable avec un horaire fixe.
- Troisièmement, le changement a porté sur le développement de contrats non-standardisés (contrats à durée déterminée, travail intérimaire). Voici l'autre grande demande du banc patronal à partir des années 1970. Au niveau législatif, la percée a eu lieu en garantissant que le contrat à durée indéterminé resterait la norme et que les démarches pour légaliser les contrats non-standardisés serviraient simplement à établir un cadre protecteur pour des situations de fait existantes. Ce cadre législatif a été progressivement assoupli. Comme exemple récent, on peut mentionner la directive sur le travail intérimaire qui oblige à un examen de toutes les restrictions afin de vérifier lesquelles sont injustifiées.[11] L'OIT n'a pas été épargnée par la vague néolibérale: avec l'abolition de la convention n° 96 et l'adoption de

---

8 H. Braverman, *Labor and Monopoly Capital. The Degradation of Work in the Twentieth Century*, New York et Londres, Monthly Review Press, 1976, 70-84 et 135-137; M. Henry, « Les conséquences de l'extériorisation pour les salariés et leurs institutions représentatives », *Dr.ouv.* 1981, 123; H. Houben, *L'évolution des systèmes de production dans l'industrie automobile: du fordisme au toyotisme*, Louvain-la-Neuve, CIACO, 1996, 55-59.

9 B. Coriat, *Penser à l'envers*, Paris, Christian Bourgois, 1991, 43; K. Dohse, U. Jürgens et T. Nialsch, « From Fordism to Toyotism? The Social Organisation of the Labor Process in the Japanese Automobile Industry », *Politics Society* 1985, nr. 2, 120; B. Baudry, « L'impact des nouvelles régulations de quasi-intégration sur la gestion de l'emploi des fournisseurs: la question des frontières de la firme » dans H. Petit et N. Thèvenot (éds.), *Les nouvelles frontières du travail subordonné*, Paris, La Découverte, 2006, 134 parle d'« *une polyvalence imposée* »; A. Thébaud-Mony, *Travailler peut nuire gravement à votre santé*, Paris, La Découverte, 2007, 84; à voir également le documentaire *La mise à mort du travail* (http://programmes.france3.fr/mise-a-mort-du-travail).

10 Même si le cadre législatif n'a donc pas changé. Cette évolution a été plus généralement problématisée et située dans le cadre du marché du travail libéralisé par Rigaux (M. Rigaux, *Tussen burgerschap en sociale concurrentie*, Anvers-New York-Oxford, Intersentia, 2004, 207).

11 En son article 4.

la convention n° 181, le travail intérimaire est désormais considéré comme licite.[12] Tant au niveau européen qu'au niveau international, le changement de paradigme est manifeste: on ne se fonde plus sur un principe de protection des travailleurs mais sur les exigences d'une organisation de travail flexible.

Bien que ce rapide état des lieux puisse déjà impressionner, la flexibilité externe, et la sous-traitance en particulier, permet d'encore mieux illustrer les conséquences du changement du mode de production. En ce qui concerne cette forme de flexibilité, un cadre législatif est largement inexistant mais nécessaire.

III. FLEXIBILITÉ EXTERNE: L'EXEMPLE DE LA SOUS-TRAITANCE

Pour pouvoir fonctionner dans un environnement *just-in-time*, la sous-traitance est devenue l'instrument de flexibilité privilégié, « la formule célèbre »: la liste des « mérites » est longue, on dirait même inépuisable.

Cependant, pour les travailleurs du donneur d'ordre et pour ceux des sous-traitants, les nouvelles structures de l'entreprise ont des conséquences importantes sur leur statut juridique.

La raison en est que le droit du travail est encore principalement lié à la notion juridique d'employeur. Que le travailleur exécute ses prestations de travail dans le cadre d'une entreprise (élargie) n'est, pour l'application de la législation du travail, qu'une donnée accessoire de peu d'importance. L'implication du travailleur est réduite aux limites de ce qui peut être convenu par contrat.[13] Globalement, le droit collectif suit cette même voie.

Je me permets d'illustrer cette thèse sur base de la loi belge. Ainsi, la loi sur les conventions collectives de travail du 5 décembre 1968 utilise la notion juridique d'employeur.[14] Le modèle d'entreprise retenu dans cette législation, qui est toujours en vigueur, correspondait au type habituel ou dominant de l'entreprise qui se manifestait dans la réalité socio-économique.[15] Il convient toutefois de signaler

12 L. Vosko, « Legitimizing the Triangular Relationship: Emerging International Labour Standards from a Comparative Perspective », *Comp Lab Law and Policy J* 1997, nr. 19, 44.

13 M. Jamoulle, *Le contrat de travail*, t. 1, Liège, Faculté de droit, 1982, 7; M. Rigaux, « De arbeidsovereenkomst: grendel op de betrokkenheid van de werknemer bij het ondernemingsbeleid » dans M. Rigaux, *Standpunten over arbeidsrecht*, Anvers, Université d'Anvers, s.d., 35.

14 Ceci a été confirmé par un arrêt du Conseil d'Etat jugeant que, en vertu de la loi sur les conventions collectives de travail, le Roi ne pouvait pas faire référence au groupe d'entreprises dans la définition des compétences d'une commission paritaire (Conseil d'Etat 30 avril 1996, *JTT* 1996, 373).

15 M. Van Putten, *Het arbeidsrecht en de onderneming. Proeve tot (meta)juridisch onderzoek naar de betekenissen van arbeid en onderneming in en voor het arbeidsrecht als elementen voor een geactualiseerde reconstructie van dat recht*, Anvers, Intersentia, 2009, 186.

que les lois qui instaurent les organes de concertation au niveau des entreprises[16] apportent une correction à cet état des choses (par le biais de l'unité technique d'exploitation), bien que cette correction reste très limitée.[17]

Ce « choix contractuel » a pour résultat que des entreprises qui, dans la réalité économique, travaillent en étroite collaboration, sont considérées comme des entreprises distinctes en droit du travail.

Cette thèse peut être illustrée par une comparaison entre l'entreprise intégrée et l'entreprise réseau. En général, les travailleurs de l'entreprise intégrée bénéficient tous des mêmes rémunérations et des mêmes conditions de travail, alors que pour les travailleurs des entreprises réseau les rémunérations et les conditions de travail sont différentes parce que le sous-traitant relève de conventions collectives de travail d'entreprise et de secteur autres que celles du donneur d'ordre.[18] Contrairement aux travailleurs de l'entreprise intégrée qui ont la même représentation, les travailleurs de l'entreprise réseau ont souvent une représentation distincte (si les seuils de représentativité sont atteints). C'est ainsi que les collectifs de travail se fragmentent.[19] Alors que les représentants des travailleurs de l'entreprise intégrée reçoivent de l'information au sujet de tous les travailleurs de cette entreprise, les représentants des travailleurs du donneur d'ordre et ceux du (des) sous-traitant(s) n'ont pas droit à l'information sur l'autre partie et ne sont pas consultés. C'est ainsi que les droits du travail collectifs fondamentaux (information et consultation, représentation[20], négociation collective) sont gravement menacés.

---

[16] La loi portant organisation de l'économie du 20 septembre 1948 et la loi relative au bien-être des travailleurs lors de l'exécution de leur travail du 4 août 1996.

[17] Par exemple, les réseaux d'entreprises n'entrent en principe pas en ligne de compte dans ce concept d'unité technique d'exploitation, voy. à ce sujet J. Buelens, *Collectief overleg in (onder) aannemingsverhoudingen*, Bruges, die Keure, 2012, numéros 121-124.

[18] Dans la jurisprudence belge, il n'est que rarement question d'entreprises réseau. Les dernières années dans la plus haute juridiction, le concept a fait son apparition concernant une nouvelle définition de la compétence du CP 149.04 (voir Cass. 23 mai 2011, AR S.10.0042.F (commentaire J. Buelens et M. Jourdan, « Aspects de la jurisprudence belge », *NAB/NRT* 2012, 82-83) et explicitement trib. trav. Bruxelles 2 février 2012, *JTT* 2012, 252). La forme modifiée des entreprises a ainsi été prise en considération pour déterminer la commission paritaire applicable.

[19] J. De Maillard e.a., « L'éclatement de la collectivité de travail: observations sur les phénomènes d'extériorisation de l'emploi », *Dr.soc.* 1979, 323; J. Magaud, « L'éclatement juridique de la collectivité de travail », *Dr.soc.* 1975, 525; G. Caire, *Le travail intérimaire*, Paris, PUF, 1993, 65-66.
Quelques garanties ont toutefois été prévues pour le cas d'un transfert d'une entreprise, mais un tel transfert ne doit pas nécessairement se faire vers un sous-traitant et de plus, ces garanties sont limitées dans le temps.

[20] Bien que la représentation soit une notion absente de la plupart des catalogues de droits fondamentaux, il s'agit bien d'un droit fondamental découlant de la liberté syndicale (M. Rigaux, *Droit du travail ou droit de la concurrence sociale*, Bruxelles, Bruylant, 2009, 98-99). Au niveau de la CE/UE, nous trouvons quelques indices de reconnaissance de l'existence de la représentation comme droit (fondamental) (indépendant). Dans un contexte concernant le sort des organes de concertation lors d'un transfert d'entreprise, la Cour de justice a reconnu récemment « *un droit à la représentation* » (CJCE 29 juillet 2010, C-151/09, *UGT-FSP*, ov. 45). En 2003, Van Peijpe écrivait encore que, sauf en cas de restructuration, le droit CE n'avait

Cette atteinte aux droits collectifs a des retombées sur le statut juridique individuel du travailleur d'un sous-traitant. Etant donné que d'autres conventions collectives de travail lui sont applicables, il lui manque les garanties individuelles suivantes. Les possibilités de formation et de recyclage sont plus limitées. Sa protection sociale et sa situation de bien-être sont sous pression parce que dans les cas de la sous-traitance, les risques en matière de sécurité et de santé sont insuffisamment connus ou même pas connus du tout. Le nombre d'accidents du travail (avec suite mortelle) est sensiblement plus élevé chez ces travailleurs. Ce travailleur ne jouit que peu ou pas de la sécurité d'emploi[21] et l'employeur est souvent en position de force pour établir unilatéralement les conditions de travail, en tout cas si le travailleur n'a pas d'autre possibilité d'emploi.[22] Lors d'une restructuration, les travailleurs d'un sous-traitant sont moins bien lotis que ceux de l'entreprise principale, parfois aucun plan social n'est convenu pour eux.[23] Dans bien des cas, la solvabilité du sous-traitant est médiocre et il peut y avoir des problèmes pour se faire payer. La Cour de cassation française a conclu qu'en cas de sous-traitance, suite à une externalisation, le travailleur est dépouillé de son statut de travailleur permanent, de la convention collective de travail de l'entreprise qui l'emploie de fait, de sa participation aux organes élus dans l'entreprise et du bénéfice des avantages sociaux.[24]

---

pas reconnu le droit à la représentation, mais qu'il n'y avait pas de raison pour ne pas le faire (T. Van Peijpe, « Industrial relations processes » dans J. Malmberg (éd.), *Effective enforcement of EC Labour Law*, La Haye, Kluwer Law International, 2003, 106). Selon Bercusson aussi, le développement de la représentation collective des travailleurs est un élément fondamental du droit du travail européen (B. Bercusson, *European Labour Law*, Cambridge, Cambridge University Press, 2009, 62 et 318).

21 L. Vosko, « Legitimizing the Triangular Relationship: Emerging International Labour Standards from a Comparative Perspective », *Comp Lab Law and Policy J* 1997, n° 19, 47; W. Nienhüser et W. Baumhus, « 'Fremd im Betrieb': Der Einsatz von Fremdfirmenpersonal als Arbeitskräftestrategie » dans A. Martin et W. Nienhüser (éds.), *Neue Formen der Beschäftigung – neue Personalpolitik?*, München et Mering, Rainer Hampp, 2002, 91-93.
Certaines formes de sous-traitance sont un « *retour à l'insécurité* » (A. Thébaud-Mony, *Travailler peut nuire gravement à votre santé*, Paris, La Découverte, 2007, 11-12; G. Caire, *Le travail intérimaire*, Paris, PUF, 1993, 65-66, qui était en effet « *le mot clé de la vie d'ouvrier* » au dix-neuvième siècle (J. Le Goff, *Du silence à la parole: une histoire du droit du travail des années 1830 à nos jours*, Rennes, Presses universitaires de Rennes, 2004, 103)). Comme le dit Castel: « *pour beaucoup l'avenir est marqué du sceau de l'aléatoire* » (R. Castel, *Les métamorphoses de la question sociale. Une chronique du salariat*, Paris, Fayard, 2006, 11).

22 C.J. Smitskam, *Flexibele arbeidsrelaties*, Deventer, Kluwer, 1989, 2-3; E. Algava et S. Amira, « Sous-traitance: des conditions plus difficiles chez les preneurs d'ordres », *Dares Analyses* février 2011, 4-6.

23 M.-L. Morin, *Sous-traitance et relations salariales. Aspects de droit du travail*, Paris, La Documentation Française, 1993, 83; J.-C. Dupuis, « La responsabilité sociale de l'entreprise: gouvernance partenariale de la firme ou gouvernance de réseau? », *Revue d'économie industrielle* 2/2008, 67-86.

24 Cass. Crim. 28 octobre 1980, *Dr.ouv.* 1981, 155; voir aussi TGI correct. Paris 17 décembre 1980, *Dr.ouv.* 1981, 156; pour une application plus récente en matière de « *privation du statut permanent* »: Cass. Crim. 5 septembre 2006, n° 05-86.531, comme cité par D. Guirimand, « L'intervention du juge pénal en droit du travail », Paris, Rencontre annuelle des juristes du travail, 8 décembre 2006, www.afdt-asso.fr/fichiers/publications/enm2006/ENM2006 GUIRIMAND.pdf, 12.

Le statut juridique des travailleurs chez le donneur d'ordre est également compromis. Leur sécurité d'emploi est menacée. Le fait de tolérer (implicitement) la sous-traitance a donné lieu à une véritable « *vague de substitution* »: certains salariés de donneurs d'ordre ont été remplacés par des travailleurs de sous-traitants. Les autres travailleurs du donneur d'ordre sont ainsi incités à modérer leurs revendications pour éviter une extension de la sous-traitance. De plus, la sous-traitance alourdit le travail, puisqu'il n'existe plus chez le donneur d'ordre d'« *emplois légers* » – appelés « emplois relax » –.[25] Enfin, l'expérience des travailleurs du donneur d'ordre et du donneur d'ordre lui-même disparaît (au profit des travailleurs des sous-traitants sans expérience), ce qui peut avoir des répercussions sur le bien-être.[26]

Plus fondamentalement, cette situation cause une certaine tension/concurrence entre les travailleurs du donneur d'ordre et les travailleurs du (des) sous-traitant(s)[27, 28], qui peut donner lieu à une véritable "*discrimination*".[29] Cette « *discrimination* » est étroitement liée à la nature de la sous-traitance qui implique

---

25 M.-L. Morin, *Sous-traitance et relations salariales. Aspects de droit du travail*, Paris, La Documentation Française, 1993, 95; P. Humblet, « De collectieve rechten van de werknemers in de 21ste eeuw: is de regressie (on)omkeerbaar? » dans X, *5 années après Lisbonne: le droit du travail sous pression européenne*, Bruxelles, Documentation Progress Lawyers Network, 2005.

26 Des témoignages pratiques montrent que les contrôles de qualité ne peuvent remplacer la connaissance acquise, certainement pas pour l'entretien d'installations fonctionnant (partiellement) (V. Pereira, « Le point de vue d'un ancien secrétaire de CHSCT d'une entreprise pétrochimique » dans M. Héry (éd.), *La sous-traitance interne*, Les Ulis Cedex, EDP Sciences, 2009, 339-340); voir aussi M. Lallier, « La sous-traitance de site. Exemple du nucléaire » dans M. Héry (éd.), *La sous-traitance interne*, Les Ulis Cedex, EDP Sciences, 2009, 364.

27 H.-J. Bauschke, « Die so genannte Fremdfirmenproblematik », *NZA* 2000, 1201 et 1206; T. Kreuder, *Desintegration und Selbststeuerung. Betriebsverfassung in der fraktalen Fabrik*, Baden-Baden, Nomos, 1998, 51-53; W. Nienhüser et W. Baumhus, « 'Fremd im Betrieb': Der Einsatz von Fremdfirmenpersonal als Arbeitskräftestrategie » dans A. Martin et W. Nienhüser (éds.), *Neue Formen der Beschäftigung – neue Personalpolitik?*, München et Mering, Rainer Hampp, 2002, 86-87; L. Willemez, *Le droit du travail en danger. Une ressource collective pour les combats individuels*, Bellecombe-en-Bauges, Éditions du Croquant, 2006, 70-71; M. Rigaux, *Droit du travail ou droit de la concurrence sociale*, Bruxelles, Bruylant, 2009, 23-24 et 54.

28 Les sous-traitants sont aussi mis en concurrence les uns contre les autres. Chaque année, les donneurs d'ordre exigent une réduction des frais (F. Eyraud et D. Vaughan-Whitehead (éds.), *The evolving world of work in the enlarged EU*, Genève, OIT, 2007, 15) et celui qui ne donne pas satisfaction est remplacé (E. De Banville et J.-J. Chanaron, « Les relations d'approvisionnement » dans J.-H. Jacot (éd.), *Du fordisme au toyotisme? Les voies de la modernisation du système automobile en France et au Japon*, Paris, La Documentation française, 1990, 94-96; cela vaut en général pour la sous-traitance, voir P.-Y. Jonnet (éd.), *Les conséquences sociales de l'externalisation et de la sous-traitance*, Bruxelles, ORSEU, 1998, 28; H.-J. Bauschke, « Die so genannte Fremdfirmenproblematik », *NZA* 2000, 1202).

29 Ici, la notion de « *discrimination* » est employée plutôt dans un sens sociologique que juridique.

une différenciation des statuts.[30] Parfois, cette situation est initiée ou encouragée par les donneurs d'ordre.[31]

D'une manière plus générale, on peut considérer que le recours à la sous-traitance est un moyen pour échapper à toute responsabilité[32], tout en recueillant les fruits du travail accompli. Contrairement à ses propres salariés, le donneur d'ordre ne paie pas de salaire aux travailleurs des sous-traitants, parce qu'il paie un service.[33] Le donneur d'ordre ne doit, en outre, pas se faire de soucis pour d'éventuels « *obstacles* » sur sa route. Si le sous-entrepreneur présente de mauvais résultats, il est remplacé, inexorablement.[34] Mettre fin à un contrat commercial est très simple, bien plus facile que mettre fin à un contrat de travail.[35] Etant donné que pour le sous-traitant le maintien de son contrat avec le donneur d'ordre est essentiel, il sera prêt à aller très loin pour répondre aux exigences du donneur d'ordre. Si une entreprise se trouve dans une situation de subordination par rapport à une autre entreprise, cette situation de subordination est encore plus vraie pour les travailleurs de cette sous-entreprise.[36] L'instabilité potentielle du contrat commercial a une influence sur la situation juridique des travailleurs.[37]

---

30 J. De Maillard, e.a., « L'éclatement de la collectivité de travail: observations sur les phénomènes d' « extériorisation de l'emploi » », *Dr.soc.* 1979, 324.

31 N. Jounin, « L'illégalité sous-traitée? Les conséquences du recours à des employeurs intermédiaires dans le secteur du bâtiment », *Dr.soc.* 2007, 43-44; Y. Chalaron, « Pour un nouveau concept pénal de marchandage », *Dr.soc.* 1980, 511.

32 M. Henry, « Les conséquences de l'extériorisation pour les salariés et leurs institutions représentatives », *Dr.ouv.* 1981, 122; A. Lyon-Caen, « À propos de l'entreprise éclatée », *Dr.ouv.* 1981, 127 ; A. Thébaud-Mony, *Travailler peut nuire gravement à votre santé*, Paris, La Découverte, 2007, 11 parle d'une « sous-*traitance des risques* ».

33 Ceci peut avoir comme effet que pour des travaux à haute intensité de travail, comme les travaux de nettoyage, le prix est plus bas que le salaire d'un travailleur intérimaire (P.-Y. Jonnet (éd.), *Les conséquences sociales de l'externalisation et de la sous-traitance*, Bruxelles, ORSEU, 1998, 25); C.J. Smitskam, *Flexibele arbeidsrelaties*, Deventer, Kluwer, 1989, 2-4; voir le rapport du Comité de l'emploi et du travail du VIIIe plan (1978), cité par G. Caire, *Le travail intérimaire*, Paris, PUF, 1993, 65-66.

34 H. Houben, *L'évolution des systèmes de production dans l'industrie automobile: du fordisme au toyotisme*, Louvain-la-Neuve, CIACO, 1996, 215.

35 Il n'y a pas d'indemnité de licenciement à payer, sauf s'il s'agit d'une rupture de contrat illicite. En théorie, il est conseillé de laisser un temps de réflexion raisonnable (W. Goossens, *Aanneming van werk: het gemeenrechtelijk dienstencontract*, Bruges, die Keure, 2003, 1070). La question est de savoir si tous les donneurs d'ordre en tiennent compte et si les entrepreneurs exigeront effectivement le paiement de cette indemnité.
Ce problème a été posé à plusieurs reprises dans la doctrine française: J. De Maillard, e.a., « L'éclatement de la collectivité de travail: observations sur les phénomènes d' « extériorisation de l'emploi » », *Dr.soc.* 1979, 324; A. Lyon-Caen, « À propos de l'entreprise éclatée », *Dr.ouv.* 1981, 127 (« *une telle relation d'affaires est marquée d'instabilité* »).

36 F. Pichault et V. Xhauflair, « Le dialogue social face aux nouvelles formes de sous-traitance dans le secteur de la construction » dans É. Arcq, e.a. (éds.), *Dynamiques de la concertation sociale*, Bruxelles, CRISP, 2010, 337.

37 A. Lyon-Caen, « À propos de l'entreprise éclatée », *Dr.ouv.* 1981, 127.
Se défaire des risques et les faire porter par les travailleurs est une nouvelle tendance dans les « *nouvelles relations de travail* » (J. Bélanger, A. Giles et G. Murray, « Vers un nouveau modèle de production: possibilités, tensions et contradictions » dans G. Murray e.a. (éds.),

Cette autre face de la médaille est peu mise en avant. Traditionnellement, on se limite à évoquer les cas d'abus. N'oublions cependant pas que des milliers de travailleurs se retrouvent dans des relations de sous-traitance. Même si les situations sont très différentes, il reste qu'ils se retrouvent dans une situation de double dépendance, d'un côté à l'égard de leur employeur, de l'autre, à l'égard de l'utilisateur.

Il faut donc des solutions appropriées. Jusqu'à présent, ces solutions ne sont pas (suffisamment) rencontrées par le droit du travail. Comme on l'a exposé, le droit du travail existant est largement construit autour du travail standardisé et de l'entreprise intègrée.

Ainsi, le droit du travail collectif s'est construit autour de l'employeur juridique, même s'il a essayé de tenir compte de certaines évolutions, comme l'apparition des groupes d'entreprises. Cependant, comme l'ont montré des éminents juristes français, ces solutions restent cantonnées dans le concept de l'entreprise et n'offrent donc pas de solutions pour des réseaux[38] dont la sous-traitance est un exemple et où la domination ne s'opère en principe pas par un lien capitalistique mais seulement par un lien contractuel.

A ce sujet, il importe de souligner que le droit du travail a été amené a découvrir l'existence des groupes. Cette recherche n'a pas eu lieu dans tous les pays (de la même façon), mais à tout le moins au niveau européen. Dès lors, actuellement, il me semble nécessaire de repenser le traitement différent des groupes et des réseaux, d'autant plus qu'en réglementant les groupes, on a vu un glissement des groupes vers des réseaux.

Une autre dichotomie qui est au centre du débat me semble également peu défendable. La différence entre le traitement juridique du travail intérimaire et celui de la sous-traitance pose problème. Même si les droits des travailleurs ne sont pas toujours respectés dans le cas du travail intérimaire[39], il existe néanmoins un cadre juridique. Mis à part en France et de manière partielle, ce cadre n'existe pas en ce qui concerne la sous-traitance. Au niveau européen, il n'existe qu'un début très prudent avec les débats autour de la responsabilité solidaire, mais il

L'organisation de la production et du travail: vers un nouveau modèle?, Québec, Presses de l'université de Laval, 2004, 42). Ce nouveau modèle est reconnu tant par des économistes que par des juristes (H. Petit et N. Thèvenot, « Introduction » dans H. Petit et N. Thèvenot (éds.), *Les nouvelles frontières du travail subordonné*, Paris, La Découverte, 2006, 17 avec renvois).

38 A. Supiot, « Groupes de sociétés et paradigme de l'entreprise », *RTD com* 1985, 626-631; M.-L. Morin, « Le droit du travail face aux nouvelles formes d'organisation des entreprises », *Rev.int.Trav.* 2005, 7-11 ; E. Peskine, *Réseaux d'entreprises et droit du travail*, Parijs, Lavoisier, 2008, 126.

39 Il s'agit d'un euphémisme.

faut compter avec le fort lobbying des employeurs, orienté vers des « solutions » de *soft law*.

Un angle d'approche intéressant est celui de la reconstitution des « collectifs de travail », c.-à-d. la création de structures d'interconcertation pour tous les travailleurs concernés qui se retrouvent sur un même site et, à terme, pourquoi pas dans la même chaîne de valeurs.[40]

Ces structures ne sont pas des inventions du moment. En France, divers *intercomités* furent créés (sous des appelations différentes). Déjà en 1976, ils furent créés dans la construction, ensuite dans l'industrie nucléaire et les sites Seveso.[41] On créa ensuite des délégations responsables de toutes les industries dans un seul domaine.

Il me semble opportun d'essayer de lier ces structures en premier lieu à la problématique du bien-être au travail (santé et sécurité). Tout d'abord, il s'agit d'un domaine où le droit fondamental à la vie se traduit dans le monde du travail et qui est donc ressenti par les travailleurs de manière physique et vitale. Il n'est donc pas surprenant qu'en ce domaine « *la prise en compte de la sous-traitance interne est sans doute à la fois la plus originale et la plus efficace* ».[42]

Par une telle recherche, nous rejoignons un courant qui a déjà été formulé il y a trente ans par le professeur Lyon-Caen dans ces termes: « *une orientation ne tend pas à saisir le pouvoir au niveau le plus élevé; elle se propose de reconstituer, en un lieu donné, une organisation collective entre les salariés écartelés entre plusieurs employeurs. C'est principalement pour la représentation du personnel et les conditions de travail que cette reconstitution, autour de l'établissement ou du site, est à la fois nécessaire et possible.* »[43]

Trente ans sont passés, le constat reste … mais le passage à l'action tarde à venir.

Fondamentalement, cette piste de réflexion peut donc mener à la reconstruction de collectivités de travailleurs, dont la nécessité a été appuyée depuis les années 1970 principalement par la doctrine[44] et l'Etat[45] français. Cette piste de réflexion a

---

[40] T. Coutrot, « Face au despotisme de marché, quelles stratégies syndicales? » dans H. Petit et N. Thèvenot (éds.), *Les nouvelles frontières du travail subordonné*, Paris, La Découverte, 2006, 211.

[41] J. Buelens, *Collectief overleg in (onder)aannemingsverhoudingen*, Bruges, die Keure, 2012, n° 273.

[42] N. Guillemy, « Sous-traitance et droit du travail » dans M. Héry (éd.), *La sous-traitance interne*, Les Ulis Cedex, EDP Sciences, 2009, 29.

[43] A. Lyon-Caen, « À propos de l'entreprise éclatée », *Dr.ouv.* 1981, 130.

[44] J. Magaud, « L'éclatement juridique de la collectivité de travail », *Dr.soc.* 1975, 526; J. De Maillard, e.a., « L'éclatement de la collectivité de travail: observations sur les phénomènes d'extériorisation de l'emploi », *Dr.soc.* 1979, 323; A. Lyon-Caen, « À propos de l'entreprise éclatée », *Dr.ouv.* 1981, 127.

[45] Voir particulièrement le *Rapport Auroux* (J. Auroux, *Les droits des travailleurs, Rapport au Président et au Premier ministre*, septembre 1981, Paris, La Doc. fr., 1982, 82p.) En France, début 1980 dans le cadre des *Lois Auroux* en découlant, une série d'expériences a été faite sur

comme avantage qu'elle peut servir de levier pour des réglementations ultérieures sur le plan du droit du travail individuel. L'existence de droits individuels suppose, en effet, un cadre dans lequel ces droits peuvent être exercés.[46] Bien qu'il existe une interdépendance entre les deux éléments du droit du travail, le droit du travail collectif est d'autant plus important pour des travailleurs dans des situations vulnérables. Concrètement, la voix des travailleurs dans des relations de sous-traitance pourrait se faire entendre par la création d'un forum.

La sous-traitance est sans nul doute un des grands défis pour le droit du travail, et par extension pour tout le tissu social. Bien que des amorces aient été données pour réfléchir à des solutions effectives, cette réflexion reste trop isolée pour produire des effets forts ou a trop peu été réalisée dans la pratique. En développant une concertation territoriale collective supplémentaire fondée sur le modèle proposé, on pourrait avoir prise sur des relations qui en ce moment, ne sont presque pas traitées par le droit. Ce n'est que de cette façon qu'on arrivera à combler le fossé qui sépare la réalité économique - où les entreprises qui se trouvent dans une relation de sous-traitance collaborent - et la réglementation du travail qui considère ces entreprises comme des entreprises séparées et leurs travailleurs comme des travailleurs séparés.

Last but not least, les organisations syndicales aussi doivent adapter leurs stratégies. L'élaboration du syndicalisme de réseau est une *conditio sine qua non* pour donner forme aux nouvelles structures.

---

le plan de l'implication des travailleurs. Celle-ci est traitée dans une certaine mesure dans ma thèse (*délégués du site, accord interprofessionnel local, comité de groupe*).

46 E. Peskine, *Réseaux d'entreprises et droit du travail*, Paris, Lavoisier, 2008, 62; voir aussi M. Rigaux, « De rechtshomogene benadering van de collectieve arbeidsverhoudingen » dans G. Cox et M. Rigaux (éds.), *De grondrechtelijke onderbouw van het collectief arbeidsrecht*, Malines, Kluwer, 2005, 21-34; L. Wedderburn, « Common law, labour law, global law » dans B. Hepple (éd.), *Social and labour rights in a global context. International and comparative perspectives*, Cambridge, Cambridge University Press, 2002, 28; T. Van Peijpe, « Industrial relations processes » dans J. Malmberg (éd.), *Effective enforcement of EC Labour Law*, La Haye, Kluwer Law International, 2003, 78 signale l'importance des négociations collectives pour le droit individuel du travail.

LE DROIT DU TRAVAIL ET LES MODIFICATIONS APPORTÉES AU MARCHÉ DU TRAVAIL

Esteban MARTINEZ*

I. LES CHANGEMENTS DE LA NORME SOCIALE DE L'EMPLOI

Les transformations observées dans le fonctionnement du marché du travail depuis les années 1980 se mesurent par référence à la norme sociale de l'emploi qui s'est affirmée au cours des « trente glorieuses » (1945-1975). Si le régime d'emploi du rapport salarial fordiste s'est érigé en norme sociale, c'est dans la mesure où les comportements que celle-ci impliquait sont devenus majoritaires, visibles au plan juridique et légitimes aux yeux des acteurs sociaux. Comme le signale Carlos Prieto (1999), la norme sociale de l'emploi qui s'est construite progressivement dans la période de croissance fordiste avait un caractère universel et consensuel dans les pays européens occidentaux, en dépit de spécificités sociétales : « [Dans tous les pays européens] prédominait l'emploi salarié, stable, à temps complet, adossé à des conventions collectives de branche, avec des perspectives de promotion, inscrit dans une tendance à une certaine homogénéisation et universalité des conditions de travail et lié à des mesures de protection sociale. Le cycle de vie au travail majoritaire était long et sans interruptions du début de la vie professionnelle jusqu'à la retraite ou avec des interruptions purement « frictionnelles » (comme l'était le taux de chômage) ». La norme traduit dès lors la vérification de régularités statistiques, reflétant des pratiques sociales homogènes, et un cadre juridique institué, mais elle comporte également « une dimension de prescription positive et de légitimité » (Bouffartigue et Bouteiller, 2003 : 3). Cette fonction prescriptive n'excluait pas pour autant des pratiques sociales différentes et des écarts par rapport à la norme juridique, mais ceux-ci étaient rangés dans l'informel ou l'atypisme. Ce modèle d'emploi, désigné en termes de *Standard Employment Relationship* (Müchenberger, 1989) relève d'un compromis social historique, par lequel les travailleurs assuraient les employeurs de leur coopération dans le champ de l'organisation du travail en échange de

* Université Libre de Bruxelles, Belgique.

garanties salariales directes et indirectes, d'une stabilité de la relation d'emploi et d'une délimitation du temps de travail.

Le constat de l'érosion de la norme d'emploi fordiste ne paraît pas contestable : l'emploi à temps plein assorti d'horaires collectifs et stables est à présent quantitativement moins dominant, en raison de l'extension du travail à temps partiel et d'horaires diversifiés et variables ; diverses formes d'emplois précaires se sont développées au détriment du contrat à durée indéterminée ; et des situations transitoires se sont multipliées au cours de la vie professionnelle, rompant ainsi avec une division ternaire du cycle de vie. On s'accorde à présent pour reconnaître, à partir de l'évolution des réglementations et des pratiques sociales, l'émergence d'une norme, sociale et juridique, flexible, qu'il est cependant difficile de qualifier de manière univoque, dans la mesure où précisément celle-ci se caractérise par la diversification des formes d'emploi et des régimes temporels et se décline, de manière différenciée, selon les contextes sociétaux, les branches d'activité, les catégories sociales et professionnelles (Prieto, 1999 ; de Terssac & Tremblay, 2000 ; Linhart & Moutet, 2005).

II. LA MOBILISATION FLEXIBLE DES TRAVAILLEURS

Ces transformations du système d'emploi traduisent les effets conjugués de la conversion des entreprises à la flexibilité et des politiques publiques de l'emploi, en matière de gestion des flux de main-d'œuvre et de réglementation du travail, qui ont accompagné les révisions de l'organisation du travail depuis le début des années 1980. Dans l'industrie, les systèmes de production en flux tendus, répondant aux principes du juste à temps et de la minimisation des stocks, font du temps de travail mobilisé la variable d'ajustement privilégiée pour faire face aux variations de la demande et garantir une utilisation optimale des équipements. Et c'est encore davantage dans les activités de services, en croissance dans les économies contemporaines, que se vérifie la diffusion de régimes horaires atypiques et singulièrement du travail à temps partiel. La relation de service a ceci de particulier que les temps de production et de consommation doivent coïncider. De ce fait, l'amplification des plages de disponibilité du service apparaît comme un critère de qualité et le recours à la flexibilité du temps de travail comme un moyen privilégié pour répondre aux flux irréguliers de la clientèle. Partout, l'argument économique de la compétitivité et de la recherche d'avantages concurrentiels s'est ajouté aux raisons techniques, liées à la nature de l'activité, qui depuis longtemps justifiaient l'adoption de régimes de travail particuliers comme, par exemple, dans la sidérurgie ou encore les hôpitaux où la production ne peut pas être interrompue.

La mobilisation flexible des travailleurs est dès lors devenue le crédo managérial. Alors que précédemment, dans les entreprises, les branches d'activité et sur un plan interprofessionnel, l'initiative de la revendication émanait le plus souvent des syndicats, les accords sociaux étant sous-tendus par la perspective d'une amélioration de la productivité et d'une paix sociale, ce sont désormais les employeurs qui avancent des exigences de flexibilité, comme préalable à la négociation de garanties d'emploi. Dans le contexte d'un chômage massif et permanent, les orientations de la politique publique de l'emploi vont s'accorder avec les stratégies de recherche de flexibilité des entreprises en favorisant la mobilité sur le marché du travail et à travers la mise en place d'une réglementation permissive en matière de temps de travail. Pour les pouvoirs publics, il s'agira de remédier au problème du chômage prioritairement à travers des mesures individuelles de redistribution du travail disponible (temps partiel, interruption de carrière, départ anticipé à la retraite), de combattre les rigidités du marché du travail afin d'adapter l'emploi et le temps de travail aux fluctuations de la production (travail intérimaire, annualisation du temps de travail, ...) et de contenir la progression salariale de manière à préserver la compétitivité des entreprises (modération salariale, réduction du sursalaire pour les dépassements aux limites normales du temps de travail).

Il ne paraît pas approprié toutefois de décrire les évolutions observées en termes de « dérégulation », ce qui laisserait entendre que le marché du travail n'est plus régulé. Mais il est certain que le relâchement des règles encadrant l'aménagement du temps de travail et la multiplication des formes d'emplois ont considérablement accru les marges laissées aux entreprises pour adapter le mode de gestion de la main-d'œuvre aux caractéristiques économiques, technologiques et organisationnelles qui leur sont spécifiques. A l'ordre fordiste caractérisé par une « normativité formelle et substantielle » supposant l'existence ex ante d'un ensemble cohérent de règles applicables en toutes circonstances a donc succédé un modèle procédural de régulation caractérisé par l'adaptabilité des règles aux situations spécifiques (De Munck et Verhoeven, 1997). A travers l'extension d'une logique dérogatoire en matière de réglementation du travail et la priorité donnée à des mesures individuelles de réduction du temps de travail, l'action publique a privilégié la « souplesse contractuelle ». C'est en ce sens que l'on peut parler d'un processus de déréglementation et mettre en exergue la transformation du mode de régulation du marché du travail, que l'on observe dans plusieurs pays européens (Alaluf et Prieto, 2001) : on est ainsi passé d'un mode de régulation assurant aux salariés des protections de portée générale à un système de flexibilité négociée au sein des branches d'activité ou des entreprises.

Au niveau de l'entreprise, la panoplie des instruments de flexibilité s'est considérablement élargie. Aux modalités de la polyvalence et de la mobilité fonctionnelle préconisées dans les années 1970 par le courant psycho-sociologique de l'organisation du travail comme alternative au travail « taylorisé », se sont ajoutées d'autres modes de flexibilité moins répandues auparavant. Le travail à temps partiel est ainsi devenu le support principal de la flexibilité dans des secteurs tels que la grande distribution, la restauration ou le nettoyage de bureaux. En matière d'aménagement du temps de travail, les mécanismes de l'annualisation prolongent ou remplacent le recours classique aux heures supplémentaires et au chômage économique. Les possibilités d'appel-rejet de la main-d'œuvre se sont étendues à travers le recours à diverses modalités de contrats temporaires. La division fonctionnelle du travail s'étend, au-delà de l'entreprise, aux réseaux de sous-traitance et à des prestataires de services, en particulier à l'appel de travailleurs mis à disposition par les agences de travail intérimaire.

Tableau 1. Typologie de la flexibilité

	Quantitative	Qualitative
Flexibilité interne	Temporelle : aménagement du temps de travail, temps partiel, chômage économique, heures supplémentaires, ...	Fonctionnelle : polyvalence, mobilité fonctionnelle, ...
Flexibilité externe	Numérique : contrats à durée déterminée, durée des préavis, ...	Productive : sous-traitance, prestations de services, travail intérimaire (entreprise-réseau)

Au niveau du fonctionnement du marché du travail, le modèle des marchés transitionnels formalisé initialement par les travaux de Gunther Schmid (1995) tend à se substituer à celui d'une division ternaire du cycle de vie marquant des ruptures franches entre les phases d'éducation, de travail et de retraite. Les marchés transitoires abritent des situations très différenciées du point de vue des contrats de travail, de la durée des prestations de travail et des logiques qui président à leur classement. Il faut donc souligner la polysémie de la notion de transition, mais dans l'ensemble, celle-ci vise à désigner des catégories de travailleurs « employables », présents sur le marché du travail, bien que leur position les place aux marges des formes de l'emploi « standard ».

En tout état de cause, il convient d'insister plus particulièrement sur les effets de normalisation de l'emploi et de conditions de travail atypiques que véhiculent les modèles de marchés transitionnels. Au-delà de leur intérêt descriptif, ceux-ci relèvent d'une démarche prescriptive, dans la mesure où l'objectif est de fonder analytiquement des recommandations de politique de l'emploi (Michon, 2006). Ils sont mobilisés dans le cadre de la Stratégie européenne de l'emploi où ils s'accordent avec les orientations de la « flexicurité » visant, comme l'indique ce néologisme, à concilier flexibilité et sécurité. Les modèles de marchés transitionnels se proposent d'aménager les règles du marché du travail afin de sécuriser et de valoriser des positions transitoires définies comme « des périodes de vie au cours desquelles le temps de travail diverge de la norme » (Schmid, 1995). Les transitions se réfèrent dès lors à des situations intermédiaires entre l'emploi rémunéré à temps plein et des situations d'éducation/formation, de chômage, d'activités domestiques ou personnelles, de retraite. Il s'agit, selon Bernard Gazier (1998 : 339), d'un « aménagement systématique et négocié de l'ensemble des positions d'activité au sens large traditionnellement considérées aux « marges » de l'emploi et qui deviennent ici des transitions : période de formation ou de congé parental, mi-temps tout court ou combiné à un autre mi-temps, associatif par exemple, pré-retraite à temps partiel, etc. Ces périodes et ces occupations ont pour trait commun d'associer des activités jugées socialement utiles à une garantie temporaire de rémunération (...) et de constituer des passerelles vers d'autres positions sur le marché du travail. Il s'agit donc, par leur développement, de renouveler les bases de la sécurité économique des travailleurs, salariés ou non ».

Cependant, tout comme l'amélioration des protections sociales est subordonnée à l'impératif de la compétitivité, la valorisation des périodes de transition est subordonnée aux nécessités de la mobilité. Les marchés transitoires sont, en effet, perçus comme des « réserves-tampons » de main-d'œuvre qui auraient capacité à se dilater en période de récession et à se rétracter en période d'expansion. La perspective du retour au plein emploi, promue actuellement à travers les objectifs d'augmentation des taux d'emploi, est envisagée dans le cadre d'une réactualisation de la notion d'emploi normal. La mobilité de la main-d'œuvre est ainsi posée comme une condition majeure de l'efficacité productive. Celle-ci impose en particulier le renouvellement des compétences et la formation tout au long de la vie active. Il faudrait fluidifier le fonctionnement du marché du travail, en améliorant les garanties collectives, pour réduire les « résistances au changement », de manière à ce que les individus tirent avantage des « transitions ». Selon Bernard Gazier, une telle approche définit un modèle social-démocrate flexible, censé s'opposer au modèle social libéral.

III. L'AFFAIBLISSEMENT DES PROTECTIONS LIÉES AU CONTRAT DE TRAVAIL SALARIÉ

Le contrat de travail, en reconnaissant le caractère asymétrique de la relation salariale, fonde le programme de protection des salariés assigné au droit du travail. C'est en ce sens que la reconnaissance du lien de subordination par le droit est apparu comme une conquête sociale, dissipant ainsi l'illusion de contrats entre égaux. La stabilité de la relation salariale, la délimitation du temps de travail, l'identification et l'unicité de l'employeur en tant qu'interlocuteur patronal dans le champ de la négociation collective comptent parmi les spécifications les plus déterminantes du contrat de travail pour limiter l'arbitraire patronal et construire un rapport de force favorable aux salariés. A l'inverse, les tendances à la précarité de la relation d'emploi, à la perméabilité des frontières du temps de travail et à la dilution de la fonction d'employeur dans l'entreprise organisée en réseau, autant de traits qui caractérisent la norme flexible émergente, constituent des facteurs essentiels de l'affaiblissement des protections sociales associées au contrat de travail.

A. L'ENJEU DE LA RELATION D'EMPLOI

Il faut commencer par souligner l'importance que revêt aujourd'hui comme hier la stabilité de la relation d'emploi au sein de l'entreprise dans la formation d'un rapport de force favorable aux travailleurs pour négocier les salaires et les conditions de travail. En première analyse, la précarité de l'emploi est associée à des situations marquées par une discontinuité de la relation salariale (Cingolani, 2005). On se réfère alors au travail temporaire qui prend la forme de contrats à durée déterminée, du travail intérimaire, de stages divers ou d'emplois subsidiés temporairement. La multiplication de ces situations définit une catégorie hybride d'actifs, entre l'emploi et le chômage, qu'il convient de distinguer des « surnuméraires » du marché du travail, en situation de chômage récurrent, et des « stables » dont la position n'est pas pour autant assurée. Les contours de la précarité de l'emploi doivent cependant être questionnés. D'une part, il faut également prendre en compte le travail à temps partiel, qui concerne très majoritairement les femmes et plus encore lorsque la quotité de temps de travail est faible, en dessous du mi-temps. C'est bien de précarité qu'il s'agit même lorsque le temps partiel est associé à une certaine garantie d'emploi. Du point de vue de la durée effective de travail, le contrat à temps partiel et le contrat temporaire présentent des inconvénients à certains égards comparables en termes de rémunération et de protection sociale : à un temps de travail réduit correspond un salaire réduit. D'autre part, si les spécifications du contrat de travail définissent bien l'horizon temporel de l'emploi, elles ne garantissent pas pour autant la continuité de la relation, tout spécialement dans les entreprises en restructuration ou les branches d'activités où, moyennant des durées de préavis courtes, la main-d'œuvre est gérée à coups d'embauches et de licenciements en fonction des besoins de la production, comme par exemple dans le nettoyage industriel ou la sécurité privée.

D'une façon générale, les analyses de la segmentation du marché du travail ne conduisent pas à accréditer la thèse d'une dualisation de l'emploi qui cloisonnerait les « précaires » d'un côté et les « stables » de l'autre. De même que les pressions exercées sur les chômeurs, poussés à accepter les emplois disponibles quelles que soient leurs qualités par le biais des politiques d'activation, finissent par déstabiliser l'emploi, le développement d'un emploi précaire aux marges de l'entreprise pèse lourdement sur le pouvoir de négociation des composantes de l'emploi réputées stables (Alaluf et Martinez, 1999). C'est à présent la légitimité même de la revendication d'un emploi stable qui est remise en cause à travers l'orientation de la flexicurité qui sous-tend de façon plus ou moins explicite la Stratégie européenne de l'emploi. À certains égards, les modèles de marchés transitionnels et les stratégies de « flexicurité », s'inscrivent dans une même perspective du point de vue de la politique de l'emploi. Ces approches se présentent comme des formes de gestion sociale de la précarité, car elles laissent entendre qu'il convient de promouvoir la flexibilité de l'emploi non seulement pour les besoins de l'économie mais également dans l'intérêt des personnes qui seraient à la recherche de marges de liberté (Ramaux, 2000). La flexibilité et la mobilité étant considérées comme des préalables, il s'agirait par conséquent de reconstruire des garanties statutaires, au-delà de celles conférées par l'occupation d'un emploi stable, à temps plein, auprès d'un employeur unique et clairement identifiable, que ce soit à travers l'instauration d'un statut professionnel adossé à toutes les formes de travail (Supiot, 1999) ou à travers l'amélioration de la couverture sociale et la valorisation des phases de transition qui peuvent, par exemple, être mises à profit pour améliorer l'employabilité (Gazier, 1998). De fait, le principe de flexicurité est clairement orienté vers la flexibilité externe quantitative, c'est-à-dire l'ajustement du volume de l'emploi par l'extension des possibilités d'engager et de licencier. La sécurité d'emploi n'étant plus assurée par le contrat de travail, ce sont les institutions du marché du travail qui devraient veiller à l'employabilité des personnes et sécuriser les parcours professionnels à travers l'offre de formations et des mesures d'activation. Au fond, de même que les formes actuelles de l'organisation du travail, misant sur l'autonomie, le management par les objectifs et la satisfaction des clients, tendent à reporter sur les travailleurs la pression provenant des marchés, l'optique de la flexicurité tend à dédouaner l'entreprise en reportant sur l'action publique la charge d'assurer la sécurité de l'emploi (Keune & Jepsen, 2007).

B. TRAVAILLER SANS LIMITES

Dans les relations de travail, la référence au temps remplit une double fonction. Au plan collectif, elle permet de synchroniser le travail et donc de fixer des disciplines et des solidarités. Au plan individuel, elle constitue le moyen d'évaluer la prestation, autrement dit de mesurer le travail et, sur cette base, de fixer la rémunération du travailleur. Dans sa formulation juridique, elle permet de délimiter le temps de la subordination, de manière à « borner l'emprise patronale sur la vie du salarié » selon l'expression d'Alain Supiot (1995).

Dans la configuration émergente d'une norme d'emploi flexible, les rapports entre temps et salaires tendent à se polariser autour de deux solutions contrastées de rentabilisation du coût salarial, deux solutions qui s'écartent chacune à sa manière de la définition juridique du temps de travail.

Tableau 2. L'enjeu salarial

Temps de travail forfaitaire	Temps de travail effectif
Déconnexion du salaire et du temps pour maximiser le travail total fourni	Ajustement des heures de travail sur la demande pour maximiser l'effort productif
Figure du cadre « qui ne compte pas son temps »	Figure du travail peu qualifié, à temps partiel, ou du travail intérimaire

Source : librement adapté de Rubery et al., 2005.

La première solution consiste à déconnecter le salaire d'une mesure précise du temps de travail. Lorsque le travail n'est plus mesuré en temps mais soumis à des obligations de résultat, l'entreprise n'a plus à se soucier de cette ressource puisqu'elle ne lui est plus portée en compte. C'est alors une notion de « temps forfaitaire » qui tend à se diffuser, parmi les cadres tout d'abord, mais plus largement au sein d'un salariat intermédiaire répondant au management par les objectifs. Et également dans des formes particulières d'organisation du travail, comme dans le télétravail : la journée de télétravail est réputée avoir une durée forfaitaire correspondant à la norme en vigueur dans l'entreprise quelle que soit la durée réelle du travail. Dans tous ces cas, les dépassements de l'horaire de travail, à la différence de la prestation d'heures supplémentaires, ne sont jamais sanctionnées par le paiement d'un sursalaire.

A l'opposé de ce modèle, pour les catégories les plus vulnérables du salariat, soumises à des temps de travail réduits, dans le nettoyage, l'hôtellerie-restaurants, la grande distribution ou l'intérim, le temps de travail est strictement compté. C'est alors une notion de « travail effectif » qui paraît s'imposer : seules les heures effectivement travaillées sont payées. Or, dans la définition juridique du temps de travail, cette notion d'effectivité du travail, présente initialement dans la réglementation de 1921, avait été progressivement écartée (Jamoulle et al., 1997) : l'employeur paie le temps pendant lequel le salarié met ses capacités à la disposition de l'employeur, en ce compris les périodes où aucun travail effectif n'est réalisé. A cette forme d'intensification du travail s'ajoute une exigence de disponibilité au travail : ce n'est en effet généralement qu'à travers le dépassement des limites contractuelles, par le cumul d'emplois à temps partiel, la prestation d'heures complémentaires, la succession de missions d'intérim et l'acceptation d'horaires incommodes qu'*in fine* un salaire jugé acceptable peut être atteint.

Par conséquent, le relâchement de la réglementation du temps de travail autorise deux variantes de la maximisation de la plus-value, selon la terminologie marxienne, l'allongement de la journée de travail et l'intensification du travail. Dans les organisations flexibles, la coordination de l'activité repose ainsi sur la disponibilité temporelle des salariés. Le temps de travail réel déborde des limites formelles définies a priori par la réglementation. Si le temps de travail peut être considéré comme un produit échangé dans un marché régulé, la disponibilité de temps se présente comme un service rendu par le salarié, consistant à donner l'assurance que le travail sera accompli, le cas échéant en dehors des temps normaux de travail (Callejo, 2004).

C. UNE PLURALITÉ D'EMPLOYEURS

Pour l'entreprise convertie à la flexibilité, l'adoption de nouvelles structures organisationnelles est justifiée par la nécessité d'un recentrage sur le cœur de l'activité. La généralisation de la sous-traitance et l'extériorisation d'activités de plus en plus nombreuses, qui deviennent des « prestations de service », donne consistance au modèle de l'entreprise-réseau, un modèle d'entreprise où les différentes activités qui constituent la chaîne de valeur, autrefois regroupées au sein d'une même entité patrimoniale, sont désormais distribuées dans une multitude d'entreprises qui se présentent comme une nébuleuse de donneurs d'ordres, fournisseurs, sous-traitants, franchisés, prestataires de services, entreprises de travail intérimaire, ... Ce qui caractérise d'abord l'entreprise-réseau c'est précisément la disjonction croissante entre l'entreprise, définie au sens juridique, et l'espace organisationnel au sein duquel se côtoient des groupes de travailleurs aux statuts divers et inégaux.

Dans ce contexte, à côté des caractéristiques intrinsèques de l'emploi, le mode de représentation collective des salariés constitue un facteur déterminant de la qualité de l'emploi. Le cas du travail intérimaire est emblématique à cet égard. Dans ce cas, l'autorité patronale est transférée à l'entreprise-utilisatrice. Mais il faut bien constater que les intérimaires pâtissent d'un déficit de représentation sur les lieux de travail : d'une part, ils ne participent pas aux élections sociales bien qu'ils entrent en ligne de compte pour le calcul des mandats à pourvoir dans les organes légaux et, d'autre part, leur représentation auprès de la firme de travail intérimaire revêt un caractère purement théorique. A travers la généralisation de la sous-traitance, de plus en plus de salariés se trouvent dans une situation comparable, bien que l'entreprise-cliente ne détienne formellement aucune autorité sur les travailleurs de la sous-traitance. La gestion de la main-d'œuvre est déplacée vers des firmes extérieures qui sont tenues par des obligations de résultats, dans le cadre de contrats commerciaux. Dans cette configuration, le travail prend la forme d'un projet à réaliser dans des temps impartis à un coût fixé par le cahier des charges. Les rapports de force entre le client-donneur d'ordre et le prestataire de services ont alors des conséquences multiples sur les salaires et les conditions de travail des salariés. Face à une pluralité d'employeurs ou à tout le moins à une dilution de la fonction d'employeur, en tant qu'interlocuteur patronal, les marges de négociation des salaires et des conditions de travail se trouvent réduites dans la mesure précisément où les travailleurs de la sous-traitance sont insérés, *de facto*, à des degrés divers, dans des relations de travail triangulaires, faisant intervenir une entreprise tierce (donneur d'ordre, firme cliente ou utilisatrice, franchiseur) par dessus la relation contractuelle bilatérale classique qui unit le salarié à son employeur.

On voit que la précarité du travail ne provient pas uniquement des caractéristiques du contrat de travail, elle recouvre plus largement « des situations où les travailleurs qui participent à la production ne sont pas les salariés de l'entreprise, des situations où l'employeur *de jure* n'est pas l'unique prescripteur du travail » (Thébaut-Mony, 2001). En d'autres termes, les protections qu'apporte classiquement la représentation collective des travailleurs comme complément nécessaire à l'asymétrie de la relation salariale sont partiellement annihilées en raison du « droit d'ingérence » (Sobczak et al., 2008) sur les conditions de travail des salariés de la sous-traitance que s'octroie la firme-pivot à partir de la définition du cahier de charges et du contrat commercial.

IV. CONCLUSIONS

Les analyses juridiques et statistiques, ainsi que de nombreuses études empiriques convergent sur le constat d'une diversification des systèmes d'emploi et des modes d'organisation du travail. Les changements apportés dans ces domaines, depuis les années 1980, sont interprétés généralement en termes d'éclatement et de fragmentation du salariat. Le relâchement des réglementations du travail de portée générale au profit d'une flexibilité négociée dans les branches d'activité et les entreprises, une certaine décentralisation des relations professionnelles, la redistribution des activités qui constituent la chaîne de valeur des produits au sein de réseaux de sous-traitants et de prestataires de services, la multiplication des formes d'emploi et la diversification des temps de travail, ... sont autant d'évolutions observables qui accentuent considérablement les divisions au sein du monde du travail et qui mettent au défi les organisations syndicales dans leur capacité à reconstruire des solidarités.

Il convient cependant de relativiser le constat de l'épuisement de la norme sociale de l'emploi fordienne, car les changements de comportement des entreprises et les orientations actuelles de la politique de l'emploi ne suffisent pas à justifier que l'on élève au rang de norme sociale le principe de flexibilité. Il faut à tout le moins faire la part entre les discours managériaux et les pratiques sociales. Malgré des évolutions manifestes, des compromis sociaux continuent à se nouer dans les branches d'activité et les entreprises autour des caractéristiques de la norme fordienne en termes de garanties d'emploi, de progression salariale, de contrôle du temps de travail. D'autre part, précisément parce que les régimes flexibles sont diversifiés et inégaux, ceux-ci ne font pas nécessairement l'objet d'un consensus social qui conduirait à les légitimer.

Mais à l'encontre du diagnostic d'une individualisation croissante des relations de travail, il convient de mettre en évidence des facteurs de convergence. Tout d'abord, en dépit de la diversité des statuts, des contrats et des temps de travail, l'emploi continue à se développer avec un dénominateur commun, dans le cadre institué de la relation salariale. Au fond, la condition salariale se diversifie au fur et à mesure que de nouvelles activités et de nouvelles couches de la population intègrent le cadre de l'emploi régulé par le droit du travail et en particulier par les conventions collectives de travail. Les dynamiques du syndicalisme et des relations professionnelles revêtent dès lors une importance toute particulière, quand elles conduisent à intégrer dans les organes de concertation les travailleurs intérimaires, les emplois de service ou les travailleurs des secteurs non marchands qui pouvaient précédemment en être exclus. Ensuite, dans le prolongement des analyses de la segmentation du marché du travail, des études récentes mettent en évidence un phénomène de polarisation des régimes de travail autour de l'affirmation de deux normes flexibles idealtypiques que presque tout sépare (Bouffartigue & Bouteiller, 2003 ; Rubery et al, 2005; Martinez, 2010) : une norme flexible « autonome » qui prend comme figure emblématique celle du « cadre » disposant d'une stabilité d'emploi relative et d'un certain autocontrôle sur son temps de travail et ses tâches et une norme flexible « hétéronome », correspondant au travail salarié intermittent, intérimaire ou à temps partiel subi, dont les conditions d'emploi et de travail demeurent contestées tant par les syndicats que par les salariés concernés.

BIBLIOGRAPHIE

Alaluf M. & Martinez E. (1999), « Bélgica: el empleo desestabilizado por el desempleo. Empleo precario y desempleo activo », in Prieto C., *La crisis del empleo en Europa*, Germania, Alzira, 37-63.

Alaluf M. & Prieto C. (2001), *Collective bargaining and the social construction of employement*, Brussels, ETUI.

Bouffartigue P. & Bouteiller J. (2003), « A propos des normes du temps de travail. De l'érosion de la norme fordienne aux normes émergentes », *Revue de l'IRES*, 42.

Callejo J. (2004), « Disponibilidad temporal corporativa y género: aproximaciones empiricas », *Anduli*, 4.

Cingolani P. (2005), *La précarité*, Paris, PUF, Que sais-je ?

De Munck & Verhoeven (ed.) (1997), *Les mutations du rapport à la norme. Un changement dans la modernité ?*, Paris/Bruxelles, De Boeck Université.

De Terssac G. & Tremblay D. G. (dir.), *Où va le temps de travail ?*, Toulouse, Octarès.

Gazier B. (1998), « Ce que sont les marchés transitionnels », *Cahiers du Centre d'Etudes de l'Emploi*, 37.

Jamoulle M. et al. (1977), *Le temps de travail*, Bruxelles, CRISP.

Keune M. & Jepsen M., « Not balanced and hardly new : the European Commission's quest for flexicurity », in Jørgensen H. & Madsen P.K. (eds), *Flexicurity and Beyond*, Copenhagen, DJØF Publishing, 2007.

Thébaud-Mony A. (2001), « L'impact de la précarité et de la flexibilité sur la santé des travailleurs », *BTS Newsletter*, 15-16.

Linhart D. & Moutet A. (dir.) (2005), *Le travail nous est compté. La construction des normes temporelles de travail*, Paris, La Découverte.

Martinez E. (2010), *Les salariés à l'épreuve de la flexibilité*, Bruxelles, Editions de l'Université de Bruxelles.

Michon F. (2005), « Cinquante ans de socio-économie du travail en France », in Sylin M. (éd.), *Cinquante ans d'évolution du travail. De la semaine de 5 jours á la Directive Bolkestein*, Bruxelles, Institut des sciences du travail, ULB, 65-97.

Mückenberger U. (1989), « Non-Standard Forms of Work and the Role of Changes in Labour and Social Security Regulation », *International Journal of Sociology of Law*, 17.

Prieto C. (1999), *La crisis del empleo en Europa*, Germania, Alzira.

Ramaux Ch. (2000), « L'instabilité de l'emploi est-elle une fatalité ? », *Droit social*, 1.

Rubery J., Ward K., Grimshaw D. et Beynon H. (2005), « Working Time, Industrial Relations and the Employment Relationship », *Time and Society*, 15, 1.

Schmid G. (1995), « Le plein emploi est-il encore possible ? Les marchés du travail « transitoires » en tant que nouvelle stratégie dans les politiques d'emploi », *Travail et Emploi*, 65.

Sobczak A., Rorive B., Havard C. (2008), « Comment réguler les relations triangulaires de travail ? La RSE face au droit dans le travail intérimaire et les centres d'appels », *Travail et Emploi*, 111.

Supiot A. (1995), « Temps de travail : pour une concordance des temps », *Droit social*, 12.

Supiot A. (1999), *Au-delà de l'emploi. Transformations du travail et devenir du droit du travail en Europe*, Paris, Flammarion.

LABOUR LAW AND COMPETITION

Wolfgang DÄUBLER*

I. INTRODUCTION

I would like to thank the editors of this volume for choosing a subject that goes beyond the traditional frontiers of labour law. This way, we return to the old insight that a field of law cannot be analysed without considering the underlying social reality. If we would limit ourselves to strict interpretations of the law we would risk cultivating a garden without paying attention to the quality of the soil, the sunshine or the floods of rain that will come in the near future.

My specific topic deals with the coexistence of social values and competition. Both seem to be in contradiction; their coexistence might endanger the homogeneity of the existing legal order. We shall see whether this contradiction really exists and if so, whether or not it can be overcome.

II. COMPETITION

The principle of competition is based on specific value assessments. On the market, the individual follows exclusively his own interest. In order to be successful, he has to be better than his competitors. Being "better" can mean that the individual is able to realise innovative ideas, offer new products. In most cases, it means increasing the quality of existing products or lowering prices or both.

Competition forces an entrepreneur to reduce costs. This can be achieved through better organisation, lower purchase prices of raw materials but also through reducing wages. Especially in the services sector, lower wages are the main instrument of acquiring a better position on the market. Innovation plays more or less a secondary role.

However, market behaviour is not completely free, certain rules have to be observed by everybody, especially the very detailed principles of fair competition

* University of Bremen, Germany.

in all industrialised countries. In many cases, antitrust laws are applicable too. These prohibit certain forms of cooperation with other enterprises, especially agreements about prices and quantities of sale. A merger between big undertakings needs to be approved by the antitrust authority; the legislator wants to prevent the establishment of a dominant position on the market which would be dangerous to competition.

Competition is thought of as a mobiliser of energies and creativity. It seems to be the productive alternative to bureaucratic decision making which was characteristic of the Soviet Union and the States of Eastern Europe before 1990. The fact that they were obviously economically weaker made the general evaluation even more convincing: competition leads to better results for everyone. The invisible hand guides us to success. The problem of different starting points in Eastern Europe played no role whatsoever.

Competition does not only exist on the market of goods and services. One can find competition on the labour market too – if two or three persons apply for a vacant post or if a promotion to a better position is only possible for one person among ten people, their relationship will become competitive. Competition also affects private life – who has the bigger car? Who was mentioned in the newspaper? Who travelled around the world in a luxury boat? This is not the moment to criticise these phenomena – we just have to look at the facts.

III. LABOUR LAW

The value assessments on which labour law is based are quite different because they concern the protection of workers – health and safety, respect of privacy, minimum income, prohibition of discrimination, right to organise. The core labour standards defined by the ILO are well-known but only describe a kind of minimum. Regarding labour law as a whole, you may call its main values "decent work" and "decent wages", both of which enable workers to have a decent life. Collective labour law gives individuals the right to "cooperate" with other workers, build unions or other organisations in order to improve working and living conditions. Collective labour law gives workers the right to take charge of their own fate.

Cooperation fits in with the solidarity principle which goes beyond the immediate common interests of people working together. You can support workers in another part of the economy or in another country by way of a solidarity strike. You can even boycott the sale of commodities produced by child labour in a country far away from Europe – in order to improve the situation of those exploited labourers. The core principle, however, is the cooperation as such – leading to collective negotiations dealing with wages and working conditions in an enterprise or in a part of the economy; as a result of these negotiations, collective agreements come about. This action does not need a spirit of solidarity – it is based on the direct interests of the individuals involved, it is the only way to improve their situation.

These solidarity values of labour law are contrary to the individualistic values of competition. For instance, the compulsory protection of health and safety established by law takes an important element out of competition: no undertaking can obtain economic advantages by giving less protection to its workers in this field. The same goes for minimum wages. The contradiction is most obvious when it comes to collective bargaining and collective action. People coming together in a union or another form of organisation do no longer compete. Some economists would call their organisations "cartels" acting on the labour market.

But the principles of cooperation and solidarity do not comprise the entire labour market: only certain conditions are fixed, the market as such remains open and still contains – as the examples of recruitment and promotion have shown – important elements of competition. If you are looking for a different model in the Western world you have to go back to the journeymen living and working in Europe between the 14th and the 18th century, who are called "Handwerksgesellen" in German: their movement was often able to dominate an entire regional market. A craftsman (who was a kind of employer in the modern sense) was "discredited" and no journeyman could work for him (without being discredited, too) if he did not accept certain conditions established by the journeymen's organisation.[1] The craftsmen of an entire city were boycotted once because they did not accept the conditions – this was an extreme case of a regulated labour market, which cannot be a model for today but which shows us that the actual forms of cooperation have a relatively limited effect.

IV. CONFLICT OR COEXISTENCE?

A. THE U.S. EXPERIENCE

In the United States, the principle of competition has always played a dominant role. In the famous *Lochner* case, the US Supreme Court held that the "liberty of contract" was implicit in the "Due Process Clause" of the 14th Amendment and decided that a New York law limiting the working time of bakers to 10 hours a day and 60 hours a week was in contradiction with this principle. It was called an "unreasonable, unnecessary and arbitrary interference with the right and liberty

1 See Däubler, in: Däubler (ed.), *Arbeitskampfrecht*, 3rd ed., Baden-Baden 2011, § 1 Rn 6, 7 including further references.

of the individual to contract."[2] But that was not the only ruling. The principle of competition was recognised by the Sherman Act of 1890. In "Danbury Hatters" the Supreme Court decided that the antitrust laws applied to labour.[3] The Clayton Antitrust Act of 1914 tried to exclude unions from the scope of competition law, but in "Duplex" the Supreme Court[4] found a way to circumvent this decision of the legislator.[5] Unions had to overcome big difficulties before collective bargaining was no longer considered to be a restraint of trade. The Wagner Act of 1935 brought a kind of breakthrough; without the election of new judges to the Supreme Court this would probably not have been possible. The freedom of association is still limited by the majority rule: the minority has no right to form its own organisation. This is no direct consequence of the principle of competition, but it may be considered as a way of limiting the influence of collective power.

B. THE GERMAN EXPERIENCE

In Germany, the development was quite different. During the 19th century and the first half of the 20th century there was no legal rule establishing and guaranteeing free competition on the market. Of course, a right to free enterprise has existed in § 1 of the "Gewerbeordnung" since 1869, but restrictions on trade were not prohibited. One enterprise could conclude contracts with another one and fix common prices or share the market by fixing certain "quota". The German Supreme Court (Reichsgericht) acknowledged such agreements as an emanation of the freedom of contract.[6] Unionisation and collective bargaining could not be restricted by referring to antitrust laws – the German legislator and the courts used police law in a broad sense to fight against the developing labour movement.[7] It was no less difficult to overcome these obstacles than in other countries where the principle of competition played a central role. However, antitrust laws were only implemented after the Second World War in Germany, i.e. during a time when collective bargaining was already well-established.

C. COEXISTENCE AFTER THE SECOND WORLD WAR IN WESTERN EUROPE

After the Second World War, there was a kind of stable coexistence between competition and labour law. Social protection and collective bargaining were

2 198 U.S. 45 (1905).
3 208 U.S. 274 (1908).
4 254 U.S. 443 (1921).
5 For details S. Gould, *A Primer on American Labor Law*, 3rd ed., 1993, Chapter 2.
6 RGZ 38, 155 – *Sächsisches Holzstoffkartell.*
7 Details at Däubler (note 1) §§ 2 and 3.

recognised in all Western European countries (except for Spain and Portugal); they were a kind of dominant framework that limited competition within the labour market. Of course, the scope of collective agreements could rarely cover 100 per cent of the workers, but competition in relation to wages and working conditions is very limited if 90 per cent of all workers are protected by collective agreements: the legal possibility of the remaining 10 per cent to make their own kind of contracts (at a lower level than the collective agreement) could normally not be used. Especially qualified workers would join the union or even leave the enterprise in order to get the "normal" conditions enjoyed by the 90 per cent. Another important element was that all employees were covered by social insurance in case of accident, illness, invalidity, old age and unemployment; only very few people, especially self-employed persons, were not covered.

The market of goods and services was not completely based on the principle of competition. Especially basic needs like water and energy supply, public transport, radio and television, health services and education were offered to all individuals by the State. This kind of welfare state seemed to be superior to the Eastern models of a socialist economy which offered the same but often at a lower quality and which could not develop all the innovations one could find in Western enterprises.

Sometimes problems of delimitation arose. Are public authorities entitled to run a business which could yield a certain profit? In some countries the law explicitly permitted it. In France, state-owned enterprises played an important role in the modernisation of the economy.[8] In Germany, the prevailing opinion was that there are strict limits to public profit-making.[9] On the other hand, there was a problem regarding how far collective bargaining can go. Is it possible to conclude a collective agreement about the opening hours of all supermarkets in a certain region? Would that not be a market rule which has nothing to do with the protection of workers? The German Federal Labour Court decided in a way that seemed acceptable to both sides: it is possible to fix the end of the working time at 6 p.m. even if the supermarkets could not continue and had to be closed at 6 for lack of personnel.[10] In Italy, investment decisions were regulated by collective agreements: Fiat had to invest in Southern Italy and had to build specific cars that were useful to the majority of the population.[11] This signalled a big change – labour law institutions penetrating the essence of the economy. The reality,

---

8 Wagenknecht, *Freiheit statt Kapitalismus*, 3rd ed. 2011, p. 279 ff.

9 Siedentopf, *Grenzen und Bindungen der Kommunalwirtschaft*, 1963.

10 BAG (=Federal Labour Court) 31 August 1982 – 1 ABR 27/80 – AP No. 8 zu § 87 BetrVG 1972 Arbeitszeit = RdA 1983, 189.

11 Details in Runggaldier, *Kollektivvertragliche Mitbestimmung bei Arbeitsorganisation und Rationalisierung*, 1983.

however, did not tally with the collective agreements. Today those rules seem to come from an ancient past, certain people in Italy would say: from a paradise lost.

To end this chapter, let me give an example of the peaceful coexistence between competition and labour law. If an enterprise does not observe a binding collective agreement, it may be able to pay lower wages and therefore offer lower prices to its customers. But is this not an unfair advantage based on illegal behaviour? In Germany, there have been a lot of court decisions asserting that it is a real case of unfair competition.[12] Another enterprise that faithfully applies the collective agreement could sue its competitor for damages and force it to end this behaviour. The same right is given to consumers' associations. Trade unions could act in the same way as they have the right to register themselves as consumers' associations. In practice, they do not use this possibility as it is out of their comfort zone.

V. THE GROWING IMPORTANCE OF THE PRINCIPLE OF COMPETITION

Since the beginning of the 1980s, the situation has been changing. Many public services were privatised, a strategy which was intensified after 1990. Would a privately run company not be much more effective than the state with its civil servants who never take any initiative? The presumption was quite polemic but it was nevertheless accepted by a big part of the population. Decades of privatisation created the prevailing opinion in European societies that private enterprises are more efficient. The markets were increasingly organised according to the competition model – a tendency which was much supported by the emerging globalisation. The nation states did not organise resistance against the world-wide free market. This was an understandable attitude in the case of exporting nations like Germany or in the case of the U.S., but in case of other countries it was difficult to understand since they lost a lot of their (economic) sovereignty. It became more and more difficult to tax enterprises because they would have a disadvantage in terms of international competition and perhaps leave the country to go to another one with more benevolence towards their interests.

If the markets of goods and services are completely organised according to the competition model, collective bargaining becomes, to a certain degree, a disturbing factor in the economy. Since 1990, the trade union movement has been losing strength in most European countries. The number of unionised people has been decreasing – to a different extent across the European nations (and the U.S.),

[12] BGH NJW 1988, 2471, 2473; BGH AuR 1993, 377; OLG Hamburg NJW 1987, 1651; OLG Köln GRUR 1991, 59; see also Kocher GRUR 2005, 647 ff.; Zwanziger DB 2005, 2318; Däubler, *Arbeitsrecht 1*, 16th ed., 2006, Rn 441 ff.

but the decrease as such is universal except for in Belgium and the Scandinavian states. To give just one example: The Unions of the German Confederation of Labour had 11.3 million members in 1993, as opposed to only 6.2 million now.[13] At the same time the coverage rate of collective agreements went down – from 90 per cent to less than 60 per cent in Germany. The level of protection provided by the agreements decreased, too. In some sectors, a full-time job covered by a collective agreement is paid so poorly that the people involved have to get supplementary social aid in order to reach at least the (modest) minimum living standard guaranteed by law for everybody. Collective agreements of this kind, recognising the "working poor" as a group and legitimatising their status, make the union still less attractive and prevent people from joining. Less members equals less successful bargaining – a race to the bottom. It will be difficult, but not impossible to stop this downward. It will require intelligent offers from the unions to new groups of workers like IT specialists and other white-collar workers and – if possible – new forms of action.[14]

VI. ATTACKS ON LABOUR LAW

The high status of competition values is supported by the neo-liberal ideology. The coexistence between competition on one side and labour law, i.e. social protection and collective bargaining, on the other side becomes more and more precarious. Why not banish labour law to an island for it does not fit into "modern times"?

Neo-liberals seem to be developing a strategy. First point: the attack on collective bargaining is easier accomplished than the attack on social protection, especially when it comes to rules concerning health and safety. Second point: it is more comfortable to use the legal framework of the European Union instead of national law. EU law is based on fundamental economic freedoms – right of establishment, right to provide services, free movement of goods, free movement of capital, free movement of workers – which are all comprehensively protected. Originally these were pure prohibitions of discrimination, now they are entrepreneurial freedoms, restrictions of which have to be justified.[15] Even if domestic and foreign companies are affected in the same way, this is contrary to the fundamental freedom in question. Furthermore, the freedom of establishment not only prohibits measures which make it impossible to start a business, or substantially impede

13 Http://de.statista.com/statistik/daten/studie/5837/umfrage/mitgliederzahlen-der-gewerkschaften/.

14 For new forms of collective actions see Renneberg, *Die Arbeitskämpfe von morgen? Arbeitsbedingungen und Konflikte im Dienstleistungsbereich*, 2005; Däubler (*supra* note 1) §§ 27–31.

15 See ECJ 30 November 1995 – C-55/94 – ECR 1995, I-4165.

establishment, it is sufficient if establishment is made "less advantageous".[16] Specific justification is required to promote or defend social values. They are no longer an ordinary part of the established order but an exception to the rule. In a way, they are pushed into in a secondary position. This corresponds to the wording of the Treaties which have developed the market rules much more than social values. This is an important difference in comparison to most national constitutions.

In 1999, the European Court of Justice still refused to apply competition rules to the labour market. In the Albany case it accepted that the social partners were entitled to determine the enterprise offering and organising an additional pension scheme.[17] The wording was clear:

> "It is beyond question that certain restrictions of competition are inherent in collective agreements between organizations representing employers and workers. However, the social policy objectives pursued by such agreements would be seriously undermined if management and labour were subject to Art. 81 par. 1 of the Treaty when seeking jointly to adopt measures to improve conditions of work and employment."[18]

This leads to the following conclusion in par. 60:

> "It therefore follows from an interpretation of the provisions of the Treaty as a whole, which is both effective and consistent, that agreements concluded in the context of collective negotiations between management and labour in pursuit of such objectives must, by virtue of their nature and purpose, be regarded as falling outside the scope of Art. 81 par. 1 of the Treaty."

In 2007, the court applied in *Viking*[19] and *Laval*[20] the fundamental economic freedoms of the Treaty to collective bargaining and strike. It found that this was no contradiction to its decision in the Albany case using arguments that were not very convincing – to put it politely.[21] If the exercise of a fundamental economic freedom becomes less attractive because of a collective agreement or a strike the union and the workers need special justification. If the workers defend their own workplaces their action will probably be considered to be legal, but a solidarity action like in the ITF cases would probably not be permitted. Collective

16 ECJ 3 October 2000 – C-58/98 – ECR 2000, I-7919 – *Corsten* par. 33.
17 ECJ 21 September 1999 – C-67/96 – DB 2000, 826 – *Albany.*
18 ECJ op. cit. par. 59.
19 ECJ 11 December 2007 – C-438/05 – NZA 2008, 124.
20 ECJ 18 December 2007 – C-341/05 – NZA 2008, 159.
21 See A.C.L. Davies, *Industrial Law Journal* 37(2008) 126, 134; Däubler AuR 2008, 409, English translation in: Ver.di (ed.), *ITF campaigns against flags of convenience vessels – inconsistent with EC law?*, Berlin 2009.

bargaining has an open flank now. Its importance is not yet clearly defined but the discussion has some similarity with the situation in the US before the Wagner Act.

VII. COUNTERATTACKS?

On the legal level, changes have occurred with the Lisbon Treaty: the EU Charter of Fundamental Rights has become an official part of primary union law. In Article 28, the Charter guarantees collective bargaining and "collective actions". These principles are now on the same level as the fundamental economic freedoms, which should lead to a "balancing" in a case of conflict. There is no longer a relationship between rule and exception. Nobody knows, however, whether the case law of the European Court of Justice will actually put collective bargaining and collective actions on the same level as the economic freedoms.

In Article 52 § 3 the Charter refers to the European Convention on Human Rights:

> "In so far as this Charter contains rights which correspond to rights guaranteed by the Convention for the Protection of Human Rights and Fundamental Freedoms the meaning and scope of those rights shall be the same as those laid down by the said Convention. This provision shall not prevent Union law providing more extensive protection."

In this way, the rules of the ECHR become a kind of minimum standard for the EU. This is of special importance as to the case law of the European Court of Human Rights concerning trade union activities laid down in Article 11 of the Convention. In *Demir* and *Baykara*[22] and in *Enerji Yapi-Yol Sen*[23] the European Court of Strasbourg recognised collective agreements and the right to strike as an inherent element of the fundamental right guaranteed by Article 11. For this court, each kind of restriction needs a justification – the relationship of rule and exception is reversed. Filip Dorssemont and Giovanni Orlandini will deal with this subject in a more profound manner in their contribution.

On the political level, many individuals and some organisations have recognised that the free competition fostered by neo-liberalism has brought a lot of harm to the European peoples. Inequality in income and fortune has increased in an unprecedented way. Even in rich countries like Britain and Germany poverty has reappeared; you can now once again find people who queue up to get a hot meal once a day.

---

[22] ECHR 12 November 2008 – 34503/97 – AuR 2009, 269 ff.

[23] ECHR 21 April 2009 – 68959/01 – AuR 2009, 274 ff.

Despite all fine declarations, the competition as such is falsified. In many cases the winner will not be the better but the established one. This is obvious in many sectors including the financial industry. If there is no real competition, there will be no innovation. That might explain why the growth of European economies has been rather modest during the last ten years.[24]

Furthermore, increasing inequality creates a lot of additional problems. Wilkinson and Pickett have compared the situation in rich states like the U.S., Canada, Western Europe, Japan and the Scandinavian states by putting the accent on the degree of inequality.[25] The results of a lot of empirical studies they quote were quite convincing: the higher the degree of inequality the higher the crime rate, the number of unhappy individuals, the percentage of ill persons. Life expectancy was the highest in countries like Sweden where there is less inequality. Wilkinson and Pickett have also compared different federal states within the U.S. and have come to the same result: the quality of life is worse in those states where inequality is highest.

During the financial crisis, market forces have created a catastrophic situation. Unlike in China, there was no regulation framework limiting the hunt for profits. The mechanisms to fight against the current debt crisis make the nation states and the European Union even weaker, depriving them of the means they need to re-establish a modernised welfare state.

But the crisis also creates opportunities. The neo-liberal idea has suffered a big defeat. This fact should be mentioned more and more and it should be treated as self-evident by the public opinion. To admit the fact that the neo-liberal idea has taken a beating would clear the way for a free discussion about alternatives regarding the current market economy. The experiences of the last years can be used as an important argument in developing new forms of social solidarity and in revitalising collective bargaining. Labour lawyers should sometimes look beyond their traditional domain of expertise and deal with the structures and the decision makers outside of the labour market. There is no reason to remain among those who do nothing but fight the worst evils market forces have produced. Let us go to the roots of injustice. More equality guarantees a better life for everybody.

---

24 See Stiglitz, *The Price of Inequality: How Today's Divided Society Endangers Our Future*, 2012, Chapter 3.

25 Wilkinson and Pickett, *The Spirit Level. Why More Equal Societies Almost Always Do Better*, London 2009; German translation under the title: *Gleichheit ist Glück. Warum gerechte Gesellschaften für alle besser sind*, 3rd ed., Berlin 2010.

MARKET RULES AND THE RIGHT TO STRIKE: A DIFFERENT APPROACH

Giovanni ORLANDINI* and Filip DORSSEMONT**

INTRODUCTION

It is widely agreed that the *Viking* and *Laval* judgements[1] represent a watershed in the process of European integration, as with these two cases the Court of Justice of the European Union (CJEU) provoked a sort of neo-liberal change in its case law favouring economic freedoms over social objectives. At the same time Viking and Laval are the outcome of decades of case law interpreting the free movement provisions in order to provide them with the highest degree of effectiveness. Accordingly, these two cases have deep roots and cannot be considered an absolute innovation in the case law of the CJEU. They rather function as a kind of "clarification" of the principles of European Union (EU) law on economic freedom, on the basis of the new problems emerging from the process of integration: the originality of *Viking* and *Laval* lies in the application of settled principles to new situations.

It is appropriate to investigate whether it is possible for the CJEU to revise Viking and Laval without contradicting its previous case law on economic freedoms. If this is not the case, only a reform of EU primary or secondary legislation could justify a new relationship between market rules and social norms within the EU legal order, more respectful of social prerogatives.

The numerous authors who commented critically on the "Laval Quartet" provided different answers to this question. Among these authors there is widespread support for the need to identify a different balance between the right to strike and economic freedoms, capable of preserving the equilibriums of domestic industrial

---

* University of Siena, Italy (Orlandini is the author of Chapter I).
** Université Catholique de Louvain, Centre interdisciplinaire de Droit, Entreprise et Société, Belgium (Dorssemont is the author of Chapters II and III. The introduction and conclusions have been written by both authors).
1 Case C-438/05 *ITF v. Viking Line Abp* [2007] ECR I-10779; case C-341/05 *Laval v. Svenska Byggnadsarbetareforbundet* [2007] ECR I-11767.

relations. Less attention, however, has been given to the issue of the so-called horizontal direct effect of Treaty provisions protecting economic freedoms: an issue that is the logical premise of the balancing judgement between economic freedoms and social rights. A *revirement* of the CJEU on this point would lead to the negation of the possibility of applying the rules of the internal market to industrial actions of the kind dealt with in the Viking and Laval cases, and such a change would exclude *tout court* the necessity of a balancing judgement between trade union rights and economic freedoms. On the contrary, once the CJEU considers the rules of the internal market applicable to industrial action, it becomes extremely difficult to imagine a relationship between trade union rights and economic freedoms that does not involve to a certain extent the erosion of such rights as recognised and regulated in domestic legal systems; unless we envisage a balancing judgement where the right to strike (as regulated by domestic legal systems) always prevails over internal market rules.

In our opinion, the argument used by the CJEU to deal with the issue of horizontal direct effect is the weakest part of the judgements, if read in the light of the previous case law of the Court. In fact, we believe that it would be possible to solve the problem of applicability of the common market rules to "private" relationships differently so as to avoid the balancing judgement between the right to strike and economic freedoms.

The question to what extent a case could be built for a judicial overruling of the infamous *Viking* and *Laval* judgements will be assessed in a first part. This solution does not require a modification, neither of EU primary law nor of EU secondary law. It could be qualified as a *de iure condito solution*. It only presupposes that a domestic judge would submit preliminary questions to the CJEU and leave it to the wisdom of the Court to overrule its previous case law.

Another option might be a modification of secondary EU Law *(de iure condendo)*. This option has nearly been lifted, as is evidenced by the communication of the so-called Monti II proposal, which was withdrawn by the Commission as a response to the "yellow card" procedure. This proposal was drafted by the European Commission with the intention to respond to a sense of unease which was generated by the Laval judgement and its interpretation of the Posting of workers Directive. Unexpected political and intellectual leaders have in fact paid lip service to this unease deeply rooted within the trade union movement. On 15 September 2009, Barroso, for instance, held a memorable speech at the EP during his campaign to be re-elected, stating:

> "I have clearly stated my attachment to the respect of fundamental social rights and to the principle of free movement of workers. The interpretation and the implementation of the *posted workers Directive* falls short in both respects. That is

> why I commit to propose as soon as possible a Regulation to resolve the problems that have arisen".

At the request of Barroso, Professor Mario Monti wrote a report regarding "A new Strategy for the Single Market".[2] The former Commissioner also referred to the necessity to adopt secondary EU legislation. Contrary to Barroso, he explicitly referred to the case law of the CJEU.

> "Between 2007 and 2008 the European Court of Justice decisions in the Viking, Laval, Rüffert and Commission vs Luxembourg cases revived an old split that had never been healed: the divide between advocates of greater market integration and those who feel that the call for economic freedoms and for breaking up regulatory barriers is code for dismantling social rights protected at national level. The revival of this divide has the potential to alienate from the Single Market and the EU a segment of public opinion, workers' movements and trade unions, which has been over time a key supporter of economic integration".

The proposal on the exercise of the right to take collective action in the context of the freedom of establishment and the freedom of expression will be studied underneath.[3]

This failed legislative solution will be studied in the second part.

Last but not least, there is a more structural solution which could be envisaged, *id est* a constitutional solution. In this respect, the question arises whether the Lisbon Treaty, which entered into force after the two judgements, provides some scope for a judicial overruling. Furthermore, the question arises how a modification of primary EU law should be drafted in order to overcome *Viking* and *Laval.*

---

2 Http://ec.europa.eu/bepa/pdf/monti_report_final_10_05_2010_en.pdf.

3 COM 2012 (130) final. For comments, see inter alia: G. Orlandini, "The Monti II proposal for the regulation and the right to strike in post-Lisbon Europe", *European Journal of Social Law*, 4, 2012, 228 ff.
K. Ewing, "Draft Monti II Regulation: An Inadequate Response to *Viking* and *Laval*" (www.lcdtu.org/eu-employment-rights-professor-keith-ewing-on-monti-11%E2%80%B3/); Niklas Bruun, Andreas Bücker, Filip Dorssemont, "Balancing Fundamental Social Rights and Economic Freedoms: Can the Monti II Initiative Solve the EU Dilemma?", *IJCLLIR*, Issue 3, pp. 279–306; M. Rocca, "The proposal for a (so-called) Monti II Regulation on the exercise of the right to take collective action within the context of the freedom of establishment and the freedom to provide services", *European Labour Law Journal*, 2012.

I. A JUDICIAL REAPPRAISAL OF MARKET RULES AND THE RIGHT TO STRIKE

A. REFORMULATING THE ISSUE OF HORIZONTAL EFFECT

For Alan Dashwood the issue of the so-called horizontal direct effect (HDE) concerns "*the possibility for an individual to enforce a right arising under a Community provision against another individual on whom a correlative duty has been imposed*".[4] It is well known that this is one of the most controversial questions of EU substantive law of the internal market. This is why it is surprising that in the Viking and Laval cases the CJEU decided to deal with it in a confused way and proposed an argument that does not include adequate motivation. The CJEU inferred the possibility of enforcing the right of the company against the trade unions involved in the collective dispute from its previous case law on non-governmental regulatory bodies. It is obvious, however, that the cases mentioned by the CJEU to support its argument relate to situations rather different from the ones dealt with in the Viking and Laval cases, both in terms of the type of bodies involved (trade unions and not "merely" professional associations) and the type of act adopted (collective source of regulation and not collective direct actions).

The reasoning of the Court is based on two closely related analogies: (1) collective action aimed at the conclusion of a collective agreement is equivalent to a collective agreement restricting the exercise of economic freedom, that is to say that collective action has the same restrictive effects on the internal market;[5] (2) industrial actions and collective bargaining can be considered equal to the exercise of public authority if exercised by actors empowered by the State to have an impact on the dynamics of the internal market (that is, if industrial actions are carried out in accordance with domestic law).[6]

The common element of the two analogies is the Court's consideration of the effects of the industrial action on the dynamics of the internal market, as Harm

---

[4] A. Dashwood, "*Viking* and *Laval*: Issue of Horizontal Direct Effect", (2008) 10 *Cambridge Yearbook of European Legal Studies* 525–526.

[5] As is well-known, thanks to the evolution of the case law of the CJEU, not only discriminatory measures but also all measures preventing or substantially hindering market access can limit economic freedoms protected by EU internal market law (for all, see C. Barnard, *The Substantive Law of the EU – The Four Freedoms* (OUP, 2010)).

[6] *Viking*, para 34–37 and 60–62; in *Laval*, para 98, the CJEU merely states that "*The abolition, as between Member States, of obstacles to the freedom to provide services would be compromised if the abolition of State barriers could be neutralized by obstacles resulting from the exercise of their legal autonomy by associations or organizations not governed by public law*", referring to previous case law on non-governmental bodies.

Schepel clearly showed.[7] In other words, the Court maintains that in terms of EU law it is irrelevant that the action is taken by a private actor if the action produces an effect on the internal market comparable to the effect that would be brought about by the action of a public actor.[8]

Following the approach suggested by the Court, the question of the applicability of the free movement rules to the acts of private individuals can therefore be divided into two parts: the assessment of the existence of a restriction to free movement (namely, a restriction to an economic freedom) and the attribution of liability (namely the identification of the person who is responsible for the violation of EU law).[9] This person could be the State or the private person or body. The issue of horizontal direct effect strictly concerns only the second part of the assessment, namely the identification of the responsible party. The application of the rules of the internal market to a private act depends on its classification as an obstacle to free movement, that is on its equivalence with measures adopted by public authorities in terms of the effects produced on the internal market.

According to Prechal and de Vries, the CJEU's statements concerning the right to strike in relation with the principles of the internal market is not surprising: considering the broad definition of "obstacle" adopted in its previous case law it was inevitable to consider a strike as a barrier to free movement.[10] In our opinion, however, the definition of obstacle used in Viking and Laval is not derived from the previous case law cited by the Court in support of its conclusions.

B. PRIVATE SOURCES VERSUS PRIVATE ACTIONS

Since the *Walrave* case[11] the CJEU has acknowledged that obstacles to the exercise of economic freedoms may also derive from private sources of regulation adopted by professional regulatory bodies, such as a Bar Council[12] or a national[13] and

---

7 H. Schepel, "Constitutionalising the Market, Marketising the Constitution, and to Tell the Difference: On the Horizontal Application of the Free Movement Provision in EU Law", (2012) 18 *European Law Journal* 187.

8 See also J. Baquero Cruz, "Free Movement and Private Autonomy", (1999) 24 *European Law Review* 618 and J. Snell, *Goods and Services in EC Law*, (OUP, 2002) 150–151.

9 The same approach is followed by S. Prechal and S. de Vries, "Seamless web of judicial protection in the internal market", (2009) 34 *European Law Review* 7 ff.

10 Prechal and de Vries, above n. 9, 9; this conclusion is also shared by C. Barnard, "Viking and Laval: an Introduction", (2008) 10 *Cambridge Yearbook of European Legal Studies* 474.

11 Case 36/74, *Walrave and Koch* [1974] ECR 1405.

12 Case 71/76 *Thieffry v. Conseil de l'ordre des avocats à la cour de Parsi* [1977] ECR 765; Case C-309/99 *Wouters* [2002] ECR I-1577.

13 Case 13/76 *Donà v. Mantero* [1976] ECR 1333 on free movement of services and Case C-176/96 *Lehtonen and Castors Canada Dry Namur-Braine ASBLE v. Fédération royale belge des sociétés de basket-ball ASBL (FRBSB)* [2000] ECR I-2681 on free movement of workers.

international[14] sports association; this because a collective autonomy cannot be allowed to do what is not permitted to public authorities.[15] As shown by the Viking and Laval cases, the analogy between public and private sources is extended to industrial action because the Court considers it as a premise to the adoption of a private source of regulation (the collective agreement). Such an analogy, however, cannot be justified if we look at the reasons why a private source can be considered as being equivalent to a public source of regulation.

Private sources of regulation are comparable to public ones if and when they determine mandatory conditions (discriminatory or not)[16] of access to the domestic market for anyone who intends to exercise a specific activity. In fact, all CJEU judgements relating to "non-governmental bodies" concern cases in which a person (worker or company) can access the market of another Member State only under the conditions imposed by the private rules. The equivalence with public sources consists of the fact that those private rules also "authoritatively" prevail over the will of the holder of the economic freedom who is evidently exposed to a *vulnus.*[17] In other words, private acts are relevant insofar as domestic law recognises their effectiveness as legally binding sources of regulation.

In this perspective, there is no doubt that trade unions, in the exercise of their collective autonomy, must respect the same legal restrictions as any other private organisation. The fact that a collective agreement cannot regulate a specific economic sector in a way that creates obstacles to those who hold a freedom recognised by the EU is perfectly in line with the rationale behind European market integration. This applies, for instance, to the case of a foreign company wishing to provide services on the territory of another Member State, as in the *Olympique Lyonnais*[18] and *Commission v. Germany* cases.[19]

In Commission v. Germany the balancing judgement between economic freedom and the trade union right (in this case, collective bargaining) is fully justified, because the CJEU had to assess the legitimacy of a collective agreement that

14 Case C-415/93 *Bosman* [1995] ECR 1333, I-4921 on free movement of workers and Case 36/74 *Walrave* on free movement of services.

15 Case C-309/99, *Wouters*, para. 120.

16 The vexed issue on the distinction between discriminatory and non-discriminatory obstacles created by private persons to free movement, is not dealt with here; the issue we intend to clarify deals with the possible equivalence between private sources of regulation and collective actions, regardless of the kind of obstacles they create.

17 As Dashwood, above n. 4, 529 rightly observes: "*In all of these cases the analogy with restriction on free movement of persons resulting from measures taken by national authorities is compelling. Action by non-governmental regulatory body had the effect of restricting access to a section of the employment market or of the market for certain category of services, or of preventing the establishment of a certain kind of business*".

18 Case C-325/08, *Olympique Lyonnais* [2010] ECR I-2177.

19 Case C-271/08, *Commission v. Germany* [2010] ECR I-7091.

prevented pension funds (other than those determined by the agreement) to be selected by local authorities through a public procedure. There is no doubt about the fact that the collective agreement constitutes an obstacle to the access of foreign companies to the German market. By referring to Article 28 of the Charter of Fundamental Rights in this case, the Court[20] and AG Trstenjak[21] aimed at balancing the economic freedoms of foreign companies and the right to collective bargaining of German trade unions. Even if the way in which the balancing judgement was conducted can be questioned, it is certain that such a judgement was necessary.

Having described the reasoning of the Court with regard to private sources of regulation, it is not possible to use that logic in order to qualify a collective agreement voluntarily signed by the holder of the freedom of movement as an obstacle to that freedom. As a consequence, the industrial action aimed at the conclusion of the same agreement cannot be considered as an obstacle to free movement. There is no correspondence between the two situations since the effects they produce on the exercise of the economic freedom are completely different.[22] Market access is not limited by the obligation to respect private rules if the same person to whom they apply negotiated such rules. The holder of the economic freedom is not a "third party" with respect to the organisation that created the private rules: these are self-imposed restrictions[23] and therefore lack the "authoritative" element, which is the only element that can justify the equivalence between private and public sources of law.

The freedom of contract of an employer who is bound by a collective agreement is clearly limited. This is not the case, however, if the employer signs the collective agreement, since he thereby exercises his own freedom of contract. By maintaining otherwise, as the Court did in *Viking* and *Laval*, a conflict is created between two sides of the same economic freedom and the freedom of contract (that is, the freedom to negotiate the content of a contract with the other party) is considered as a restriction to the freedom of movement.[24]

---

20 Ibid., para 38.

21 *Commission v. Germany*, Opinion, para 79.

22 Prechal and de Vries, above n. 9, 14 recognise that "Viking *and* Laval, *however, concerned a phase* before *the introduction of those rules. After all, in both cases the trade unions were taking collective action in order to get foreign employers to sign or apply a certain collective agreement*"; however, they do not consider this point relevant for the qualification of the actions as obstacles to free movement.

23 F. Dorssemont, "The Right to Take Collective Action V. Fundamental Economic Freedoms in the Aftermath of Laval and Viking-Foes are forever!", in M. De Vos (ed), *European Union Internal Market and Labour Law: Friends or Foes?* (Intersentia, 2009), 87.

24 Risk that the horizontal application of the general principles of the EU would infringe the very core of private autonomy, M. Safjan and P. Miklaszewicz, "Horizontal Effect of the General Principles of EU Law in the Sphere of Private Law", (2010) *European Review of Private Law*, 485 ff.

C. EMPLOYERS' BEHAVIOUR VERSUS TRADE UNIONS' ACTIVITIES

In the *Angonese* case[25] the CJEU adopted a very broad notion of obstacle, since it considered the behaviour of a private bank which asked for a certificate of bilingualism, issued by the local authority, as a condition for employment, to be in contrast with the internal market rules. The CJEU, referring to its seminal *Defrenne II* decision,[26] explicitly stated that "*the prohibition of discrimination applied equally to all agreements intended to regulate paid labour collectively, as well to contracts between individuals*". By doing so, the Court included within the scope of the rules on the common market also acts between private individuals, directly or (as in the case at issue) indirectly discriminatory.[27] The reasoning followed in *Angonese* was confirmed by the subsequent *Raccanelli* case,[28] in which the Court recognised that a private research centre may infringe the freedom of movement of a national of another Member State, discriminating him or her regarding the access to work.

If the imposition by a company of certain contractual terms may violate the economic freedom of other persons, it could be argued that this should apply *a fortiori* when such conditions are imposed through collective action by a trade union. In the cases *Angonese* and *Raccanelli* the CJEU seemed to reach conclusions that could not be inferred from its case law on private sources of regulation, namely that the rules of the Treaty protecting economic freedoms shall be applied between the parties of a contract also. Both cases, however, concerned the free movement of workers, hence the need to clarify their relevance for the other economic freedoms as well.

In legal literature there is no unanimity of opinion on the possibility of transferring what the Court stated in *Angonese* to the other free movement provisions.[29] There is no doubt, however, about the fact that the *Angonese* principle cannot apply to the free movement of goods, because, as Oliver and Enchelmeier rightly observed, "*the right of natural and legal persons to choose their trading partners is the very*

25 Case C-281/98, *Angonese v Cassa di Risparmio di Bolzano* [2000] ECR I-4139.

26 Case 43/75, *Defrenne II* [1976] ECR 455, para 39, where, with reference to Article 141 ECT (now Article 157 TFEU) the CJEU stated that "*the prohibition on discrimination between men and women applies not only to the action of public authorities, but also extends to all agreements which intended to paid labour collectively, as well as to contracts between individuals*".

27 It is still questioned whether the *Angonese* principle is applicable to non-discriminatory obstacles; in *Bosman* the CJEU applied provisions on free movement of workers to non-discrimination measures, but the case concerns private collective sources of regulation (see S. Van den Bogaert, "Horizontality: The Court Attacks?", in C. Barnard and J. Scott (eds), *The Law of the Single European Market* (Hart pub., 2002), 126–129).

28 Case C-94/07, *Raccanelli v Max-Planck Gesellschaft (MPG)* [2008] ECR I-5939.

29 For different opinions see Van den Bogaert, above n. 27, 146 ff and P. Oliver and W.-H. Roth, "The Internal Market and the Four Freedoms", (2004) 41 *Common Market Law Review* 407 ff.

stuff of free markets".[30] If this is true, we do not see why the same should not apply to the freedom to provide services as well: within the internal market of services, the market freedom is represented by the right to choose a service providing company and to establish by contract the conditions to do so.

In the *Sapod Audic* case on free movement of goods, the CJEU expressly recognised that "*a contractual provision cannot be regarded as a barrier to trade for the purposes of Article 30 of the Treaty since it was not imposed by a Member State but agreed between individuals*".[31] This judgement did not provide proof that the Court takes two different approaches to the problem of horizontal direct effect with respect to the free movement of goods and the free movement of services.[32] In fact, even if the reasoning behind the *Sapod Audic* decision could be opposed to the one in the *Angonese* decision,[33] this judgement did not contradict the case law on the freedom to provide services because the CJEU has never denied the possibility of two persons (receiver and provider of a service) contractually regulating their relations by providing restrictive conditions that would not be legal if provided by a binding rule (private or public). In addition, the case law on goods does not exclude that a private source of regulation (such as a regulation of a sports federation imposing on its members not to use balls produced in a particular State[34]) can be considered contrary to Article 34 TFEU (former Article 28).

This is not the place to further discuss the coherency of the basic principle of the economic freedoms. It is sufficient to observe that the Court's finding in *Sapod Audic* is in accordance with a general principle of law of the Common Market, that also applies to the freedom to provide services. That general principle states that what is freely agreed upon by the parties of a contract cannot harm the fundamental economic freedoms.

The situation is substantially different if we consider the freedom of movement of workers. The main difference between the freedom of movement of workers and the other economic freedoms is that the former concerns relations between "unequal" persons, only one of which (the employer) has the power to decide on the content of the contract and to subordinate its conclusion to certain conditions. The other economic freedoms concern contractual relations between companies or between persons with the same bargaining power. This fundamental difference

---

30 P. Oliver and S. Enchelmaier, "Free Movement of Goods: Recent Developments in the Case Law", (2007) 44 *Common Market Law Review* 662.

31 Case C-159/00, *Sapod Audic v Eco Emballages SA* [2002] ECR I-5031, para 74.

32 Such a different approach can be inferred from other judgements (see widely J. Snell, 'Private Parties and the Free Movement of Goods and Services', in M. Andenas and W.-H. Roth (eds), *Services and Free Movement in EU Law* (OUP, 2002), 211 ff).

33 Schepel, above n. 7, 180 and Oliver and Enchelmaier, above n. 30, 664.

34 The example given by Oliver and Enchelmaier, above n. 30, 663–664.

explains why EU secondary legislation regulates the freedom of movement of workers (and only this freedom), providing the nullity of discriminatory clauses of the individual contract, imposing constraints on the freedom of contract of the employer (Article 7.4 Regulation 1612/68, now Regulation 492/2011). Accordingly, with regard to secondary EU legislation, it is accepted that the rules protecting free movement of workers produce legal effects in the relations between individuals, which means that they also limit the freedom of contract (of the employer). According to Van de Bogaert, the CJEU could have used Article 7.4 in *Angonese*, thus avoiding to recognise the horizontal direct effect of Article 39 TEC.[35] In our opinion, the opposite seems true: Article 7.4 recognises that the employer must respect the freedom of movement of workers exactly because it is in the nature of this freedom to produce effects in the relations between individuals (that means in employment relationships). In other words, Regulation 1612/68 implements through secondary legislation a legal effect that is already produced by the Treaty norms recognising free movement of workers. The next step of the CJEU in the *Angonese* and *Raccanelli* cases was to recognise that the employer is also bound by the acts preceding the hiring.

The *Ferlini* case,[36] which does not concern an employment relationship, confirms and further clarifies the rationale that led the Court, in *Angonese*, to consider the principles of the internal market applicable to private relationships between individuals. The Court considered the fees charged by hospitals in Luxembourg to those not enrolled in the social security system contrary to the principle of non-discrimination under Article 12 TEC (now Article 18 TFEU), since such fees came from an institution which "*exercises a certain power over individuals and is in a position to impose on them conditions which adversely affect the exercise of the fundamental freedoms guaranteed under the Treaty*".[37] A patient does not have the power to negotiate the fees that are to be paid to a hospital, just like a worker cannot bargain the conditions of employment in a company: it is therefore reasonable that such conditions are considered an obstacle to free movement and that their legitimacy can be assessed in the light of the rules on the internal market, first of all with regard to the principle of non-discrimination.

From this it follows that the *Angonese* principle cannot be utilised to assess the legitimacy of trade union actions. The action of a union against a company cannot be considered equivalent to the behaviour of a company *vis-à-vis* a single worker in terms of the effects it produces on the dynamics of the market. It is evident that a company has the power to decide on the terms of access to the market whereas

[35] Van den Bogaert, above n. 27, 146 and 149 suggests to adopt a wide interpretation of Article 7.4, conflicting with the interpretation adopted by the CJEU in *Angonese* (para 23–25) which only refers to obligations laid down in the employment contract and collective agreements.

[36] Case C-411/98, *Ferlini v Centre hospitalier de Luxembourg* [2000] ECR I-8081.

[37] Ibid., para 50.

a trade union does not; the union is unable to impose unilaterally the conditions of employment on a company (or on an association of companies) but can only negotiate the conditions using its bargaining power, which implies the recourse to industrial action. The right to take collective action was created with the aim to re-establish a level playing field with respect to bargaining between employer and employee that would otherwise not exist. This is an obvious consideration, which is challengeable only if we ignore the fundamental principles of labour law. Therefore, it is equally obvious that *Angonese* and *Raccanelli* do not provide any arguments to support the *Laval* doctrine.

Angonese, *Raccanelli* and *Ferlini* do not contradict the principles established by the CJEU in its case law on private sources of regulation. Actually, the cases fully confirm the previous case law. In fact, even a single company can be considered as a private organisation endowed with regulatory power, namely the ability to determine unilaterally the conditions of employment and occupation of workers.[38] Accordingly, the measures put in place by an employer towards a worker can be considered equivalent to the acts of a "non-governmental regulatory body" in terms of the effects they produce on the domestic market. Even if the scope of application of the acts of the former is clearly narrower than that of acts produced by the latter (not an entire economic sector or profession, but a single company), this is the case. On the other hand, the collective agreement remains a "conventional" source of regulation for workers when it is concluded at company level or national level: for the workers (and only for them) a plant collective agreement counts as a private source of regulation like the agreements negotiated at a higher level. So, if a company is an "organisation" able to dictate the conditions of employment for a range of persons (workers or job-seekers) there is no doubt that such a company has to respect the workers' freedom of movement,[39] following what emerges from the case law on private rules.

---

[38] Dashwood, above n. 4, 530 observes that a bank cannot "*be described as an 'association' or 'organisation'*"; of course that is generally true, but a bank, as an employer, undeniably has "regulatory" powers over the workers employed, as it is able (just like an organisation) to adopt rules that must be respected.

[39] The conclusions drawn by *Angonese* case, proposed in the text, definitely conflict with those of Schepel, above n. 7, 183–184 which, following Dashwood's opinion, denies that a single undertaking could "*plausibly be accused of being granted the 'legal autonomy' to engage in 'collective regulation'*"; a statement which implicitly excludes that a code of conduct adopted by an undertaking or an agreements signed at plant level could be considered a collective source of regulation.

D. COLLECTIVE AGREEMENT, COLLECTIVE BARGAINING AND COLLECTIVE ACTIONS

Novitz and Syrpis suggest to revise the *Viking* and *Laval* doctrine, considering that private parties, including trade unions, are bound by free movement provisions (only) when they are exercising regulatory tasks which otherwise would be exercised by public authorities.[40] The two authors give the example of a collective agreement establishing minimum pay at national level, as opposed to a plant collective agreement. This reasoning is acceptable, as it is based on the effects produced by private acts on the functioning of the market, but could be rephrased in simpler terms, distinguishing between generally binding collective agreements and collective bargaining: only the former can be an obstacle to economic freedom, never the latter. A plant collective agreement can never be a barrier to the economic freedom of the company because, as in the case of an individual contract, it is signed voluntarily as a product of the bargaining process with the trade union. The same can be said for a collective agreement at the sectoral or local level if its application is not mandatory by law but depends on the result of the negotiation with trade unions. This distinction between collective agreement (as a private source of regulation) and collective bargaining (as an expression of freedom of contract) is self-evident, yet it was ignored by the CJEU in *Viking* and *Laval*. In fact, the Court applied the principles used to assess the legitimacy of a collective agreement to collective action and collective bargaining, without providing any justification. This is even more surprising if we consider that this distinction is expressly recognised by Directive 96/71. On the one hand the Directive considers the collective agreement as a "source" of regulation of labour relations when its application is imposed on foreign companies by the law of the Host State (that is, if it is made generally applicable by law); and Article 3.8 provides the conditions to make its application compatible with the principle of the internal market. On the other hand, paragraph 22 of the Preamble clarifies that the rules laid down by the Directive do not concern the exercise of collective action.[41] This is equivalent to saying that in fact only a collective agreement (as a source of regulation) can restrict the freedom to provide services, not the industrial action supporting the exercise of collective bargaining. Accordingly, we cannot explain why paragraph 22 of the Preamble was considered irrelevant by the CJEU when deciding on the *Laval* case.

---

40 P. Syrpis and T. Novitz, "Economic and Social Rights in Conflict: Political and Judicial Approaches to their Reconciliation", (2008) 33 *European Law Review* 421.

41 More explicitly, Directive 2006/123/EC excludes from its scope of application "*the right to negotiate, conclude and enforce collective agreements and to take industrial action in accordance with national law and practices which respect Community law*" (Article 1.7), and it even states that "*rules laid down in collective agreements negotiated by the social partners shall not as such be seen as requirements within the meaning of this Directive*" (Article 4).

Paragraph 22 also implicitly confirms that the industrial action does not affect the "will" of the employer to conclude a collective agreement and, for this reason, it cannot harm his economic freedom. A different conclusion would imply the denial of the function of the industrial conflict in labour relations.

Filip Dorssemont notices that the "*Court erroneously denied that collective agreements which are concluded due to the exercise of economic power need to be construed as self-imposed restrictions*".[42] Tonia Novitz formulates a similar concept when she observes that "*the actions of trade unions would appear to be treated by the Court primarily as a constraint on the employer's freedom of movement, which has a coercive aspect*".[43] This is a decisive criticism to the approach of the Court because such a coercive aspect is not compatible with the recognition of the right to strike as a fundamental right. It follows that the recognition of strike actions as a fundamental right in the EU legal system is relevant not only for the balancing judgement but also to exclude that strike can be qualified as an obstacle to economic freedoms. In other words, as a result of Article 28 of the Charter of Fundamental Rights the possibility of balancing the right to strike and economic freedoms is excluded.

By recognising the right to strike in Article 28 of the Charter of Fundamental Rights, the EU legal system implements what is already accepted in domestic legal systems, namely that the social conflict is not a form of undue pressure on the freedom of contract. In labour relations industrial conflict is a normal tool that makes negotiation between social partners possible. Accordingly, the right to strike does not vitiate in any way the consent and will of the party against whom it is exercised. Collective bargaining supported by strike is equivalent to the bargaining activity preceding the conclusion of a contract between individuals, who are free to regulate their relations on the basis of mutual interests and to use their bargaining power to do so.

If in the Laval case the obligation to respect the collective agreement had been agreed between the contractor and the subcontractor, as a condition of execution of the contract, no obstacle to the freedom to provide services would have been conceivable. In the Laval case, the only difference with this situation was the tool used to enforce the compliance of the service provider with certain conditions of employment: collective autonomy (in the form of a strike) of the union, rather than individual autonomy of the company. By treating the two situations differently and by only identifying an obstacle to free movement in the first case, the right to strike is implicitly denied.

42 F. Dorssemont, above n. 23, 88.

43 T. Novitz, "A Human Rights Analysis of the Viking and Laval Judgments", (2008) 10 *Cambridge Yearbook of European Legal Studies* 551.

E. RESTRICTIONS ON COLLECTIVE ACTIONS: NON-DISCRIMINATION AND PROTECTION OF THIRD PARTIES

From the case law on free movement of services and workers it results that "private" sources of regulation (including collective agreements) and the acts and behaviour of a company towards a job-seeker can be considered as obstacles to free movement. This does not apply to collective actions. Before *Viking* and *Laval* the CJEU had dealt with collective actions only in its case law on free movement of goods in the *Commission v. France* case (Spanish strawberries or rioting farmers case)[44] and in the *Schmidberger* case.[45] In both cases, the Court denied the horizontal direct effect of the provisions of the Treaty, thus assigning the responsibility for the obstacles created between private actors to Member States. However, what concerns us here is to clarify what kind of collective action is considered by such case law as an obstacle to the functioning of the EU market.

In Commission v. France, the Court had to assess, in the light of the Treaty, the legitimacy of the actions of French farmers aimed at boycotting and destroying goods (strawberries) imported from Spain. The actions were intended to materially impede the access of foreign goods to the national territory, that is, to exclude the possibility of exercising an economic freedom recognised by the EU.[46] To exemplify an industrial action producing similar effects on the service market, we can look at the case of strikes and blockades organised to prevent workers of a foreign company from entering national territory to carry out their activity; in this case, the objective of the collective actions is not to negotiate the terms of the exercise of the employer's economic freedom but to prevent its exercise.

The *Schmidberger* case concerned road blockades caused by a protest at the Brenner Pass. A trade union action can produce analogous effects on the functioning of the internal market when the workers taking part in it in order to put pressure on the employer or the public authorities impede or obstruct the exercise of the freedom of movement of third parties, namely other citizens or other workers who do not take part in the strike.

The examples above demonstrate that the rationale that led the Court to consider the collective actions in the *Schmidberger* and *Commission v. France* cases as "obstacles" to the freedom of movement is not in contradiction with the rationale

---

44 Case C-265/95, *Commission v France (Spanish strawberries)* [1997] ECR I-6959.

45 Case C-112/00, *Eugen Schmidberger Internationale Transporte und Planzüge v Austria* [2003] ECR I-5659.

46 As A.G. Lenz observes in its Opinion in *Commission v France* (C-265/95), para 14 "*Pillaging and destroying goods from other Member State is one of the most serious forms of restriction on imports imaginable. It is nothing short of the negation of free movement of goods*".

underlying the case law on private sources of regulation. Just like a collective agreement, a collective action can produce effects on the legal position of private individuals who cannot affect the conditions to access the market of another Member State: this is because they are third parties with respect to the parties in conflict (*Schmidberger*) or because the objective of the action is not to negotiate with the other party, but simply to prevent its entrance to the country (*Commission v. France*). Again, there is a clear difference with the industrial actions in the *Viking* and *Laval* cases, which were expressions of the contractual freedom.

The difference between collective actions aimed at negotiation with the person who is exercising the freedom of movement and collective actions that are not motivated by this objective follows from the principles governing the internal market. The first situation does not interfere with the economic freedom of others because it has the objective of regulating a private relationship through a contract. In the second situation the industrial action (even in the form of a strike) may constitute an obstacle to the functioning of the internal market that has to be justified under the proportionality principle.

Boycotts and campaigns of information against companies can also be included among the types of collective behaviour that can affect the economic freedoms. This stems from the *AGM* case, in which the Court recognises that public statements made by an official to the media, which negatively affect the marketing of a product, may constitute a breach of EU law.[47] In this case, the right to compensation for the holder of the economic freedom is deduced by the fact that the statements were attributable to the State since they were made by a public official.[48] The Court denied that the trade union that encouraged the circulation of negative publicity could be held responsible.[49] This is a reasoning, however, that relates to legal liability and not to the possibility of certain behaviour harming an interest protected by EU law. What concerns us here is that the *AGM* judgement has an underlying logic similar to that in *Schmidberger* and *Commission v. France*: private action is unlawful because in terms of EU law the action is aimed at damaging the holder of the economic freedom. Due to its purpose, a private action becomes an obstacle to free movement; in Viking and Laval the collective

---

47 In Case C-470/03, *A.G.M.-COS.MET srl v Suomen Valtio, Tarmo Lehtinen* [2007] ECR I-2749 a Finnish official warned against the safety risks of vehicle lifts manufactured by an Italian company; the CJEU admitted that "*Since the statements at issue described the vehicle lifts, in various media and in widely circulated reports, as contrary to standard EN 1493:1998 and dangerous, they are capable of hindering, at least indirectly and potentially, the placing on the market of the machinery*" (para 65).

48 Case C-470/03, *A.G.M*, para 86.

49 The Metalworkers' union (Metallityöväen Liitto ry) adopted a memorandum in which it stated that there were problems with AGM's vehicle lifts and demanded in a regional newspaper "*the ban on use of dangerous vehicle lifts' and the subheading '150 fitters in danger every day Trade unions*" (Case C-470/03, *A.G.M.*, para 33).

actions pursued a different purpose and are for this reason not considered as obstacles to free movement.

Following the logic of the *Schmidberger* and *Commission v. France* cases we can identify a legal restriction on the exercise of collective action for the protection of economic freedoms that is extremely different from the one stemming from Viking and Laval: the internal market leaves social partners free to negotiate the employment conditions of workers but it restricts the use of collective action that prevents access to a national market (that is a mere protectionist purpose) or infringes the freedom of movement of third parties not involved in the negotiations.

The outcomes of the two cases, however, are significantly different since only in the *Schmidberger* case the Court considered the obstacle to free movement created by the protesters to be justified. The different conclusion in *Commission vs France* stemmed from the directly discriminatory nature of the collective action designed to block the import of Spanish goods to the French market. An additional criterion can be derived from this to assess collective actions; a criterion that is also consistent with the principle of non-discrimination as stated in general terms in Article 18 TFEU. The general principle of non-discrimination can always be invoked between private persons, as well as by an employer against trade unions' actions;[50] and the obstacles that discriminate directly can hardly be justified if created by individuals, because they can be acceptable only through the express derogations listed by the Treaty (public policy, public health, public security) which clearly refer to public powers. Obstacles which are indirectly discriminatory or which do not have a discriminatory nature are created (in a legal sense) by trade unions only if their actions damage third parties other than the employer; and may be justified for reasons of public interest or because they are an expression of a fundamental right.[51]

In conclusion, *Schmidberger* and *Commission vs France* allow the identification of criteria alternative to those applied by the Court in *Viking* and *Laval* to assess the compatibility of the trade union's action with the rules of the internal market. First, social actors are also obliged to respect the principle of non-discrimination laid down in Article 18 TFEU, which is one of the foundations of the EU legal order. This means that a collective action that aims to prevent the exercise of

[50] The seminal Case C-555/07, *Kücükdeveci v Swedex GmnH* [2010] ECR I-365 confirms that the general principle of non-discrimination has the character of a fundamental right, and as a consequence it creates obligations for private individuals, giving rise to full horizontal direct effect. In this sense, see also Prechal and de Vries, above n. 9, 16–18, who suggest limiting full horizontal direct effect only to discrimination on grounds of nationality; for a different opinion, see also Schepel, above n. 7, 180–183.

[51] See widely, Barnard, n. 5, 480 ff.

the freedom of movement of an individual who comes from another Member State is to be considered in contrast with EU law. Accordingly, any industrial action aiming to create obstacles to the execution of a contract of service by a company based abroad for the sole purpose of defending national companies (and employees) should be considered discriminatory. It is evident that this kind of industrial action not only affects the economic freedom of the company, but also creates a discriminatory obstacle to its workers who are prevented from carrying out work in another Member State.

The *Lindsey* case could fall within the hypothesis described above even if its contours are not clear.[52] In the *Lindsey* case the objective of the British workers' collective action was to preclude the execution of a service contract in the Lindsay Oil Refinery by a sub-contractor, an Italian company (IREM) employing mainly Italian workers. The slogan "British jobs for British workers" was a clear indication of the protectionist (an therefore discriminatory) nature of the action; in the same vein the support given to the action by the British National Party in the name of the protection of employment of British workers manifested its protectionist intent. However, it is significant that the union (GMB and Unite) justified the action from the beginning onwards with the necessity to impede social dumping, and not to exclude foreign workers from the British market.[53]

In addition to the general prohibition of discrimination, trade union actions are restricted so as to avoid damages to individuals who are not part in the conflict. In this respect, the legitimacy of the action depends on the balancing judgement conducted in the light of the principle of proportionality that implies the assessment of the terms and duration of the action and of the severity of its effects on the dynamics of the EU internal market. The balancing of economic freedoms and the right to strike should never focus on the counterpart of the industrial action (as happened in *Viking* and *Laval*) but always on third parties because it is only with respect to them that collective action can be qualified as a non-discriminatory or indirectly discriminatory obstacle to the access to another Member State's market.

---

[52] C. Barnard, "'British Jobs for British Workers': The Lindsey Oil Refinery Dispute and the Future of Local Labour Clauses in an Integrated EU Market" (2009) 38 *Industrial Law Journal* 245 ff.

[53] Barnard, n. 52, 259: the ACAS (Advisory, Conciliation and Arbitration Service) also called for an inquiry on the dispute, and observes in its report that "*It is important to emphasise that the unions were not seeking to have Italian workers made redundant, nor were they seeking exclusive jobs for UK workers*" (ACAS, Report of an Inquiry into the Circumstances Surrounding the Lindsey Oil Refinery Dispute, 16 February 2009, 5).

F. HORIZONTAL DIRECT EFFECT OR INDIRECT STATE LIABILITY?

So far we have attempted to show that *Viking* and *Laval* do not represent the logic of the previous CJEU case law and are not the consequence of the application of the principles of the internal market. On the contrary, a different reading and application of such principles not only is possible, it is also more in line with the rationale of the rules governing the dynamics of the market.

This reading is based on the distinction between a collective agreement (a source of regulation) and collective action (necessary to enforce collective bargaining); the first can be considered as an obstacle to free movement if it is binding for foreign companies entering the national market; the second is not an obstacle if it is directed to the other contractual party (the employer). A collective action can become an obstacle to the functioning of the market if it is directly discriminatory (that is, if it is intended to prevent access to the domestic market) or if it affects the economic freedom of third parties (stakeholders other than the employer); in the latter case it is necessary to evaluate the justification of the action through a balancing judgement between rights also recognised in the EU legal system (the right to strike and the right to economic freedom).

As mentioned at the beginning of this contribution, the issue of horizontal direct liability arises only at this point, namely after having clarified what an "obstacle" to the freedom of movement is under the principles of the internal market: it remains in fact unclear who is legally liable for the acts impeding the free movement between Member States.

The problem does not really arise in the case of an infringement of the economic freedom produced by a collective agreement. In fact, the collective agreement will be disapplied, as would happen with any other source of regulation (public or private) that produces such effects on the internal market. A private organisation cannot be held legally responsible for the production of a contractual source of regulation that is inconsistent with EU law because the legal consequence of this is simply the removal of the incompatible source. It follows that the State is still responsible for the obstacle created by a private source of regulation and its legal system must ensure the legal effect imposed by EU law: the nullity of the contractual clause or disapplying in the specific case.

The problem of horizontal direct effect arises when the (unjustified) obstacle to the freedom of movement is caused by an industrial action. In the *Viking* and *Laval* cases the CJEU did not clarify the possibility of direct liability of trade unions. As is known, Swedish judges solved the issue by condemning the unions to pay damages, thereby applying domestic legislation on liability for illegal strikes to the *Laval* case.[54]

The criteria for assessing the liability of private individuals for breaches of EU law are ambiguous, since the principles developed by the CJEU concern infringement of competition law that is *ab origine* directed to private persons.[55] Assessing direct liability of trade unions is even more problematic because the determination is affected by the diversity of the national industrial relation systems. In countries where a strike has the nature of an individual right (as in Italy) it is even doubtful that it would be possible to assign such liability.[56]

In general, horizontal direct effect presupposes the existence of a private body to which the liability for the damages caused by the action is attributable, on the basis of the domestic law of the Member State. It is no coincidence that in *Schmidberger* and *Commission v. France* the Court did not contemplate the possibility of considering the individuals who created the obstacle liable since it was impossible in both cases to identify the persons who could be held responsible for the actions. Admitting the existence of horizontal direct effect would create a situation in which only some collective actions that affect the functioning of the internal market would be actually punishable, depending on the persons who organised the actions and the Member State where it happened.

The problems associated with the recognition of horizontal direct effect suggest we need to follow the approach the CJEU used in *Commission v. France* and *Schmidberger.* In this case, responsibility for the obstacles created by private individuals was assigned to the Member States on the basis of the duty of loyal cooperation under Article 10 of the EC Treaty (now Article 4.3 TEU), following the traditional perspective that the EU norms on competition are directed to companies and that the EU norms on internal market are addressed to public authorities.[57] This conclusion is also based on the need to preserve the consistency of the principles of the internal market: it is not clear why the indirect liability of the State should only apply within the context of free movement of goods

[54] U. Bernitz and N. Reich, "Case No. A 268/04. The Labour Court, Sweden (Arbetsdomstolen) Judgment No. 89/09 of 2 December 2009", (2011) *Common Market Law Review* 603 ff.

[55] K. Apps, "Damages claims against trade unions after Viking and Laval", (2009) 34 *European Law Review* 141 ss.

[56] A. Lo Faro, "Responsabilità e sanzioni per sciopero illegittimo: cambia qualcosa in Italia dopo Laval?", (2011) 131 *Giornale di diritto del lavoro e di relazioni industriali* 419 ss.; similar situation in France (see Robin-Olivier, Pataut, "Europe sociale ou Europe économique (à propos des affaires Viking et Laval)", (2008) *Revue du Droit de Travail* 85).

[57] See also Schepel, above n. 7, 200, who suggest to return to the 'traditional' distinction between free movement and competition rules, whereby only the latter is binding to private persons, in order to avoid the unsolvable problems created by the horizontal direct effect theory.

(governed by Regulation 2679/98) whereas in the case of the other fundamental freedoms private persons should be directly liable.

The approach based on indirect state liability is certainly more respectful of the equilibrium of domestic systems of industrial relations and of the exercise of collective autonomy.[58] However, the question as to which measures should be taken by the State in order to avoid responsibility remains an open one. Given that States enjoy a wide margin of discretion in the choice of measures to be taken (as the Court acknowledged in *Schmidberger*), it is obvious that the absence of appropriate instruments in the domestic legal system to avoid collective actions that are harmful to economic freedoms cannot constitute a justification.[59] From this follows the conclusion that indirect liability may also imply the need for States to change the rules of industrial conflict in order to make them compatible with the principles of the internal market.[60] Such reforms, however, would not lead to the erosion of domestic industrial relations because the reforms would not affect the bargaining autonomy of the unions and their activities of collective bargaining. The restrictions to union activity would enable the prevention of protectionist trade union actions and avoid disproportionate negative effects on third parties (workers or companies other than the opposite party of the collective action) who are exercising their freedom of movement within the internal market. If in this second objective we can see the price that trade unions have to pay for market integration, the first objective can only create advantages for the European trade union movement, the growth of which is primarily obstructed by the protectionist temptations still present in national trade unions.

II. A FAILED LEGISLATIVE ROAD *DE IURE CONDENDO*: THE MONTI II PROPOSAL

A. LEGAL BASIS

The legal basis of the so-called Monti II Proposal is Article 352 TFEU Monti II. This article is very lenient. It allows EU intervention in order to attain one of the objectives set out in the Treaties, "if the Treaties have not provided the necessary powers". It is construed as a last resort. A legislative instrument on the basis of Article 352 can only be adopted unanimously.

The European Commission and the European Council are not required to follow the consultation procedure in respect of social partners laid down in Article 154

58 P. Oliver and W.-H. Roth, above n. 29, 426–427.
59 J. Snell, *Goods and Services in EC Law* (Oxford UP 2002) 152.
60 Prachal and De Vries, above n. 9, 22.

TFEU. Article 154 TFEU only applies to proposals in the field of social policy based on Title X. The current wording of Article 352 TFEU is different from the original version (ex Article 308 TEC). In the previous version the parliament only had to be consulted.

This legal basis had been used before in Monti I. Regulation 2679/98 has been adopted on the same legal basis. Though the choice of this Treaty article seems obvious, some critical remarks are appropriate.

First, Monti II nowhere identifies the objective the Union regulation seeks to achieve. Neither the body nor the recitals indicate the relevant policy. Monti I was more transparent on this point.[61] That regulation sought to improve the functioning of the internal market in relation to free movement of goods. The establishment of such a market is a treaty objective. According to the title, Monti II by no means relates to the operation of the internal market. It is related to the exercise of the right to collective action in the context of freedom of establishment and to the freedom to provide services. The question arises whether promoting or safeguarding the fundamental freedoms can be seen as an objective of the European Union within the meaning of Article 352 TFEU.

The only eligible "policy" in connection with such a fundamental right could be related to social policy concerns. The Title on social policy formulates some social objectives, referring in this regard to the European Social Charter and the Community Charter. Both charters refer to the right to collective action, although in a problematic way. It is absurd to assume that the European Union under Title X (Social Policy) would have wanted to promote the right to take collective action, because the most important aspects of this fundamental right are explicitly excluded from the powers specified in Title X.

The problem can be remedied by the observation that the Union has the objective to promote the values on which it is founded. Respect of fundamental rights is explicitly mentioned as a value in Article 2 TEU. Within a dynamic interpretation, the promotion of these rights could be seen as an objective in the meaning of Article 352 TFEU. The English and French versions of Article 352 TFEU do not refer to "objectives" but to policies. None of these titles as such are dedicated to the promotion of fundamental rights.

Of course it can be argued that this regulation essentially seeks to safeguard the freedom of establishment and the free movement of services. Such an argument,

---

[61] Regulation (EC) No 2679/98 of 7 December 1998 on the functioning of the internal market in relation to the free movement of goods among the Member States, OJ L 337/8 (1998); for an analysis of the influence of this regulation on industrial relations: Orlandini, *ELJ* 2000, 341–362.

however, seems problematic to us. It implies that a legal basis was available. In contrast to what is the case on the free movement of goods, chapter two (freedom of establishment) and chapter three (freedom to provide services) of the Fourth Title TFEU contain provisions which attribute legislative powers to the European Union. These provisions do not allow the adoption of regulations.

B. THE BALANCE OF MONTI II

Monti II contains two clauses that regulate the relationship between the right to collective action and economic freedoms. The first clause is inserted in a description of the scope of the draft Regulation. The second clause is central to the section "General principles". Both clauses are in our opinion internally contradictory.

The first clause is highly analogous to the clause in Monti I Regulation. This regulation codifies the obligation formulated in *Commission v. France* (Spanish strawberries) for Member States to act against obstacles to the free movement of goods, including actions of individuals. The judgement resulted from an infringement procedure by the Commission against France. The Commission criticised the French Republic for its lingering attitude against the attacks that angry French farmers deployed in true guerrilla style against the dumping of cheap exotic fruit and vegetables on the French market.

For two reasons, these guerrilla techniques could not be related to a right to collective action. Firstly, the French farmers did engage in violence against property and to a lesser extent against persons. Secondly, the collective action was not an action by workers, but rather by entrepreneurs.

Monti I also limited the doctrine developed in Spanish Strawberries. It did not aim to clarify but to correct. The regulation sought to describe exemption from the application of the rule in an explicit and unconditional manner.

It specified that these rights "also include the right or freedom to take other actions covered by the specific industrial relations systems in Member States".

At first sight, Article I of Monti II seems to repeat such an exemption mechanism in a literal manner. The formula is even more specific. Contrary to what is the case in Monti II, it explicitly states that "the right to negotiate, conclude and enforce collective agreements and to take collective action in accordance with national law and practices" is not affected either.

This clarification is extremely helpful, due to the often neglected impact of the *Viking* and *Laval* judgements in the field of collective bargaining. In both cases, the collective actions are inextricably linked with the freedom of collective bargaining. In *Viking* the ITF had blacklisted a particular ship-owner. In view of the The Flag of Convenience campaign, the ITF urged its members to exercise their negative freedom of collective bargaining in a concerted way. With the exception of the trade union of the country which financially controlled the ships, members were called upon not to conclude collective agreements with the Finnish ship-owner. The *economic* benefit of an establishment of the ship-owner in Estonia would be lost. After all, the ship-owner sought to sign a collective agreement with an Estonian union so this agreement could then be applied to the crew of the Rosella. In *Laval* another kind of boycott was undertaken. The collective action was undertaken in order to force a Latvian subcontractor to accede to a Swedish collective agreement. Unfortunately, the CJEU did not examine whether the freedom of collective bargaining was a general principle of European law that had to be weighed against the economic freedoms. It only considered the right to collective action. In *Commission v. Germany*, the Court finally recognised the freedom of collective bargaining as a fundamental principle of European Union law.

However, Monti II affirms in a subsequent provision that the rights to collective action and collective bargaining are limited by the freedom of establishment and the freedom to provide services. The exemption is therefore deficient and at least unconvincing. The observation that the economic freedoms are limited by the right to collective action seems to sugar the pill. The idea that economic freedoms and fundamental rights are mutually restrictive was previously expressed by Advocate General Trstenjak in her Opinion in *Commission v. Germany*. The CJUE did not adopt such a formula, which was clearly inspired by the intention to silence the criticism that Viking and Laval had generated.

C. PROBLEMS OF THE DISPUTE RESOLUTION MECHANISM

Article 3 of the Monti II proposal is analysed from a conceptual industrial relations and collective labour law perspective. It can be argued that the provision concerned is problematic, insofar as it is at odds with the classical understanding of industrial relations dynamics. The question is then considered whether and to what extent a supplementary layer of transnational industrial relations is being shaped or whether the Commission is actually disrupting existing layers of a domestic industrial relations system. Last but not least, an attempt is made to demonstrate that two unique opportunities to mitigate to a certain extent the "chilling effect" of the infamous *Viking* and *Laval* judgements have been lost.

The Monti II Proposal introduces a provision on dispute resolution mechanisms,[62] in contrast to the Monti I Regulation, which contains nothing on this area. The mechanisms concerned are qualified as "alternative" and "non-judicial mechanisms". The disputes concerned are qualified as *labour* disputes. The notions "industrial dispute" and "industrial action"[63] are thus avoided.

The disputes are said to "originate from the exercise of the right to take collective action, including the right or freedom to strike, in transnational situations or situations having a cross-border character in the context of the exercise of the freedom of establishment or the freedom to provide services, including the application of Directive 96/71/EC".

Contrary to the so-called Monti Report,[64] the Monti II proposal does *not* urge Member States to introduce any mechanism for the informal resolution of labour disputes. The Proposal's approach is based upon a principle of *equal* access to dispute resolution mechanisms. It does not provide for a principle of access to such mechanisms. When Member States do provide for such a mechanism, equality needs to be ensured. A principle of equality can only work in practice when the holder of a right to equal treatment and a comparator (fictitious or real) can be identified. Neither the holder nor the comparator is identified. A contextual interpretation seems to suggest that equal access needs to be guaranteed for the benefit of the holder of the freedom of establishment or the freedom to provide services. Insofar as an employer has in fact exercised his right of establishment in a Host State, the principle of non-discrimination based upon nationality might be sufficient to guarantee equality.[65] Insofar as the holder is an undertaking which is being prevented from establishing itself or a service provider prevented from providing a service, the principle might have an added value in relation to Article 18 TFEU. In theory, the workers' organisation in the state of origin that is potentially responsible for protecting the interests of posted workers should benefit from the principle of equal access as well.

The facts in the *Viking* and *Laval* cases provide evidence that Host State trade unions have not been reluctant in resorting to alternative dispute resolution procedures. In *Viking* these procedures were not followed in the country of origin. There was no need to involve any Estonian subsidiary, since the establishment had not yet taken place. Furthermore, no trade union outside Finland was involved, despite the fact that all ITF affiliates, including the Estonian trade union, had decided to respond to the circular issued by the ITF. It also seems to us that in the *Laval* case access to the Swedish mediation procedure would not have

[62] Article 3 Monti II Proposal.
[63] See e.g. Article 9 EU Regulation No. 864/2009.
[64] Mario Monti, "A new strategy for the single market", 72.
[65] Article 18 TFEU.

been of much help. The question therefore arises whether extending the existing alternative dispute procedures to foreign service providers and foreign trade unions would have made any difference to the outcome of the industrial dispute.

The Commission's approach is very much reminiscent of the equality principle enshrined in EU Regulation 492/2011 on the free movement of workers, Article 8 of which reiterates the rules of the repealed Regulation 1612/68. A worker who is a national of a Member State and who is employed in the territory of another Member State shall enjoy equality of treatment as regards membership of trade unions and the exercise of rights attaching thereto. The provision does not impede the autonomy of trade unions to draft internal rules regarding membership. However, these rules should be applied without any nationality-based discrimination of a worker moving freely from one Member State to another. The scope of trade union rights would seem to be a matter of domestic law of individual Member States. Nevertheless, a hard core of trade union rights is identified: trade union rights need to include the right to vote and the right to be eligible for the administration or management posts of a trade union. The approach of trade union rights is purely internal. It does not extend to rights related to the promotion and defence of workers' interests *in foro externo*.[66] Considering the fact that the Regulation dates back to 2011, the approach could be considered outdated.

Alternative and non-judicial dispute resolution mechanisms are often intertwined with national industrial relations systems.[67] The principle of equal access indicates a reluctance to shape a cross-border industrial relations framework. In fact, no supplementary layer is constructed, with existing national layers merely being extended to cover foreign actors.

Although the State has a potential role in promoting alternative dispute resolution mechanisms, these have often been shaped in an autonomous and voluntary way. Giving foreign service providers an enforceable right to access to an existing alternative dispute resolution mechanism on the basis of an equal treatment principle may be out of line with the purely voluntary character of such methods as mediation and conciliation. The voluntary nature of such procedures is an essential prerequisite for any mediation to be able to function. Another objection relates to a paradox. The CJEU has established an ontological and economic fallacy by stating that posted workers not recruited as agency workers have no access to

---

66 F. Dorssemont, "The right to form and joint trade unions for the protection of his interests under Article 11", *European Labour Law Journal*, 2010/2, 185–235.

67 See S. Dubled and R. De Quénaudon, "Les modes alternatifs de règlement des conflits (collectifs) du travail: généralités", in M. Rigaux and P. Humblet, *Conciliation, médiation et arbitrage*, Brussels, Bruylant, 2011, 1–49.

the Host State's labour market.[68] If this fallacy is upheld in a consistent way, it is incoherent to give their employers any kind of access to an industrial relations system closely intertwined with the functioning of such a market. Furthermore, the question could be raised whether such access to a system of industrial relations can be granted to the sole benefit of foreign service providers and not to the posted workers. Access to a Host State's industrial relations system can take many forms: posted workers participating in the election of workers' representatives in the Host State and participating in strikes organised in the Host State under the same conditions as permanent workers or Host State workers' representatives playing a role in enforcing Host State legislation applicable to posted workers. At present, the Posting of Workers Directive adopts a rather ambiguous stance on this issue, with Article 5 stating that adequate enforcement procedures should be available to workers *and/or* their representatives. The "and/or" does not seem to impose workers' representation, neither does it indicate in which State such representation needs to be situated.

Unfortunately, the CJEU has not upheld this fallacy in a consistent way either. In *Portugaia Construçoes*[69] the Court held the idea that foreign service providers should have access to the collective bargaining system of the Host State under the same conditions as employers of the Host State.

In this case, the hierarchy of collective agreements under German law was at stake. Under German law, sectoral agreements declared to be generally binding had no priority over agreements concluded at company level. Hence, there is scope for *in pejus* bargaining when a company concludes a collective agreement with a trade union. Foreign service providers were not considered to be capable of concluding such company-level agreements under German law. The CJEU ruled that such exclusion from access to the company layer of collective bargaining was discriminatory.

In sum the principle of equal access is far from unproblematic.

Another problem is of a conceptual nature. It relates to the way Monti II construes the relation between "labour disputes" and "collective action".

The Commission considers labour disputes to result from collective action. In our opinion, trade unions have recourse to collective action within a context of a labour dispute. Article 6 § 4 of the European Social Charter recognises a right to take collective action *in cases of conflict of interest*. Recourse to strike action in the

68 See CJEU, Case C-113/89, *Rush Portuguesa*, § 15 ("without at any time gaining access to the labour market of the host Member State").
69 CJEU, Case C-164/99, 24 January 2002 (*Portugaia Construcoes*).

case of a *legal conflict* is said to fall outside the scope of the Charter. Although the line between conflicts of interests and a legal conflict is a fine one, the idea is that collective action stems from conflicts of interests. Trade unions and workers have recourse to collective action in order to promote and further their interests. The only "conflicts" stemming from collective actions are legal disputes, not labour disputes, as seen in the *Viking* and *Laval* cases. These cases deal with the question of whether recourse to collective action is lawful. Alternative dispute resolution procedures are non-jurisdictional by nature since they seek to resolve a conflict of interest.

Recourse to alternative dispute resolution mechanisms might entail a mandatory or voluntary *cooling off* period. The conflicting parties would be obliged or would be willing to suspend collective action for the duration of the alternative measures. The cooling off period relates to the collective action. In Article 3 § 3 Monti II a different kind of cooling off is described. It is suggested that alternative disputes resolution procedures might help parties to cool off due to the fact that they would not have recourse to *judicial remedies*. There is a shift in focus. In a classic view, alternative dispute resolution procedures are seen as a means to avoid recourse to collective action. In Monti II they are all about avoiding, if possible, recourse to judicial remedies. The fact that *non*-judicial dispute resolution mechanisms are qualified as being "alternative" corroborates that view. In a more classic view, *judicial* intervention in the context of a labour dispute is seen as an unsatisfactory, hence alternative approach to the genuine resolution of labour disputes. A legal approach is unable to go to the heart of the matter. It can only appreciate whether the conduct of parties in the conflict was lawful or not. It does not provide a genuine solution for the conflict of interest at hand.[70] The fact that the Commission does not explicitly focus on the fact that recourse to alternative dispute resolution procedures restricts the ability to have recourse to collective action, is consistent with the lack of competence of the EU legislator in the field of strikes. It is probably for this reason that the Commission suggests that there is still scope for an autonomous agreement on the issue.[71] Although it is out of the question that such an agreement between management and labour could be implemented by a Directive, no obstacle seems to exist against an autonomous implementation according to the procedures and practices specific to management and labour of a Member State British Labour lawyers have argued that *Viking* and *Laval* have had a *chilling effect* on recourse to collective action.[72] The chilling effect relates to

70 See in this respect the observation of M. Rigaux: "le juge n'intervient qu'en marge du conflit". M. Rigaux, "L'intervention du juge dans les conflits collectifs du travail : marginale, mais essentielle", in M. Rigaux and P. Humblet, *Conciliation, médiation et arbitrage*, Brussels, Bruylant, 2011, 85.

71 See Article 3 § 2 Monti II Proposal.

72 See Ewing, Draft Monti II Regulation: An Inadequate Response to Viking and Laval, (www.lcdtu.org/eu-employment-rights-professor-keith-ewing-on-monti-11%E2%80%B3/) and L. Hayes, T. Novitz and H. Reed, "Applying the Laval quartet in a UK context: chilling,

the fact that trade unions experience a feeling of legal insecurity when planning a recourse to collective actions which might come under the scrutiny of the CJEU.

The sense of insecurity is related to two factors. First, there is unease about the fine line between collective actions which fall outside and those which fall inside the doctrine of the CJEU. In this respect, the chilling effect coincides with a spill-over effect. Trade Unions within Member States which are unfamiliar with a proportionality test in domestic law, fear that the case law of the Court might be used as an argument to submit all collective actions to such a test. Such an approach is erroneous. First, the Court has not submitted collective actions to a test of proportionality, balancing the economic interests of the parties concerned. This test of proportionality weighs fundamental rights against fundamental freedoms. Furthermore, the Court's doctrine is restricted to collective actions which interfere with the exercise of the freedom of establishment and/or the freedom to provide services. Collective actions which do not interfere with one of these economic freedoms fall outside the ambit of the case law.

Monti II refers to collective actions in transnational situations or situations having a cross-border character *in the context* of the exercise of the freedom of establishment or the freedom to provide services. In our view the *impetus* on transnationality is superfluous and confusing. Indeed, a collective action can be purely national from an industrial relations perspective, but can still interfere with free movement rules. There was nothing intrinsically transnational about the boycott in *Laval* though. The conflict did not cross the boundaries of the construction site. Swedish trade unions were in fact pressuring a Latvian company established in Sweden. This company had recourse to posted workers on Swedish soil. The mere fact that a collective action has a pan-European character does not constitute an *in se et per se* obstacle to free movement. The pan-European, indeed global, boycott based upon the circular of the ITF did fall within the ambit of the Court's scrutiny, since the Court considered it to be an obstruction to the freedom of establishment.

The previous draft of Monti II contained an explicit warning against such a spill-over effect. A provision stated that "where cross border elements are lacking or hypothetical, any collective or industrial action shall be assumed prima facie not to constitute a violation of the freedom of establishment or the freedom to provide service and therefore in principle legitimate and lawful under EU law".[73]

---

ripple and disruptive effects on industrial relations", in *Reconciling Fundamental Social Rights and Economic Freedoms after Viking, Laval and Rüffert*, 195–244 (Bücker/Warneck eds.) Baden-Baden, Nomos, 2011. The discourse on the chilling effect has been triggered by the BALPA case See K.D. Ewing and J. Hendy QC, *The new spectre haunting Europe*, pp. 68–72 (Institute of Employment Rights 2011).

73 See Article 3 of the Draft Proposal.

The formula was unfortunate since it suggested that the presumption could be rebutted. In our view, such a collective action would not interfere with fundamental freedoms and could for this reason not be challenged under EU law. The formula has been improved in Monti II, clearly suggesting that the assumption could not be rebutted. Unfortunately, this clear-cut signal has not been distinctly conveyed in the explanatory memorandum.

The legal insecurity also stems from the fact that there is a risk of the lawful character of the collective action being assessed, to a great extent, by a Court which is not characterised by proximity to the labour conflict. In *Laval* the question whether the collective action was lawful was in fact tackled high up at the Kirchberg. The judges ruled that the collective action did not serve a legitimate purpose. This approach did not even leave any scope to assess whether the collective action passed the proportionality test. If the aim of the collective action is qualified as illegitimate, the game is over. Hence, a *Viking* approach allowing the national referring judge to assess the proportionality test is less intrusive. It would provide more scope for respecting divergences in systems of industrial relations. The previous draft of Monti II did prescribe an appealing PIL rule related to the competent judge at domestic level. A provision provided that the court of the country in which the industrial action had started or was planned had jurisdiction. This preference for the *locus actus* as opposed to the *locus damni* is reminiscent of the approach in Regulation no 864/2007 regarding the law applicable to non-contractual obligations. In this regulation a specific PIL rule was introduced. Article 9 states that the law applicable to non-contractual obligations in respect of the liability of a person, in the capacity of a worker or an employer or the organisations representing their professional interests, for damages caused by an industrial action, pending or carried out, shall be the law of the country where the action is to be, or has been, taken.

In Monti II the Commission completely shifts its focus. Rather than stressing the importance of a division between the role of the Court of Justice and that of the domestic judges, it focuses on the division between the role of the institutions and actors responsible for the alterative non-judicial dispute mechanisms and that of national courts. In the previous draft the Court distinguished between the role of the Court of Justice and that of national courts "ultimately" assessing the proportionality test.[74]

The sensitive issues of the division between the role of the CJEU and that of the national courts are addressed in the Explanatory Memorandum.[75] The Commission pays tribute to the idea that competent national authorities enjoy

[74] See Article 3 of the Draft Proposal.
[75] See p. 13.

a wide margin of discretion to apply the proportionality test. It breaks down the test into an assessment of appropriateness, necessity and reasonableness. The Commission is mute on the quintessential issue of which court deals with the assessment of the lawful character of the aim of the collective action. It does take the opportunity to repeat the idea that the proportionality test needs to be operated in both ways. Despite the reference to Trestenjak's opinion, no trace of the *converse* proportionality is found in Article 3 § 4 of the Monti II proposal.

D. CRITIQUE ON THE ALERT MECHANISM

Monti II does not just copy the "exemption" clause of Monti I, it also pays tribute to the alert mechanism. Despite this obvious inspiration, there are important differences between the alert mechanism and the information obligations under Monti I.[76]

The information obligation under Monti I cannot be dissociated from the more far-reaching core obligation for Member States to "take all necessary and proportionate measures so that the free movement of goods is assured in the territory of the Member State in accordance with the Treaty".[77]

This more comprehensive obligation is a codification of a duty the CJUE considered to flow from the loyalty to the Union in the landmark case *Spanish strawberries*. In this case the French state was condemned for its omission to act against the collective actions French farmers undertook over a decade against the dumping of imported fruit and vegetables on the French market. Monti I defines such an omission or inaction as "the case when the competent authorities of a Member State, in the presence of an obstacle caused by actions taken by private individuals, fail to take all necessary and proportionate measures within their powers with a view to removing the obstacle and ensuring the free movement of goods in their territory".

In sum the information obligations are part of a monitoring procedure related to Member States' obligations. In Monti II such a State's obligation is not laid down. Neither *Viking* nor *Laval* allows to construe such an obligation.[78] In this respect, Monti II does not go beyond the State obligations enshrined in Monti I. However, as far as the information obligations are concerned, it can be considered that Monti II imposes more severe obligations. The information obligations

[76] See especially G. Orlandini, "The free movement of goods as a possible community limitation on industrial conflict", *European Law Journal* 2000, 341–362.

[77] See Article of Regulation No. 2679/98.

[78] See in this respect the observations of G. Orlandini, "The Monti II proposal for the regulation and the right to strike in post-Lisbon Europe", *European Journal of Social Law*, 4, 2012, 228 ff.

under Monti II were subjected to conditions which have been phrased differently, whereas these obligations are essentially cumulative in Monti I. Furthermore, the conditions are different. Indeed, the obligations under Monti II arise as soon as "serious acts or circumstances affecting the effective exercise of the freedom of establishment or the freedom to provide services *which could cause* grave disruption to the proper functioning of the internal market and/or *which may cause* serious damage to its industrial relations system or create serious social unrest in its territory or in the territory of other Member States arise". The conditional nature of the impact which is described differs from the approach in Monti I, which focuses on more immediate "obstacles". It might be argued that information obligations under Monti II arise "in monte", *id est* at a prior stage.

The reference to "serious damages to industrial relations systems" or "a serious social unrest" is puzzling. In fact, it could be argued that collective actions do not provoke such serious damages or social unrest. It is the other way around. In *Viking* and *Laval*, it was the exercise of the economic freedoms in a way that led to social dumping that disturbed a system of industrial relations of the Host State. The collective actions did not provoke social unrest, they were a symptom of social unrest. In sum, the Commission once more seems to confuse cause and result.

Another difference concerns the structure of the information procedure. In Monti I, the Commission had to be informed and subsequently had to inform all the other Member States itself. In Monti II the Commission and the Member States need to be informed simultaneously. Furthermore, the obligation to inform the Member States is restricted to the Member States concerned.

In our view, the information obligation is being disconnected from a State obligation to intervene in a collective conflict. Information should serve some purpose. It has an ancillary role. In industrial relations systems, information is used to facilitate a more predominant procedure. It might thus facilitate a process of bargaining or consultation. An isolated approach to information is puzzling.

The question arises whether Monti II is capable of meeting the objectives it sets out. To answer such a question, those objectives must be pre-identified. In contrast to other instruments of secondary Union law, they have not been put forward, not in the recitals nor in the body of the text. The objective of the draft regulation has only been explained in the Memorandum. The proposal is qualified as a measure to clarify the interaction within the EU between the exercise of social rights and the exercise of the Treaty freedom of establishment and freedom to provide services. "It was explicitly not the intention to invalidate the case law of the Court."

In no way does the proposal invalidate the case law of the Court. The relationship between the right to collective action and economic freedom has not been altered. A flaw which is inherent in the EU Treaties can never be remedied by adopting secondary EU Law, neither can the adoption of a regulation alter "constitutional" case law of the CJEU. For that reason, the ETUC has consistently advocated a solution that had to be enshrined in primary EU Law.

It seems to us that the Viking and Laval judgements do not suffer from a lack of clarity. The mere fact that the social partners could reach a consensus on the scope of those judgements in their joint report is illustrative. They did not disagree on the meaning of the content, but on the substance of the judgement.

This proposal, formulated by Monti, was meant to help the European trade union movement accustom to the process of economic integration. It is clear that this attempt completely failed. The Executive Committee of the ETUC expressed a very negative view in its resolution of 19 April 2011.

The ETUC stated:

> "It (Monti II) restricts the right to take collective action;
>
> It does not ensure that economic free property does not take priority over fundamental social rights and that, in case of conflict, fundamental social rights will take precedence;
>
> It enforces the pure proportionality test as developed by the CJEU in the Viking case, which leaves it up to the national courts and the CJEU to decide ultimately if collective action is necessary;
>
> It reinforces the interpretation given by the CJEU in Viking and Laval and does not solve the problems".

Ewing said in an analysis of the draft for the British Institute of Employment Rights, that "there is nothing of merit in the Draft Monti II Regulation".

Perhaps some elements of the proposal could be saluted. It seems to us that the proposed mutual restriction of economic freedoms and fundamental rights of employees, as proposed in line with AG Trstenjak's reasoning, is a symbolic improvement. Its potential should not be overestimated. The test developed by Trstenjak did not safeguard the freedom of collective bargaining.

The fact that Monti II refers to the benefits of mechanisms of conciliation and mediation is important. They are in our opinion the most appropriate way of dealing with collective conflicts in a satisfactory manner. However, The Commission, in our view, did not provide evidence of a proper understanding of the nature of these procedures. Indeed, it appears that the foreign service providers' access to systems of industrial relations is in stark contrast to that of the posted workers. The foreign service provider and its employees are not supposed to seek entry to the labour market of the host country, but the service provider is in fact given access to a system of industrial relations that also regulates that labour market.

The private international law approach to the issue of competence in the case of transnational collective actions was refreshing. This approach was, however, abandoned in the final proposal. The more restrictive formula even entails a risk of modifying Monti I, which may have serious consequences for activists who do not have the formal status of employees.

A qualitative legal text should be deprived of internal contradictions. It seems to us that Articles 1 and 2 of the Monti II proposal are internally contradictory. Whereas Article 1 seems to give equal status to collective action and the freedom of collective bargaining as the status of economic freedoms, Article 2, however, submits those workers' rights to a proportionality test. Such contradictions give the impression of window dressing. The exemption rule is in fact hidden in a section which governs the scope.

III. A CONSTITUTIONAL PATHWAY

A. THE ACCESSION TO THE EUROPEAN CONVENTION FOR THE PROTECTION OF HUMAN RIGHTS AND FUNDAMENTAL FREEDOMS

Due to the ratification of the Lisbon Treaty, the consolidated Treaty on European Union now provides that "The Union *shall* accede to the European Convention for the Protection of Human Rights and Fundamental Freedoms."[79]

The accession of the EConvHR constitutes a more far-reaching step in the constitutional recognition of fundamental rights within the European Union. In our view, it goes beyond a recognition of fundamental rights as mere general principles of the Union's law. In fact, Article 6 § 3 TEU *as such* already recognises such an impact of the fundamental rights, as guaranteed by the European Convention on Human Rights.

Due to the accession, the status of the fundamental rights enshrined in EconvHR will differ fundamentally from those enshrined in the Charter of Fundamental Rights. At best, the rights enshrined in the Charter have the same *legal value* as conflicting fundamental freedoms enshrined in the EU Treaties. Furthermore, the Charter itself has upgraded some of the fundamental freedoms which have the potential to conflict with fundamental (workers') rights. Thus, Article 15 of

[79] Article 6 § 2 TEU.

the Charter has raised the status of the freedom of establishment and the freedom to provide services to proper "fundamental freedoms". In *Viking* and *Laval,* both freedoms have been considered to justify restrictions to the fundamental right to strike and the fundamental freedom of collective bargaining. Last but not least, Article 16 of the Charter has put the freedom to conduct a business on a pedestal. The only international court to interpret the Charter is the CJEU. For the CJEU, it will be one of many "constitutional" principles to be taken into account.

In sum, in our view, the prospects are extremely weak that the Treaty reference to the Charter of Fundamental rights might provoke a *shift* in the way the Court deals or even has to deal with potential conflicts between the right to strike and so-called fundamental (economic) freedoms. The prospects stemming from the accession to the EConvHR for changing the economic constitution of the European Union are more promising.[80] An accession to the EConvHR might tone down the flat juxtaposition of fundamental freedoms and fundamental rights integrated in one Charter. It puts genuine fundamental (workers') rights at the heart of the matter. Since the EConvHR is enforceable in a court, it will force all European institutions, including the CJEU, to abide by the judgements delivered in Strasbourg. As opposed to Luxembourg, Strasbourg will not dwell on the question of whether human rights can restrict fundamental economic freedoms. It will assess whether and to what extent these fundamental economic freedoms can actually restrict genuine fundamental rights. It will force the European institutions to justify restrictions to citizens' rights, instead of forcing citizens to justify the exercise of their human rights.

The accession to the EConvHR is by no means a fact. Although Article 6 TEU provides that the Union *shall* accede, Article 218, § 8 of the Treaty on the functioning of the European Union provides that such a decision needs to be taken unanimously by the Council. The contrast between the wording of Article 6 and Article 218 § 8 TFEU is reminiscent of a similar contrast which characterises the implementations of European (collective) agreements concluded between management and labour at Community level in the meaning of Article 139 TEC. The request of unanimity does not as such provide an argument for the Member States to question the obligatory nature of their constitutional duty under the Treaty on the functioning of the European Union to decide in favour of the accession. Article 238 § 8 TFEU does indicate that the ratification of the Lisbon Treaty as such is not sufficient to guarantee that the decision of the Council enters into force. The article provides that the decision will enter into force solely "after it has been approved by the Member States in accordance with their respective constitutional requirements".

---

80 In the same vein the impact of the Charter and the accession to the EConvHR can be compared: Ph. Syrpis, "The Treaty of Lisbon: Much ado ... But about what?", *Industrial Law Journal* 2008, 233–234.

B. PROSPECTS OF THE ACCESSION

The *Luxembourg* Court considers that the European legal order is a *supranational* legal order. It is a unique legal order. It considers EU law to prevail over domestic constitutional law. It also distinguishes EU law from ordinary international law. The Court adopts an attitude in respect of other legal orders which is fairly "dualistic". The EU legal order is characterised by a kind of impermeability. The Court does not consider legal standards of distinct legal orders in their own right, but primarily as general principles *of EU law.* Insofar as these heteronomous instruments are not recognised as the result of a legal "reception", it the Court adopts a consistent attitude and disregards the case law of the distinct legal orders from which they sprang.

The accession of the EU to the European Convention on Human Rights might provoke a more "monistic" approach of the Court. This means that the provisions of the European Convention on Human rights will be part of EU law in their own right. According to the interpretation of the Strasbourg Court, this will logically force the Court to interpret those standards as legal standards which originate from the Council of Europe. Ideally, the intervention of the CJEU could remedy a potential clash by issuing an interpretation of EU law which avoids a conflict with standards. In a recent discussion document, the CJEU seems to favour a similar stance.[81] It stated: "In order to preserve this characteristic of the Union's system of judicial protection, the possibility must be avoided of the European Court of Human Rights being called on to decide on the conformity of an act of the Union with the Convention without the Court of Justice first having had an opportunity to give a definitive ruling on the point."

Mutatis mutandis, in the relation between the Strasbourg and the Luxembourg Court, both courts should respect the principle that the CJEU remains the sole judge for the interpretation of EU Law. The 'supreme' assessment of the conformity of EU law as interpreted by the CJEU with the EConvHR should be entrusted to the Strasbourg Court. However, the CJEU seems to suggest that the European Court on Human rights cannot declare acts of the European Union to be "invalid". The scope of this observation remains unclear. It gives the impression that Strasbourg can rule that there is a lack of conformity with the European Union. The Strasbourg Court could condemn the European Union, but it could not declare that the act is null and void.

81 See "Discussion document of the Court of Justice of the European Union on certain aspects of the accession of the European Union to the European Convention for the Protection of Human Rights and Fundamental Freedoms".

It is not crystal clear to what extent the European Court on Human Rights will have the courage to adopt a progressive stance on the right to take collective action. The timid recognition of the right to strike as a corollary right which cannot be dissociated from the freedom of association only dates back to 2009,[82] the case related to a clear-cut *prohibition* of strikes in the Turkish public sector. In two judgements of the Strasbourg Court (*Unison* and *Federation of Offshore Workers' Trade Unions)* which preceded both landmark judgements the Court did adopt a broad interpretation of the conflicting private and public interests which could justify *restrictions* to the right to take collective actions. Hence, at first sight, the prospects seem bad. In *Demir and Baykara*,[83] the Court indicated that it was under an obligation to interpret Article 11 of the EconvHR in the light of "international law other than the Convention, the interpretation of such elements by competent organs, and the practice of European States reflecting their common values." If taken seriously, such a canon of interpretation will urge the Court to see whether restrictions imposed by the Signatory Parties are in fact consistent with the case law developed by the ILO's Freedom of Association Committee and that of the Council of Europe's European Committee on Social Rights. Since both previous judgements did not respect the ILO's supervisory bodies and were not in accordance with the case law of the European Committee on Social Rights, the persuasive authority of these "precedents" is poor. In this respect, it is worthwhile to recall that the European Committee on Social rights has refused to take into account mere business interests as a justified restriction on the right to take collective action. Thus, it has refuted that a "proportionality test" was compatible with the exhaustive character of the restrictions under Article 31 ESC.[84]

The later judgement *Trofimchuk v. Ukraine*[85] relating to the dismissal of a worker for participating in a "spontaneous" strike is disappointing for its total lack of dialogue with the aforementioned committees.

In sum, the prospects that accession to the European Convention on Human Rights will provoke a shift in the balance between fundamental economic freedoms and fundamental workers' rights, will also depend on the judicial activism of the European Court on Human Rights. The method of interpretation introduced in *Demir* and *Baykara* provides the necessary tools to adopt a more progressive attitude based upon the dialogue between the European Court on Human Rights and specialised supervisory bodies monitoring fundamental workers' rights.

82 ECtHR 21 April 2009, *Enerji Yapi-Yol Sen,* No. 68959/01.
83 ECtHR 12 November 2008, *Demir and Baykara v. Turkey,* No. 34503/97.
84 See in this respect: ECSR, XVI-1, Conclusion with regard to Belgium. See for the situation in Belgium: F. Dorssemont, 2009a, 167–202.
85 European Court on Human Rights, 28 October 2010, *Trofimchuk v. Ukraine,* No. 4241/03.

C. A SOCIAL PROGRESS CLAUSE

In the report of 19 March 2010 on the impact of both judgements, the European Trade Union Confederation was extremely critical about the case law, while the employers' side (Business Europe, UEAPME and CEEP) applauded. The employers' side ruled that the relationship between economic freedoms and fundamental rights was not changed by the case law. A legislative intervention was not required. The European Trade Union Confederation (ETUC) ruled that the judgements of the Court of Justice in fact established a principle of primacy of economic freedoms over the Fundamental Social Rights and that the Member States are forced to violate obligations arising from human rights treaties. ETUC argued for a structural solution. Only an adjustment to the Treaty could bring salvation. It suggested that a protocol would be added to the Treaties. In this protocol a "Social Progress clause" would have to be enshrined. That clause should provide that the exercise of the economic freedoms should harmonise with the exercise of fundamental social rights in order to do justice to the goal of social progress and the improvement of living and working conditions. The social progress clause advocated by the ETUC states that in case of an insurmountable conflict, fundamental social rights as recognised in the EU Member States and by EU law should have precedence over fundamental economic freedoms.

To some extent this protocol could be described as a constitutional Monti clause. It is different from the well-known Monti clauses enshrined in secondary EU instruments which are incapable of regulating a relation between the fundamental economic freedoms enshrined in the Treaties and conflicting social rights in the EU Member States. Furthermore, the Social Progress clause underlines that the protection of social rights is imbedded in EU law. The deliberate use of the notion Progress clause instead of safeguard clause provides evidence of this offensive strategy.

CONCLUSIONS

In the first part of this contribution we intended to show that it is not necessary to change the existing rules of the EU common market in order to avoid the new scenarios created by Viking and Laval. On the contrary, the correct application of such common market rules is the most direct and convincing way to prevent the negative effects of such judgements on national industrial relation systems.

We also suggested how the internal market principles could be applied to collective actions in a way that does not simply guarantee an "exemption" for trade unions, but that limits their collective autonomy when its exercise seriously infringes the rights of persons other than the employer and when it has protectionist purposes.

In the second and third part, this contribution aimed at finding a solution *de iure condendo*. First, the failed attempt to remedy a feeling of unease within the European Trade union movement was analysed through a legislative avenue. Last, but not least, a constitutional solution based upon primary EU law was envisaged. We did not examine the extent to which the restrictions of the right to take collective action imposed under EU law are at variance and to what extent they are incompatible with international labour standards upholding the freedom of association and the right to take collective action. Such a finding will not compel the CJEU to change its interpretation, insofar as the EU is not bound by these international standards. In this respect, the accession to the ECHR as scheduled in Article 6 § 4 TEU might provoke a shift.

Neither will the Courts or supervisory bodies be able to condemn the European Union. However, these finding will put Member States that are bound by these positions in a catch 22 position, since they will be bound to respect conflicting international standards. However, it goes without saying that these verdicts will constitute an *indirect* critique of the CJUE's position. There are signs that these pathways are gradually being explored by trade unions, which have either communicated observations to supervisory bodies or filed formal complaints.

In fact, the *Viking* and *Laval* judgements suggest a clash between the legal order of the Council of Europe and of the ILO on the one hand, and that of the European Union on the other hand. That apparent "clash" was in fact confirmed by the ILO's Committee of experts which considered that "it has never included the need to assess the proportionality of interests bearing in mind a notion of freedom of establishment or freedom to provide services".[86] The Committee considered that the "doctrine that is being articulated in these CJEU judgements is likely to have a significant restrictive effect on the exercise of the right to strike in practice in a manner contrary to the Convention".

The conclusions of the Expert Committee monitoring ILO Conventions and recommendations illustrate that the clash between legal standards finally amounts to a clash between bodies enforcing or monitoring these standards. The fact that this was not just a slip of the tongue of the CEACR is illustrated by the recent Report delivered at the International Labour Conference (102nd Session, 2013) regarding the Freedom of Association in Sweden. It severely criticises the ruling of the Laval dispute by the Swedish Arbetsdomstolen (after the preliminary questions had been answered by the CJUE). Since the collective action was considered lawful at the time of its exercise, the liability of the trade union, which was established in a retroactive way, was considered to be "a grave violation of the

[86] Report III (1A) Report of the Committee of Experts on the Application of Conventions and Recommendations, International Labour Conference 99th Session 2010, 209.

principles of the freedom of association". In sum, the CEACR rightly considers that the error of the trade unions was an insurmountable one. The Committee further analysed the legislation, which was passed after the Laval judgement and which restricted the right to have recourse to collective action against a foreign service provider in order to conclude a collective agreement which went beyond the minimum conditions in the central collective agreement. The Committee has expressed that this legislation raises concern.

These observations of the CEACR are extremely relevant in the light of the collective complaint which Swedish trade unions have brought with the ECSR, which monitors the European Social Charter, criticising the law reform as a violation of Articles 4, 6 and 19 § 4 RESC.[87]

[87] Collective Complaint No. 85/2012 *Confédération générale du travail de Suède (LO) et Confédération générale des cadres, fonctionnaires et employés (TCO) c. Suède.*

FUNDAMENTAL SOCIAL RIGHTS: AN ADDED VALUE TO THE PROTECTION OF WORKERS?

The increasing importance of fundamental (social) rights to the development of labour law?

Teun Jaspers* and Willemijn Roozendaal**

> "does the new rhetoric of social rights – as embodied in instruments such as the ILO Declaration of Fundamental Principles and Rights at Work (1998) and the EU Charter of Fundamental Rights (2000) – match the reality of the new world of market regulation and growing global inequality?"[1]
>
> (B. Hepple, Social and Labour Rights in a Global Context, CUP, 2002, p. 1–2).

I. INTRODUCTION

Since a few decades, attention for fundamental social rights as a source of protection for workers seems to have become stronger.[2] No doubt this growing attention is related to the enhanced economic competition due to globalisation during these decades. In the European region it has been the Europeanisation in economic terms that had the same effect. The creation and the actual functioning of the single market based on the four freedoms and free competition, in combination with the intensified globalisation have resulted in increased competition between and on labour markets in Member States. Moreover, due to this development,

* Utrecht University, The Netherlands.
** VU, Amsterdam University, The Netherlands.
1 B. Hepple, "Introduction", in Hepple (ed), *Social and Labour Rights in a Global Context*, CUP, 2002, p. 1/2.
2 Cf. Philip Alston (ed), *Labour Rights as Human Rights*, Oxford 2005.

competition is emerging between labour law systems of the various countries.[3] Labour law is challenged by this development.

Of course, competition is of all time. The ILO has been dealing with it since its foundation. However, the recent intensified globalisation and European economic integration have extended the national labour markets beyond their 'natural' boundaries, more than ever before. Consequently, national labour laws and even European labour law are no longer able to regulate and indeed capable of regulating the labour market(s) on their own.[4] In this respect it is interesting to see that in practice as well as in literature the invocation of fundamental principles, of fundamental (social) rights has become stronger.

Fundamental social rights did not reach the level of European Union law for a long time, except for the principle of equal treatment. The debate about a European Constitution at the beginning of this century has accelerated the process of adopting fundamental (social) rights as the basic principles of the European Union. The Treaty of Lisbon, assigning the European Charter of Fundamental Rights the status of primary European law, can be seen as a confirmation of this development. This might have seemed like good news to many advocates of stronger labour rights. Surely, fundamental rights are expected to bring stronger social protection for employees.[5] When fundamental rights are adopted on an international level, it might be possible to mitigate, remedy or even prevent the consequences of enhanced international competition.

However, this expectation can be questioned. Indeed, to what extent are fundamental social rights helpful for achieving adequate protection of workers against the consequences of increased competition, compared to the protection provided by the traditional national or international labour laws and labour regulations? In other words: to what extent can fundamental social rights have an added value?

We will start our investigation into this question with some theoretical notes on the concept of fundamental social rights, as opposed to 'ordinary' social rights (see under III). We will continue our discussion with an assessment of the value of fundamental social rights for workers in an increasingly competitive world. Our analysis will focus on European Union law (see under IV). First, we will list the

---

3 European (labour) law is trying to cope with it by proposing and adopting labour law regulations with cross-border effects. Various directives prove this. The CJEU also contributes towards this.

4 Cf. John Craig and S. Michael Lynk (eds.), *Globalization and the Future of Labour Law*, Cambridge, 2006.

5 Virginia Mantouvalou seems to take that position. See Virginia Mantouvalou, "Are Labour Rights Human Rights?", *European Law Journal* Vol. 3 (2012), No. 2, p. 151–172.

contributions made by the European legislator (see under IV.B) and in a separate paragraph we will analyse what the European Court of Justice has contributed (see under IV.C).

A distinction can be made between an emerging competition on a global level, which implies competition on the international and the European labour markets, the macro level on the one hand, and competition on the national, local labour markets, the micro, mostly individual level on the other hand. The two are interrelated in the sense that the latter is definitely influenced by the former. A primary question will be whether an invocation of fundamental rights aiming at an improvement of the protection of workers' rights, has to be assessed in a similar way on the international level as on the national level. On a more macro level, the question is to what extent fundamental social rights may function as a barrier to social dumping. With respect to the competition among individuals, i.e. the micro level, the question is whether the invocation of fundamental social rights can be helpful for achieving an adequate protection of workers compared to the protection provided by national labour laws. The case law of the European Court of Justice (ECJ) on equality rights for women will serve as a test case. Since this is the oldest and most developed example of a fundamental social right in the EU, it may be exemplary for the potential of the protection against competition between individuals (see under V). We will finish with some concluding remarks (see under VI). Before moving on to the theoretical issues however, we would like to mention some controversies that may occur (see under II).

II. CONTROVERSIAL ASPECTS

The invocation of fundamental social rights in order to preserve the main objective of labour law: protection of – vulnerable – workers has several, sometimes controversial, aspects. Below, we will draw attention to some of them.

1. Scholars as well politicians and trade unionists are advocating the appeal to fundamental social rights as a *safeguard against destruction* of labour rights, which might occur in an increasing competitive world. Fundamental social rights may combat social dumping by upholding social standards. This is seen as being in line with the increased attention to human rights as an instrument to protect people against the powerful state and corollary against powerful market players, more in particular big enterprises.[6]
2. Earlier, we raised the issue of the *globalisation* of the economy. But globalisation also has another side apart from the negative connotation:

[6] Namely extensive relocations, restructuring combined with a loss of jobs and/or a deterioration of employment conditions.

extension of the welfare state to other parts of the world where people can now benefit from an economic development based on their favourable conditions of production, 'cheaper' employment conditions and less strict labour laws.[7] The negative side is that it can endanger the level of protection of employees in more developed, richer countries: the downward spiral. An appeal to fundamental rights has two sides. It can help countries and societies to improve the situation of its citizens. On the other hand, however, countries facing more competition with regard to employment and social conditions can find it quite challenging to combine the maintenance of an adequate level of protection with an increase of their competitiveness in a globalising world.

3. An appeal to fundamental social rights is also motivated by the recognition of *unequal treatment* of persons who are in a disadvantaged position due to intrinsic personal characteristics beyond their influence. The first fields on which the principle of equality has been invoked and applied concern the discrimination of women and black people, followed by the discrimination of handicapped people and elderly persons, although this last category is quite complicated. All these groups were discriminated against on the labour market in one way or another.[8] In the field of social law the aim of invoking fundamental social rights was to activate social law that – mostly not deliberately – was discriminating these groups.[9] More in particular, in the field of discrimination the question will rise whether the fundamental social right of equality and the invocation of it have really improved the position of these groups when compared to the level of protection of the individual members of these groups. In the second part (see under V) we will come back to this when we analyse whether women, handicapped and elderly people have benefitted from the application of the equality rules provided by EU law.[10] Do the fundamental social rights add value to the protective rights that are embedded in the various labour laws (of the EU and of the MS)? The analysis will show at least some ambiguity.
4. In the European arena, the application of the *free movement principle* has triggered the debate about the value of labour law as an effective instrument of protection at the national level. In fact, as does any medal, this one too has two sides. On the one hand it is an expression of a fundamental right which entitles an individual (European) citizen to look for and to accept a job in another member state regardless of whether (s)he is a national of that country,

[7] All this combined with a low level of social security, means that these economies have a favourable competitive position.

[8] Not only negatively, however, as the example of elderly employees shows. Older employees usually benefitted from seniority rules.

[9] We will not deal with social law. There are many examples of how the law was amended in order to remedy the discrimination of women.

[10] Taking into consideration that this equality rule has a long-standing tradition in EU law. Article 119 EEC Treaty of 1950 already recognised this equality of men and women in relation to pay.

and to enjoy additional social security protection. The principle does not only allow a person to look for and accept a job, it also determines that the same terms should apply to both nationals and non-nationals. This stipulation is based on the prohibition of discrimination on grounds of nationality. It can be seen as a benefit for a lot of citizens in the European Union and its member states. These rules can be considered as the materialisation of a fundamental (social) right. The other side of the medal implies a potential drawback: the free movement principle as one of the main pillars of the European Union can also result in less protection on certain domestic markets. It can lead to or justify the application of the principle of 'equality in pejus' or in other words: a reverse equality. The outcome of some cases before the European Court of Justice (hereafter CJEU) has shown these two sides.[11] It can lead to less protection than the protection provided for by national law.

5. Another rationale for the appeal to fundamental social rights could be the possible beneficial effect on citizens in situations where the level of protection of employees or workers in the EU member states differs. When these rights become binding they can be valuable to employees or workers in countries with a low standard of protection, lower than the fundamental rights provide for. The employee can appeal to a fundamental social right provided it has obtained legal effect in the EU legal order. It can be invoked directly when the fundamental (social) right as such has a direct effect. The other option is that the fundamental (social) is recognised in general terms only. There are many examples of the fundamental (social) right having been *transposed in primary or secondary European law* and in this way having become effective.[12] The appeal to fundamental social rights that are supplementary or at least supportive to the rules of both national and European labour law can result in an extra protection that is not offered by the current law of the state concerned or by European law. The fundamental social rights have or can have a positive impact on those situations.

Taking the protective character of labour law as a basic notion,[13] we will discuss the question of whether fundamental social rights can contribute towards an effective protection of workers. Are they additions to the protective rules of

[11] Examples include the cases of *Laval*, *Viking* and *Rüffert*. Cf. more in detail Giovanni Orlandini and Filip Dorssemont in their contribution to this book. We also use the abbreviation CJEU when referring to its predecessor: the Court of Justice of the European Communities (CJE).

[12] For instance health and safety at work, information and consultation of workers, which are all laid down in various directives, as well as the equal treatment rule in the broad sense, laid down not only in directives directly related to equal treatment but also in directives on part-time work, on secondment or temporary agency work, fixed-term contracts, posting of workers.

[13] Generally, it is assumed that workers need (legal) protection due to their (assigned) weak position in their relationship to the employer. Economic dependency is one of the characteristics of any labour relation.

national laws? Can they have preference over national laws in states where the protective rights of workers are endangered as a result of intensified competition? Are fundamental rights better able to withstand the potential dangers of globalisation and the increasing competition on the national labour markets? The first question to be answered will be which functions and which effect can be attached to fundamental (social) rights.

III. THE MEANING OF 'FUNDAMENTAL' SOCIAL RIGHTS

When talking about the meaning of – an invocation of – a fundamental (social) right a threefold distinction can be made.[14] A first approach is a positivistic one: a fundamental social right is recognised as such when it has been adopted in international treaties or other sources of international law. If this is not the case, they are not considered as a fundamental social right. The second approach has a normative character.[15] It is crucial that the rights have a compelling moral weight, or as Collins has expressed: "all human beings should be accorded certain fundamental rights by virtue of their humanity. These human rights are universal and imperative, with a special moral weight that normally overrides other considerations".[16] The protection offered by the fundamental rights could be strengthened through this approach when they are considered as *human rights* because they are based on the principle of universality and indivisibility of human rights. That would imply that labour rights are better preserved and protected because they are not subordinate to other interests, in particular economic interests,[17] unless the human rights provisions themselves provide a restriction[18] Labour rights as human rights are to be considered as being of a higher level in

[14] We refer here explicitly to an article of Virginia Mantouvalou in which she elaborated on this distinction. Cf. Virginia Mantouvalou, "Are Labour Rights Human Rights?", *European Law Journal*, Vol. 3 (2012), No. 2, p. 151–172; see also Philip Alston (ed.), *Labour Rights as Human Rights*, Oxford 2005.

[15] Hugh Collins has assessed this approach: "Theories of Rights as Justifications for Labour Law", in: Davidov and Langille (eds.), *The Idea of Labour Law*, Oxford 2011, pp. 137–155.

[16] H. Collins, Theories of Rights as Justifications for Labour Law, in: Davidov and Langille (eds.), *The Idea of Labour Law*, Oxford 2011, p. 140. Collins argues that this approach is not fruitful because it can be questioned whether labour rights can be seen as human rights. Mantouvalou has criticised the opinion of Collins in her contribution (note 14).

[17] In the context of this contribution I mean employers' interests in particular.

[18] The usual wording is found in many human rights provisions in the various international sources: *in accordance with the law and when it is necessary in a democratic society in the interests of national security, public safety or the economic well-being of the country, for the prevention of disorder or crime, for the protection of health or morals, or for the protection of the rights and freedoms of others.*

the hierarchy of laws. This debate has gained relevance since the *Laval* and *Viking* cases in 2007.[19]

The third and last approach is called the instrumental one.[20] Human rights are seen as part of strategies aiming at the promotion of labour rights as human rights. It refers directly to the success of invoking human rights in order to defend against attacks on labour conditions. Labour rights have certain characteristics of human rights if "labour rights (are) really best promoted under the rubric, or within the framework, of human rights".[21] The results of the attempts of states, international organisations or civil society organisations (trade unions and NGOs) to get human rights applied to labour-related cases, are what count.[22] In this respect courts play a crucial role.

When evaluating the three approaches from the point of view of the actual value of the approaches for the effective protection of labour rights, the first approach seems to be inappropriate since the mere mentioning of the (fundamental social) right does not say anything about its actual application. Although these rights can be mentioned in a political debate, merely mentioning them is of no use in a legal debate. The two other approaches are more worthy of an analysis. The instrumental approach has gained attractiveness in legal terms since courts have recognised the interplay between labour rights and human rights.[23] In the past it has been argumented that the human rights character of labour rights will not have an unequivocally positive impact. This opinion was based on the case law of courts. The case law of the Strasbourg Court, in particular, was considered as being 'disappointing', 'individual and formalistic', and as attaching 'greater importance to the defence of individual autonomy than to collective solidarity'.[24] The case law refers to decisions of the European Court of Human Rights in the seventies and eighties of the previous century.[25] The opinion with regard to the

---

19 CJEU 11 December 2007, C-438/05 (*Viking*); CJEU 18 December 2007, C-341/05 (*Laval*). With regard to these cases, see under IV.B.

20 Cf. Virginia Mantouvalou, "Are Labour Rights Human Rights?", *European Law Journal*, Vol. 3 (2012), No.2, p. 164–165.

21 Philip Alston, "Labour Rights as Human Rights: The Not So Happy State of Art", in Philip Alston (ed.), *Labour Rights as Human Rights*, Oxford 2005, p. 3.

22 See the quotation by Bob Hepple at the top of this contribution.

23 Virginia Mantouvalou speaks of an *integrated approach* being an 'interpretative technique that reads certain social and labour rights in the provisions of the ECHR'. Cf. Virginia Mantouvalou, "Are Labour Rights Human Rights?", *European Law Journal*, Vol. 3 (2012), No. 2, p. 158.

24 In that sense K.D. Ewing, "The Human Rights Act and Labour Law", 27 *Industrial Law Journal* (1998), 0. 27; Lord Wedderburn, "Freedom of Association or Rights to Organise? The Common Law and International Sources", in Wedderburn (ed.), *Employment Rights in Britain and Europe?*, London 1991, p. 138–144; and T. Novitz, *International and European Protection of the Right to Strike*, Oxford 2003, p. 238.

25 Reference has been made to ECtHR 27 October 1975, App No. 4464/70 (*National Union of Belgian Police*); ECtHR 6 February 1976, App No. 5589/72 (*Schmidt and Dahlstrom*); ECtHR

case law of the ECtHR has changed substantially. In a number of decisions the ECtHR has applied human rights, as laid down in the ECHR, to labour cases aiming at the protection of workers.[26] However, that does not mean that such cases are always ruled in favour of the workers or the workers' organisations since some studies show that the "legal avenues presented to pursue workers' claims –by constructing them as human rights- do not always lead to optimal outcomes for workers and their organisations. On the contrary: the results have been decidedly mixed".[27]

However, what is even more interesting is that the ECtHR has moved away from the strict interpretation that only state power is involved when respecting human rights. Not only states can be forced to take measures regulating the employment relationship, ruled by private labour law, also private powers, such as employers, have to respect fundamental (social) rights.[28] To some extent the case law of the CJEU is more and more in line with this development although not all its decisions fit in with it. The case law of the CJEU concerning equal treatment is generally speaking an example of this positive development.[29]

In cases where human or fundamental rights can have a direct effect and therefore can be invoked in law suits by individuals or by representing organisations such as trade unions, the instrumental approach seems to be the more suitable approach. That is the case when subjective rights are at stake. It is only logical that in terms of an effective deployment of human rights for the protection of a worker's position the instrumental approach is preferable in order to achieve a positive result. However, that does not mean that the normative approach falls short. In the normative, or in other words in the political and ideological debate, the normative human rights approach can be highly valued. That is all the more true when economic interests are brought in, arguing that the (full) application of fundamental (social) rights jeopardises the economic position of a private entity,

---

18 October 1982, App Nos. 7601/76 and 7806/77 (*Young, James and Webster*); ECtHR 11 January 192006, App Nos. 52562/99 and 52620/99 (*Sorensen and Rasmussen*).

26 A.Ph.C.M. Jaspers, "Dutch labour law and the ECHR", *Europäische Zeitschrift für Arbeitsrecht*, 2/2013, p. 161-177, gave a number of examples in which the ECtHR ruled in favour of workers or workers' organisations, which resulted in the recognition and effective application of fundamental rights to labour conditions. These were cases relating to compulsory labour law, right to private life, right to privacy, right to work in decent conditions, collective bargaining and collective action. Cf. also K. Ewing and J. Hendy, "The Dramatic Implications of *Demir and Baykara*", *Industrial Law Journal*, Vol. 39, No. 1, March 2010, p. 2–51.

27 Colin Fenwick and Tonia Novitz, "Conclusion: Regulating to Protect Workers' Human Rights", in: Colin Fenwick and Tonia Novitz (eds.), *Human Rights at Work*, Hart, Onati 2010, p. 588.

28 Recently ECtHR 12 September 2011 (Appl Nos. 28955/06, 28957/06, 28959/06 and 28964/06 (*Palomo Sanchez*).

29 It should be noted that not all case law of the CJEU has to be unambiguously positively in terms of protection of workers, as we try to demonstrate in the second part of this contribution.

such as a company, or even of the country. Usually, the debate is not about the recognition of the right as such[30] but more often about the exercise of the right.

The normative approach is basically the only possible one when so-called programmatic rights are at stake. For that reason it is quite useful to distinguish between the various types of human, fundamental rights. Contrary to the first category of directly applicable subjective rights, the programmatic rights – usually – require interference by the state regarding their realisation. Programmatic rights are therefore hardly enforceable since they do not concern concrete rights or impose a concrete obligation. As Mantouvalou rightly argues, certain labour rights should prohibit *grave moral wrongs*.[31] They can be seen as safeguard provisions and are an expression of the general duty of respecting *human dignity*. And even when the realisation of the rights depends on the resources available or the current state of the economy of a country, these restraints have to be taken into account but that does not relieve the country from its obligation to show that it has made very serious efforts to address the core duties imposed by the human rights treaty provisions.[32]

It cannot be denied that fundamental rights play an increasingly large role in the fields of labour law and social policies as well. As mentioned above, that does not imply that an invocation and the application of fundamental rights in the field of labour are always beneficial to workers in their specific situation. When fundamental rights, internationally recognised and laid down in legal documents, are used to adapt the level of protection of workers to the lower standard as established in these documents, one can question their value. Although non-regression is generally accepted as a common principle, that does not mean that *adaptation in pejus* is excluded in practice. The development of globalisation accompanied by the intensified competition, also on employment conditions and social welfare, tends to point in that direction. One can wonder whether the current economic crisis has contributed or will further contribute to that.

---

30 Although that can be the case when it is argued that the right at stake is not covered by the treaty provision. For a long time the ECtHR took that position when judging a claim concerning the right to take collective action. Cf. ECtHR 6 February 1976, App No. 5589/72 (*Schmidt and Dahlström)* affirmed in the *UNISON* case: ECHR 10 January 2002 App No. 53574/99. Recently the court changed its opinion in the *Demir and Baykara v Turkey* case, ECtHR 12 November 2008, Appl No. 34503/97.

31 Cf. Virginia Mantouvalou, "Are Labour Rights Human Rights?", *European Law Journal*, Vol. 3 (2012), No. 2, pp. 164–165. She gives the examples of emotional and psychological humiliation by an employer, the privacy of the worker and exploitation in terms of very long working hours or no holidays or very low pay.

32 This is the standing opinion of the international supervisory committees, see the reports of the UN Committee on Economic, Social and Cultural Rights, as well as of the European Committee of Social Rights.

IV. EU LAW AND RESPECT FOR FUNDAMENTAL RIGHTS

A. INTRODUCTION

When considering the proposition that the introduction of binding social rights on an international level could help countries and societies to improve the situation for its citizens or to maintain the acquired level of protection, one can wonder whether the adoption of fundamental (social) rights in the EU would have the same, although stronger, effect. One might assume that the EU regulations in the field of social policy, to a certain extent, have prevented or at least mitigated competition between states with respect to labour conditions. The question remains whether the fundamental social rights have contributed or can contribute to this objective. Again: do they have added value? For a proper analysis we want to distinguish between the efforts made by the EU legislator and the role played by the European Court of Justice.

B. THE EU LEGISLATOR AND FUNDAMENTAL SOCIAL RIGHTS

EU law has always paid attention to – some – fundamental rights, although not explicitly. With hindsight, the equal treatment provision of the EEC Treaty of 1957 (Article 119 EEC) is an example of a human right being incorporated in the treaty, just as the prohibition of discrimination on grounds of nationality is. The economic background of these provisions[33] might have fitted perfectly in with the objective of the European Community of economic integration. Soon enough, however, that economic background was also recognised as a fundamental standard for the EC and its member states. In the *Defrenne* case the CJEU stated "that it repeatedly stated that respect for fundamental personal human rights is one of the general principles of Community law, the observance of which it has a duty to ensure".[34] The importance of the equal treatment principle in the EC and the EU has been underlined by the series of secondary law regulations in both fields. Levelling down of equal treatment protection of employees was thus effectively prevented in Europe due to primary and secondary European law.

The proclamation of the Community Charter of the Fundamental Rights of Workers of 1989, though not legally binding, was the next step,[35] followed by the

33 The CJEU explicitly points this out in the Defrenne cases as well as in later cases. Cf. Catherine Barnard, *EC Employment Law*, Oxford 2006, p. 298 ff.

34 CJEU 15 June 1978. Case 149/77, no. 26 (*Defrenne III*).

35 We leave aside the contribution of primary and secondary European law. The relevant Treaty provisions as well as the regulations and various directives have been the main instruments

EU Charter of Fundamental Rights presented in Nice in 2000. The Treaties of the European Community as well as the Treaties of the European Union of 1997 and 2002 explicitly referred to fundamental rights as laid down in the European Convention on Human Rights and/or in the European Social Charter.[36] The final phase of this development was completed with the Treaty of Lisbon at the end of 2009, by which the EU Charter got full recognition by awarding it the status of primary EU law.[37] With regard to the realisation of the EU's fundamental rights approach, it is very important that the provisions of the EU Charter meet the requirements of direct effect. It has to be mentioned that only a few provisions of the EU Charter do have direct effect.[38] Those that do, can have a real impact.

The question is what the impact can be of EU Charter provisions – as far as they can have direct effect – when it comes to supporting or strengthening workers' protection. There are two reasons why one should be careful not to attach too much value to EU Charter provisions since the Charter itself contains possible restrictions.[39] The first one is the most important one: the provision of Article 51 EU Charter containing a rule concerning its application. As Article 51 states: "The provisions of this Charter are addressed to the institutions, bodies, offices and agencies of the Union with due regard for the principle of subsidiarity and to the Member States only when they are implementing Union law". Since only 'state' institutions – either European or national ones – are addressed, this restricting provision implies an exclusion of a direct effect in horizontal relations. Therefore, it can be considered as a rejection of the enforceability of EU Charter provisions by a worker against his or her employer when the latter violates fundamental social rights of the EU Charter that are not transposed into the national law of a member state.[40] This implicates an important obstacle to the effectiveness of

for the development of social rights in Europe, also in terms of their effective recognition and application. Many directives stem from fundamental rights recognised by the EU Charter: prohibition of child labour in connection to directive 94/33 (young people), information and consultation (directives 2002/14, 2009/38 and 2001/86), family and private life (directives on parental leave and pregnancy), health and safety at work (various directives) including working time, annual paid leave and finally some aspects of privacy and freedom of expression (directive on data protection). Historically, however, the introduction of these labour law directives was not specifically inspired by the idea of fundamental human rights, except for the Directive on data protection.

36 Article 6 TEU refers to the ECHR and Article 136 EC and Article 151 TFEU refer to the ESC.

37 Article 6 § 1 TEU.

38 For instance Articles 5, 12 and 21 of the EU Charter, although Article 51 can provide an obstacle. See infra.

39 Apart from both restrictions mentioned here, the EU Charter includes another general restriction, similar to restrictions laid down in other international sources, for instance several provisions in the ECHR. See supra note 18.

40 The meaning of this restriction as to the scope is relative because primary EU law contains fundamental (social) rights that can be invoked by the individual and applied by courts.

the EU Charter and constitutes a divergence from the European Convention on Human Rights to which the EU is going to accede in the near future.[41]

A second sign that the Charter will not have a strong effect in terms of preventing decreased protection, can be found in Protocol No. 30, which contains exceptions for Poland and the United Kingdom. These countries have reserved the right to opt out of the judiciary competence of the CJEU to assess and decide on conformity of domestic law with EU law. The meaning of this opt out clause may be modest in practice,[42] it can nevertheless be seen – not only in the debates about the EU Charter – as a partial denial of the universal nature of human or fundamental rights as being generally applicable regardless of the territorial sovereignty of the states concerned.

When taking a closer look at the instrumentalist approach introduced under III, one may indeed question whether the EU Charter contributes substantially to the development of the effective impact of fundamental social rights in the field of labour law. That does not mean, however, that the introduction of the Charter of Fundamental Rights is completely effectless. The embodiment of the Charter as a source of primary EU law has induced a lively discussion about the social values of the European Union.[43] The moral value of the Charter will certainly have some influence on the position of employees in the European Union, although this influence will perhaps be difficult to trace.

C. THE CJEU AND FUNDAMENTAL SOCIAL RIGHTS

When analysing the role of fundamental social rights from an instrumental perspective, it is interesting to look at the role played by the CJEU[44] in the course

41 Cf. Saskia Peters and Teun Jaspers, "Sociale Grondrechten", in: Saskia Peters and Ronald Beltzer, *Inleiding Europees Arbeidsrecht*, Deventer 2013, pp. 60–68. See also among others Clemens Ladenburger, Paper "*Protection of Fundamental Rights post-Lisbon – The interaction between the Charter of Fundamental Rights, the European Convention of Human Rights and National Constitutions*", FIDE 2012 (not yet published). It should be noted that member states have recognised fundamental rights in their own constitutions; they can be directly enforceable if they meet the criteria stipulated by the national law of the state in question.

42 An important reason is the obligation of these countries to apply similar fundamental rights laid down in other binding international sources, such as the ECHR.

43 We only refer to the intense discussions among labour lawyers on this subject. The social European model is a major subject of the discussion not only among labour law scholars, but also in the political arena, mainly started by the European Commission. The literature is too extensive to mention here. We would only like to mention Gráinne Búrca and Bruno de Witte (eds.), *Social Rights in Europe*, Oxford 2005 and Brian Bercusson (ed.), *European Labour law and the EU Charter of Fundamental Rights*, Nomos, Baden-Baden 2006.

44 We also use the abbreviation CJEU when referring to its predecessor: the Court of Justice of the European Communities (CJE).

of time in terms of strengthening the rights of workers when the fundamental rights have been invoked.

Long before the entry into force of the EU Charter in 2009, the CJEU had taken a positive stand towards the value of fundamental social rights. As mentioned above, the CJEU referred in the *Defrenne* case to the respect for fundamental personal human rights as one of the general principles of Community law, the observance of which it has a duty to ensure.[45] The *Defrenne* decisions are important for their effects since the CJEU granted the direct applicability of the right to equal pay for men and women in horizontal relations as well. The CJEU has thereby given the prohibition of sex discrimination a firm basis, as a number of decisions dealing with the nationality issue also did.[46] Via this case law the CJEU strengthened the practice of respecting equal pay for men and women by making use of primary and secondary European law.

It took the court a long time, however, to go further along this path. In 2000 – in the BECTU case – Advocate General Tizzano pleaded for the recognition of fundamental rights as "a substantive point of reference for all those involved – Member States, institutions, natural and legal persons – in the Community context".[47] The CJEU itself explicitly referred to the Charter in its decision of 2006.[48] Apart from EU law instruments, the Court also relies on other sources containing fundamental rights, in particularly on the ECHR and *constitutional traditions common to the Member States.*[49] Moreover, although the court has no competence or power to examine the compatibility of national laws with the ECHR, it states that "the Community cannot accept measures which are incompatible with observance of the human rights thus recognised and guaranteed".[50] In case the court has to interpret whether the rules of national law fall within the scope of EC/EU law it has to be determined "whether those rules are compatible with the fundamental rights the observance of which the Court ensures and which derive in particular from the European Convention on Human Rights". The meaning of the fundamental human rights is underlined by the CJEU even when fundamental freedoms of the EC/EU, *in casu* freedom

45 CJEU 15 June 1978, Case 149/77, par. 26 (*Defrenne III*).

46 An overview of the developments, COM (2010)373 final of 13 July 2010.

47 Advocate General Tizzano in his conclusion to CJEU 26 June 2001, C-173/99 (*BECTU*), point 28. It concerned the right to paid annual leave. He concluded that this right "constitutes a fundamental right". See also Brian Bercusson, Stefan Clauwaert, Isabelle Schömann, "Legal Prospects and Legal Effects of the EU Charter", in: Brian Bercusson (ed.), *European Labour law and the EU Charter of Fundamental Rights*, Nomos, Baden-Baden 2006, p. 45.

48 CJEU 27 June 2006. C-540/03 (European Parliament), par. 38.

49 CJEU 14 May 1974, C-4/73 (*Nold*), par. 13. Since then often repeated. For a more elaborate text concerning its meaning, see Saskia Peters and Teun Jaspers, "Sociale grondrechten", in: Saskia Peters and Ronald Beltzer, *Inleiding Europees Arbeidsrecht*, Deventer 2013, pp. 57–60.

50 CJEU 13 July 1989, C-5/88 (*Wachauf*), par. 19. The prohibition to examine remains valid when the rules do not fall within the scope of Community law.

to provide services, are at stake. When assessing whether a restriction on the exercise of a fundamental freedom is justified, as stipulated by Article 56 TFEU, by invoking a fundamental right, the national court has to examine whether the imposed limitation is compatible with the fundamental right. Consequently, it seems possible to invoke fundamental rights when national (legal) measures derogate from EU law.[51] This approach has been confirmed in later decisions of the CJEU. In the *Schmidberger* case[52] the court repeats that "measures which are incompatible with observance of the human rights thus recognised are not acceptable in the Community".

The Kücükdeveci approach. Rather recently the CJEU took the debate about the extended value of opening up the possibility to invoke fundamental rights to another level.[53] As mentioned before direct effect to fundamental rights in horizontal relationships has been refused by the CJEU.[54] In the Kücükdeveci decision, the CJEU argues that when a general principle of EU law, in this case the principle of equal treatment irrespective of age[55]-, falls within the scope of EU law, a national law provision that potentially breaches that general principle can be assessed on its compatibility with EU law. If it is not compatible with EU law, it should not be taken into account.[56] This methodology is – at least for the moment – restricted to cases where a general principle of EU law can be combined with a provision of primary or secondary EU law.[57] Anyhow, the approach of the court is indirectly inclining towards direct horizontal effect. As mentioned above, according to Article 51 EU Charter member states are bound by the provisions of the Charter to respect the provisions of the article in law and in practice (that means the measures they take or envisage to take) only when they

[51] CJEU 1991, C-260/89 (*ERT*). The freedom to provide services (Article 56 TFEU) collides with the freedom of expression (Article 10 ECHR). In similar words, Advocate General Bot in his conclusion to CJEU in C-108/10 (*Scattolon*), points 119 and 120.

[52] CJEU 12 June 2003, C-112/00, (*Schmidberger*), par. 73.

[53] CJEU 19 January 2010, C-555/07 (*Kücükdeveci*). The case was a labour law case 'pur sang'. It was about dismissal and discrimination on grounds of age (framework directive No. 2000/78 on equal treatment). Cf. the elaborate analysis by Saskia Peters and Teun Jaspers, "Sociale grondrechten", in: Saskia Peters and Ronald Beltzer, *Inleiding Europees Arbeidsrecht*, Deventer 2013, pp. 70–83 and the literature mentioned.

[54] CJEU 26 February 1986, No. 152/84 (*Marshall)*, par. 48. Since CJEU 13 November 1990, C-106/89 (*Marleasing*) it is constant case law although the CJEU made serious efforts to extend the borders as much as EU law would permit; see CJEU 4 July 2006 C-212/04, (*Adeneler*) and CJEU 12 June 2008, C-364/07 (*Vassilakis*).

[55] Article 21, 1 EU Charter and Article 6, paragraph 1 TEU with the legal value of a Treaty provision.

[56] The court refers to the primacy principle of EU law; see CJEU 19 January 2010. C-555/07 (*Kücükdeveci*), par. 54. It is a confirmation of the Mangold decision: CJEU 22 November 2005, C-144/04 (*Mangold*).

[57] Since the CJEU kept silent about this alternative in its recent decision in the Dominguez case, it can be questioned whether the court will go this far in other cases. CJEU 24 January 2012, C-282/10 (*Dominguez*).

are implementing EU law. A certain link with EU law is therefore required.[58] The question that has to be answered in the future – mainly by the court – is what kind of link is required? In order to enable individuals to try and enforce the effective application of fundamental social rights, the rights have to meet the four requirements of direct effect, as explained above: a subjective right that has to be clear, unambiguous, unconditional and not subject to further legislation.

Potentially the scope can be extended when considering for instance the following fundamental rights recognised by the EU Charter: prohibition of child labour in connection to directive 94/33 (young people), information and consultation (Directives 2002/14, 2009/38 and 2001/86), family and private life (directives on parental leave and pregnancy), health and safety at work (various directives) including working time, annual paid leave and finally some aspects of privacy and freedom of expression (directive on data protection). It is more problematic if there is no link to European law, see for instance the example of the right to association.

At the end of this analysis we are still challenged by the question whether there is a positive impact of the invocation of fundamental rights on workers, individually as well as collectively, aiming at a strengthening of the protection they want and need from law. Also, if there is a positive impact, what does it entail exactly? The provisional conclusion may be that fundamental social rights in European Union law have an ambiguous character. Some of them seem to be able to prevent social dumping to a certain extent, namely in the case of equality rights. Other fundamental social rights do not really contribute to a stronger protection of workers and are therefore less effectively protective. Examples of the ambiguity on the collective level are the cases of Laval and Viking. It has been argued by labour lawyers that the right to take part in collective actions, if seen as a fundamental right, must have priority unless it violates the limitations set by the human right provision concerned.[59] The CJEU has decided otherwise. Although the court recognises the fundamental nature of the right to take collective action it did not recognise its priority.[60] Or in the words of the CJEU: "it cannot be considered that it is inherent in the very exercise of trade union rights and the right to take

---

58 See also Advocate General Trstenjak's opinion in the case *Dominguez* of 8 September 2011. Case C-282/10.

59 Cf. Filip Dorssemont en Teun Jaspers, "Collectieve actie en vrij verkeer. Eindigen grondrechten waar 'fundamentele' vrijheden beginnen?", *NJW*, no. 154 (January 2007), p. 1 ff.; Teun Jaspers, "The right to collective action in European Law", in: Filip Dorssemont, Teun Jaspers, Aukje van Hoek, *Cross-Border Collective Actions in Europe: A Legal Challenge,* Antwerp-Oxford (Intersentia) 2007, pp. 32–74; and Tonia Novitz, "A Human Rights Analysis of the Viking and Laval Judgments", in: Catherine Barnard, *The Cambridge Yearbook of European Legal Studies*, Vol. 10, 2007–2008, Oxford and Portland 2008, p. 541–562. See also Giovanni Orlandini and Filip Dorssemont in their contribution to this book.

60 The court explicitly rejected the so-called Albany approach of assigning immunity to trade union rights.

collective action that those fundamental freedoms will be prejudiced to a certain degree".[61] The right to take collective action has to be weighed against economic freedoms and then assessed via the application of the proportionality principle. It therefore cannot be seen as a safeguard against 'social dumping'.

However, even if fundamental social rights do not really contribute towards a stronger protection of workers, it should be noted that their moral weight should not be underestimated and may influence political debates in a powerful yet untraceable way.

When analysing the laws on equal treatment more precisely, we will perhaps come to a less positive conclusion. We will now turn to the question concerning the extent to which equality rights can offer protection against competition between individuals.

V. COMPETITION BETWEEN INDIVIDUALS AND EQUALITY RIGHTS

A. INTRODUCTION

It is common use to speak of 'the labour market' as the place where demand and supply of labour meet each other. The workers are the actors with the purpose of 'selling themselves' in order to get a job, an income etc. In market terms workers have to distinguish themselves from others with attractive curricula and distinctive skills. *Social competition* among individuals on the labour market is therefore a reality. In this sense the ILO statement *labour is not a commodity* must not be understood as a denial of the existence of a labour market, but as a correction of the outcome of the exchange process on the labour market. Labour law plays an important role in empowering the worker to be better protected against the consequences of the functioning of the labour market, to mitigate competition with one another.[62] Fundamental social rights may in theory even be better able to provide that protection, because of their moral weight, as opposed to market considerations or the economic interests of employers. The question dealt with in this part of the paper, is whether or not equality rights in the case law of the CJEU indeed provide protection to workers to the effect that it alters the outcome of competition between individuals. This is especially relevant in the case of 'vulnerable' individuals who will not end up being one of the 'winners' of the competition when left to their own devices.

61 CJEU 11 December 2007, C-438/05 (*Viking*), § 52.

62 The empowering of the worker to operate independently of labour market conditions is often referred to as 'decommodification'. G. Esping-Andersen, *The Three Worlds of Welfare Capitalism*, Princeton University Press 1990, p. 22.

Prima facie, there is a certain link between equality rights and vulnerability of employees. Equality rights generally protect workers who are member of a certain target group, such as the group of female workers, foreign workers, handicapped workers, older or younger workers, or religious workers. Sometimes, these groups are referred to as 'vulnerable' or disadvantaged groups on the labour market.[63] Not every individual member of that group will in fact have a vulnerable position. Women for example vary strongly in their labour market positions. Some have very highly valued skills and education, others have not. Some members of the target groups that are vulnerable, may have vulnerabilities that have no specific link to the group characteristics, such as low intelligence. Some members of the target groups, however, may have vulnerabilities that have a certain link to the group characteristics. Many women, for example, need flexible working time arrangements because of their care duties at home. Because of the biological conditions of procreation and the traditional division of care, they need these arrangements more often than men. Religious workers also may need special working time arrangements to perform their religious duties. Disabled workers may have special needs in terms of accommodations at the workplace. These workers can be called 'vulnerable' because they have a disadvantage on the labour market. They are less available than other workers, or they may be less productive than other workers. Therefore, they may need more protection than other workers. But do equality rights offer them just that? Does the CJEU interpret equality rights in such a way that these disadvantages or vulnerabilities are compensated for?

The example that is used to explore this question is the case of women with care duties. There is a substantive body of case law of the CJEU on equal treatment of men and women, which enables us to study this question in more detail. We focus on the equality of men and women, but we will add some reflections regarding age discrimination and discrimination of handicapped people.

B. PROTECTION AGAINST DISCRIMINATION ON THE GROUNDS OF SEX

Decades before people would even think of women as standing on an equal footing with men, women were protected with regard to their reproductive tasks. In the 19th century, in most European countries working time protection was first introduced for children and then for women during their pregnancy. During the first half of the 20th century, however, women retreated from the paid labour market, at least in some countries such as the Netherlands. When they reappeared

[63] E.g. Erica Howard, "The European Year of Equal Opportunities for All – 2007: Is the EU Moving Away From a Formal Idea of Equality?", *European Law Journal*, Vol. 14, No. 2, March 2008, pp. 168–185; citing communications from the Commission in which the protected target groups are called 'vulnerable'.

on the labour market from the second half of that century onwards, they entered a rather hostile environment. Unequal treatment of women was commonplace, in labour and social security legislation as well as in practices at the workplace. One can think of a few reasons why.

Firstly, the male breadwinner model "was inscribed in the structure of most post-industrial welfare states".[64] Many differences in the legal position of men and women in labour law and social security law were based on the assumption that men were breadwinners who had to provide for their spouses and children. Therefore, they needed higher wages or social security benefits and more protection against dismissal than women, whose income was supposedly a mere extra. Hence, an assumed difference in need was believed to justify a difference in treatment. Secondly, stereotypes about women worked to their disadvantage on the labour market. It was generally believed that their 'communal, warm, nurturing' characteristics made women perfect for a domestic role but not for paid labour.[65] Perceived differences in skills may therefore offer an explanation for the differences in treatment by employers. A third explanation can be found in the situation of the labour market. Employers may not have believed the stereotypes themselves nor may they have been inclined to reward differences in need between breadwinners and non-breadwinners, but they just happily benefitted from the fact that for some reason beyond their control, women were inclined to accept lower wages than men.[66] If they did, why pay more? A fourth explanation may have been that women were less available for work than men. Women sometimes needed time off during and after their pregnancy. Many wanted to work part-time, on flexible hours or only during school hours because of their domestic tasks. Some were more often absent than their colleagues because of ill children or relatives. This was not simply a stereotype or an assumed difference in need. The need for flexible working time arrangements was and still is a real need of many women that presumably makes them less attractive for employers. The question is therefore, to what extent equality law offered women protection against these reasons for an unfavourable outcome for women of the social competition between employees.

---

64 Nancy Fraser, "After the Family Wage, Gender Equity and the Welfare State", *Political Theory*, Vol. 22, No. 4, November, 1994, p. 591.

65 Alice H. Eagly and Antonio Mladinic, "Are People Prejudiced Against Women? Some Answers From Research on Attitudes, Gender Stereotypes, and Judgments of Competence", *European Review of Social Psychology*, (1994) 5:1, p. 1–35.

66 The lower 'value' of women on the labour market can be explained by stereotyping, but also by more neutral factors such as the traditional segregation of the labour market in male and female functions, which may have confined women to 'overcrowded' areas of the labour market. Nadine Taub, "Keeping Women in Their Place: Stereotyping Per Se as a Form of Employment Discrimination", 21 *Boston College Law Review* 345 (1979–1980), p. 349–350.

Since the '70s, the European Directives have effectively introduced legal norms to protect women against unequal treatment.[67] The first, very influential effect[68] of European equality law was of course the withdrawal of rules based on sex in labour law and social security law. According to the new equality principle, it was no longer accepted to use that criterion in these fields of law, with a few exceptions such as the protection of pregnant women. Hence the assumption that breadwinners were always male could not be maintained, and although the breadwinner criterion was not excluded as a relevant criterion in social assistance law,[69] the breadwinner principle was abandoned in labour law and social insurances. In the Netherlands, for example, the legislator completed the withdrawal of sexual denominators in law during the late eighties.[70] By then, female workers were officially on an equal (legal) footing with 'normal' male workers, except for the protection of pregnant women that had been created a century before.

The second effect of European equality law concerned the terms and agreements of labour relations. Roughly speaking, up till then, employers were free to use their criteria of choice to hire or reward employees. This freedom was now restricted. Since direct discrimination was forbidden, the characteristic 'male' or 'female' could no longer be used to make distinctions between employees. The prohibition of direct discrimination has improved the bargaining position of women on the labour market and in that sense it altered the outcome of undisturbed competition on the labour market.

The prohibition of direct discrimination includes unfavourable treatment on the grounds of pregnancy, as made clear by the European Court of Justice, for example in the ground-breaking *Dekker* case.[71] While the income and the health and safety of pregnant women had been protected in labour law and social security law since the end of the 19th century without any reference to the principle of equality, equality law has added the protection against the refusal to hire a woman because of her pregnancy. Also, the protection against dismissal before and sometime after pregnancy was introduced as a result of European equality law.[72] This extra protection was adopted in the Netherlands too.

---

67 Directive 75/117 on equal pay for male and female workers; Directive 76/207 on equal treatment with regard to access to employment, vocational training, promotion and working conditions; Directive 79/7 on the progressive implementation of equal treatment with regard to statutory social security schemes.

68 The analysis is restricted to 'legal' effects. Whether or not the prevalence of discrimination was in practice effected by the introduction of the Directives is outside the scope of this paper.

69 CJEU 11 June 1987, C-30/85 (*Teuling-Worms*).

70 W.L. Roozendaal, *Werk en privé*, Kluwer, Deventer 2011, par. 4.2.2. European equality law has strongly contributed to that development.

71 CJEU 8 November 1990, C-177/88 (*Dekker*).

72 The prohibition was introduced in 1976. W.L. Roozendaal, *Werk en privé*, Kluwer, Deventer 2011, par. 4.3.3.

The prohibition of direct discrimination had strong protective effects that certainly went beyond market efficiency, especially in the case of pregnancy. However, the unfavourable treatment of women on the labour market did not disappear when sex was no longer used as a relevant criterion. Employers, who were aware of the prohibition, could reach the same result by using other, seemingly neutral criteria. The concept of indirect discrimination, developed by the Court of Justice,[73] can counter this effect. Indirect discrimination is at present defined as the situation in which an apparently neutral provision, criterion or practice would put persons of one sex at a particular disadvantage compared with persons of the other sex, unless that provision, criterion or practice is objectively justified by a legitimate aim, and the means of achieving that aim are appropriate and necessary. In the wording often used by the CJEU, the provision, criterion or practice may be justified by objective factors unrelated to sex.[74] To what extent did the prohibition of indirect discrimination alter the outcome of social competition on labour markets?

In the course of time the CJEU has certainly helped plaintiffs establish their discrimination claims by shifting part of the burden of proof to the respondent.[75] The burden of proof is now regulated in Art. 19 of de Recast Directive and reads: "Member States shall take such measures as are necessary (…) to ensure that, when persons who consider themselves wronged because the principle of equal treatment has not been applied to them establish, before a court or other competent authority, facts from which it may be presumed that there has been direct or indirect discrimination, it shall be for the respondent to prove that there has been no breach of the principle of equal treatment".[76]

Due to equality law, governments and employers can therefore be forced to explain what criteria they use when distinguishing between employees and why these criteria are justified. In order to know the extent to which the effects of this duty to explain are really protective beyond the outcome of undisturbed market competition, we need to know what kind of explanation is acceptable. Which arguments justify their choices? What is a legitimate aim? What is meant by appropriate and necessary means?

The justification test seems to be less severe for governments than for parties to a collective agreement or employers. More than once, the court has stressed that member states have a broad margin of discretion and can choose the measures

[73] Starting with CJEU 13 May 1986, C-170/84, Ju 1986, p. 1607 (Bilka). Cf. C. Barnard, *EU Employment Law*, Oxford University Press 2012, p. 317.
[74] CJEU 13 May 1986, C-170/84 (*Bilka*).
[75] CJEU 27 October 1993, C-127/92 (*Enderby*); CJEU 17 October 1989, C-109/88 (*Danfoss*).
[76] Art. 2.1.b. Directive 2006/54. This clause was first introduced by Council Directive 97/80/EC of 15 December 1997 on the burden of proof in cases of discrimination based on sex.

capable of achieving the aim of their social and employment policy.[77] Employers, on the other hand, face a somewhat stricter test. They are requested to show that the measures chosen 'correspond to a real need on the part of the undertaking, are appropriate with a view to achieving the objectives pursued and are necessary to that end'.[78]

This does not mean, however, that the test is difficult to meet. Of course, employers should put in some effort to come up with an acceptable justification. It is not enough to point out that paying (mostly female) part-timers a lower wage is cheaper.[79] Also, generalisations about part-time workers, such as the believe that they are less integrated in the undertaking, are not accepted,[80] nor is the general assertion that a certain reward system disadvantageous to part-timers maintains staff motivation, commitment and morale.[81] Apart from this though, most other regular business or administrative reasons are accepted as a real need on the part of the undertaking. Personal factors such as productivity, the quality of the work done, the worker's flexibility or adaptability to hours and places of work, training or length of service are accepted as objective factors that can explain differences in pay.[82]

Hence, differential treatment is justified for as long as it is related to the comparative qualities of the workers. However, quality is not the sole relevant factor. Labour market factors can contribute to the justification of a different treatment as well. According to the CJEU the national court may take into account a shortage of candidates for a job and the need to attract candidates by means of higher pay as an objectively justified economic ground for the difference in pay between two jobs of equal value.[83] The employer can also manipulate the labour market by promoting desired behaviour. For example, the argument that part-timers were paid less in order to promote full-time work was accepted,[84] as it is accepted not to pay a yearly gratification to workers on parental leave when this gratification is meant to stimulate hard work or loyalty to the firm in the future.[85]

---

77 Barnard 2012, p. 323–324; CJEU 14 December 1995, C-317/93 (*Nolte*); CJEU 14 December 1999, C-444/93 (*Megner*); CJEU 9 februari 1999, C-167/97 (*Seymour-Smith*).

78 CJEU 13 May 1986, C-170/84 (*Bilka*).

79 CJEU 17 June 1998, C-243/95 (*Hill*), par. 40; CJEU 10 March 2005, C-196/02 (*Nikoloudi*), par. 51.

80 CJEU 13 July 1989, C 171/88 (*Rinner-Kühn*).

81 CJEU 17 June 1998, C-243/95 (*Hill*).

82 Barnard 2012, p. 318–321. For example CJEU 27 October 1993, C-127/92 (*Enderby*); CJEU 31 May 1995 C-400/93 (*Royal Copenhagen*); CJEU 11 May 1999, C-309/97 (*Wiener Gebietskrankenkasse*); CJEU 26 June 2001, C-381/99 (*Brunnhofer*).

83 CJEU 27 October 1993, C-127/92 (*Enderby*).

84 CJEU 31 March 1981, C-96/80 (*Jenkins*), par. 12.

85 CJEU 21 October 1999, C-333/97 (*Lewen*). The stimulation of full-time work at the expense of part-time work could not be maintained as a legitimate aim, however, after the introduction of the Part-Time Directive 97/81, since that directive seeks to promote part-time work. CJEU 10 June 2010 C-395/08 and C-396/08 (*Bruno a.o.*), par. 80–81.

The objective factors of flexibility or adaptability to hours and places of work, training and length of service deserve particular attention, since (mostly female) employees with care duties have difficulties to keep up with other workers in these respects. The CJEU itself has observed that women are often less inclined to attend trainings and that they are less flexible, because of their care duties.[86] This does not lead the court to oblige employers to use these criteria restrictively or even proportionally. The employer is merely required to justify the remuneration of such adaptability or training by showing it is of importance for the performance of specific tasks entrusted to the employee. The justification of rewarding length of service does not even require such specification. The CJEU considered, as a general rule, recourse to the criterion of length of service appropriate to attain the legitimate objective of rewarding experience acquired which enables the worker to perform his duties better.[87]

In conclusion, the prohibition of indirect discrimination works well (at least in theory) to combat vague, disadvantageous stereotypes about women. It is less effective, however, when it comes to disadvantageous labour market circumstances. It is virtually non-effective when it comes to real differences in objective factors between men and women, whether or not these objective factors are linked to their sex. Practically all economic or business objectives are accepted as a real need of the undertaking that can justify differences between men and women. Economically speaking, this makes good sense. It also illustrates that equality law does not always function as a correction of the outcome of social competition on the labour market. Often, it merely functions as a correction to the rules of competition on the labour market, by sieving out stereotypes and prejudices. In a sense, equality law confirms the core market value that the most valuable worker should win the competition.

C. PROTECTION AGAINST AGE AND DISABILITY DISCRIMINATION: RECONSIDERING THE PROPORTIONALITY TEST

Would an alternative have been possible? Would it have been possible to protect vulnerable workers within the framework of the justification test? There is indeed an alternative, which can be found in an extension of the proportionality test.

The objective justification test of indirect discrimination is sometimes referred to as a proportionality test. Proportionality can be used to refer to the relation

86 CJEU 17 October 1989, C 109/88 (*Danfoss*), par. 21–23.

87 CJEU 3 October 2006, C-17/05 (*Cadman*), par. 33–40.

between aim and means.[88] This relation is indeed examined in the justification test of indirect discrimination, since the respondent has to show that the means chosen are appropriate and necessary to reach his aim. Proportionality can also be defined as describing the relation between the interests concerned, i.e. the interests of the plaintiff and the respondent. This second definition of proportionality is in European Union law also known as *proportionality stricto sensu* or *proportionality in the narrow sense.*[89] According to that principle, measures must not cause disadvantages which are disproportionate to the aims pursued, even if those measures are appropriate and necessary for meeting legitimate objectives. It thus requires a balancing of interests. It is a core element in the justification of breaches of human rights in the case law of the European Court of Human Rights as well. The European Court of Human Rights often requires member states to *strike a fair balance between general interest of the community and the protection of the individual's fundamental rights.*[90]

This proportionality *stricto sensu* recently seems to have gained weight in the case law of the CJEU regarding discrimination. The Court referred to the proportionality principle in age discrimination cases, briefly in the *Mangold* case[91] and more explicitly in the *Andersen* case.[92] In *Andersen*, the question was whether severance payments to older employees could be lower in view of the fact that they would soon be entitled to old age pensions. The Court stated (in par. 32) that: "It is also necessary to ascertain (...) whether the means used to achieve those aims are 'appropriate and necessary'. In the present case it must be examined whether [the national law provision] enables the attainment of the employment policy objectives pursued by the legislature *without unduly prejudicing the legitimate interests of workers* who, as a result of that provision, find themselves deprived of the severance allowance on the ground that they are entitled to an old-age pension to which the employer has contributed".[93] In most sex discrimination cases so far the interests of the plaintiff were not included in the test as defined

---

88 It is not uncommon to exclusively define the principle of proportionality as meaning that the means have to be suitable and necessary in order to reach the goal. Cf. Tor-Inge Harbo, "The function of the proportionality principle in EU law", *European Law Journal* Vol. 16 No. 22, March 2010, p. 158–185; in particular p. 161.

89 Cf. the conclusion by Advocate General Kokott of 6 May 2010, C-499/08 (*Andersen*), par. 68; J.H. Jans, "Proportionality Revisited", *Legal Issues of Economic Integration*, 27 May 2009, Vol. 27, No. 3, pp. 239–265. According to Gerards the test is relatively rare. Cf. J.H. Gerards, "Fundamental rights and other interests: should it really make a difference?", in: E. Brems (ed.), *Conflicts between fundamental rights*, Antwerp/Oxford/Portland 2008, pp. 655–690; p. 681.

90 S. Greer, "'Balancing' and the European court of human rights: a contribution to the Habermas-Alexy debate", *Cambridge Law Journal*, 2004, 63, pp. 412- 434; p. 413. It should be noted that the ECtHR leaves quite some discretionary power to the state concerned. Cf. also Jaspers as mentioned in note 26.

91 CJEU 22 November 2005, C-144/04 (*Mangold*), par. 65.

92 CJEU 12 October 2010, C-499/08 (*Andersen*) par. 32.

93 Emphasis placed by the authors.

by the CJEU. We can find this in three relatively old decisions concerning the exceptions to the prohibition of direct discrimination.[94] So far, the interests of the plaintiff have never been explicitly included in the justification test regarding indirect discrimination on the grounds of sex.

If the plaintiff's interests were included in cases of women who were treated unfairly because of their care duties, it would have been possible for the CJEU to balance the business objectives of employers against the interests of women to combine work and care, while at the same time having access to equal wages and careers. The most favourable outcome of this balancing exercise we can think of, would have been that employers are asked to accommodate working time patterns to the needs of women with care duties, while at the same time giving them similar wages and career opportunities as they would have had without the accommodation. Possibly this outcome would have been less efficient to employers, but the essence of fundamental social rights should be that efficiency or market conformity is not the decisive consideration for the outcome of a case. Other humanitarian values such as equality of opportunities, solidarity or protection can overrule it.[95]

As observed by many scholars, European equality law as interpreted by the CJEU is based on a formal idea of equality.[96] The inclusion of a strict proportionality test could make the equality model more substantive. Of course, it would be naive to think that the extension of the justification test would automatically lead to more protective results for vulnerable workers. This is not particularly true for age discrimination, for example. In the *Mangold* en *Andersen* cases, to which the CJEU applied a high level of scrutiny, the outcome was favourable to the plaintiff. After these cases, the proportionality test *stricto sensu* has been applied to a range of other cases of direct discrimination on the grounds of age. But in these cases, the Court applies a test that is much more lenient, and the outcome is not favourable to the plaintiffs.[97] The Court gave states and parties to collective agreements wide margins of appreciation for policies that are disadvantageous to older workers as long as those disadvantages can be justified by legitimate

[94] CJEU 15 May 1986, C-222-84 (*Johnston*); CJEU 26 October 1999, C-273/97 (*Sirdar*); CJEU 19 March 2002, C-476/99 (*Lommers*).

[95] We do see this 'inefficient' outcome in the case of pregnant women, under the flag of 'the strict prohibition of direct discrimination'. Although it is clear that refusing to hire an applicant because of future pregnancy-related absenteeism makes sense as a rational business decision, it is prohibited in the name of equality.

[96] E.g. Howard 2008; Barnard 2012, p. 290.

[97] CJEU 16 October 2007, C-411/05 (*Palacios*), par. 73; CJEU 12 October 2010, C-499/08 (*Andersen*), par. 32; CJEU 12 October 2012, C-45/09 (*Rosenbladt*), par. 73; CJEU 18 November 2012, C-250/09 and C-298/09 (*Georgiev*) par. 54, CJEU 21 July 2011, C-159/10 (*Fuchs*), par. 63 and 64; CJEU 5 July 2012, C-141/11 (*Hörnfeldt*), par. 38. See for this conclusion also D. Schiek, "Age Discrimination before the CJEU, Conceptual and theoretical issues", *CMLR* 2011, 48: 777–799.

social policy aims. The Court did not closely scrutinise the appropriateness of the means to reach these aims. The legitimate aims themselves were often aims of labour market policy such as the need to plan personnel development and to give young people access to the employment market. Even a reference to age-related stereotypes was accepted in the cases of *Rosenbladt* and *Fuchs*.[98]

Besides, the case law of the European Court of Human Rights, which is not abundant on the subject of special needs at work, is not particularly friendly for workers with special needs either, despite the regular use of the proportionality test in a narrow sense by that court.

There is one recent decision of the CJEU on discrimination on the grounds of handicap, however, that shows that the proportionality test *stricto sensu* can indeed have remarkable effects. In the *Odar* case,[99] the same policy aim that could justify discrimination on the grounds of age was not sufficient in the case of handicap, precisely because the policy had more disruptive effects on disabled persons.

The fact that the entitlement to pension benefits was taken into account in the determination of a severance payment was accepted by the CJEU as an objective factor with respect to the normal pension age, but in the case of the earlier pension age for disabled workers, according to the Court, the measure disregarded the risks faced by severely disabled people: "*Severely disabled people have specific needs stemming both from the protection their condition requires and from the need to anticipate possible worsening of their condition. Regard must be had to the risk that disabled workers may throughout their lives have financial requirements arising from their disability which cannot be adjusted and/or that, with advancing age, those financial requirements may increase*". The Court concluded that the measure at issue had an excessive adverse effect on the legitimate interests of severely disabled workers.[100]

It should not come as a surprise that the proportionality test in the narrow sense is applied so generously in the case of handicapped people. The formal equality approach is much more difficult to maintain with respect to handicap, since handicapped people are very often not only disadvantaged because of stereotypes or prejudices, but they have real vulnerabilities that makes it difficult to find a

98 The government's contention in *Rosenbladt*, that older employees should not be subjected to the humiliation of being declared unfit to work, was accepted as an objective factor to justify age discrimination. In *Fuchs*, it was considered a legitimate aim of a compulsory retirement measure to prevent possible disputes concerning employees' fitness to work beyond a certain age.
99 CJEU 6 December 2012, C-152/11 (*Odar*).
100 CJEU 6 December 2012, C-152/11 (*Odar*), par. 69 and 70.

suitable job. The directive explicitly targets substantive equality for handicapped people. It is the purpose of the directive to oblige employers to a certain extent to accommodate the workplace to handicapped workers.[101] On the other hand, the directive does not oblige to engage a person that is not competent, capable and available to perform the essential functions of the post concerned or to undergo the relevant training.[102] It will be a challenge for the CJEU to develop a substantive form of equality which is not based on the objective qualities of employees or on labour market considerations, but on special needs. The *Odar* decision shows that the Court is willing to take a different turn.

VI. CONCLUDING REMARKS

The debate about a European Constitution, which started at the beginning of this century, has resulted in the insertion of the European Charter of Fundamental Rights in the Treaty as a source of primary European law in 2009. Many advocates of labour rights will have welcomed this development. Perhaps the promotion of a number of social rights to the level of 'fundamental' social rights creates the expectation that henceforth, it will be more difficult for member states to decrease the level of employee protection with respect to these rights. They serve as weapons against a destruction of workers' social rights caused by globalisation and increased competition. The recognition of social rights as fundamental rights may halt or at least slow down neo-liberal policies aiming to improve the competitiveness of national economies at the expense of worker protection.

If we look at the international and, more particularly, at the European level there is some evidence that the invocation of fundamental rights has a positive effect although it possibly only subdues the hard consequences of the process of increasing competition on the global and the European (labour) market.[103] The growing recognition of the effect of fundamental rights in labour relations, also in transnational settings, illustrates this development. Certainly, EU legislation, and more particularly the case law of both European Courts – the CJEU and the ECtHR – have contributed to this. Notably, the CJEU has taken major steps by giving direct horizontal effect to the principle of equality in the Treaty and by applying what can be called the Kücükdeveci approach.

For other fundamental social rights, included in the European Charter of Fundamental Tights, the added value to the protection of workers against

[101] See par. 6; 9; 16; 20; 21 of the considerations and Article 5 Directive 2000/78 on the duty to provide reasonable accommodation.

[102] Consideration 17 of Directive 2000/78/EC regarding equal treatment.

[103] Since the recent crisis a drawback can be seen. In some member states there is a political tendency to diminish European legislation in this field or to lower the standards.

increased competition between Member States is less clear. As for now, the added value to employees seems to depend on the impact of the moral weight of the fundamental social rights on decision makers, both at the national and the international level. Surely, the invocation of fundamental social rights is not able to eradicate competition in the social field, but it can mitigate the excesses of unlimited and uncontrolled competition between labour markets and individuals on the markets. So there is an added value, we would conclude, but a rather modest one.

With regard to the second part of our analysis, our conclusion is even more modest. European equality law often does not function as a correction to the outcome of social competition between individuals on the labour market. Compensation of vulnerabilities is not part of the regular objective of European law as interpreted by the CJEU, when it comes to discrimination on the grounds of sex or age. As we have derived from our analysis, there are two exceptions. In both cases, the formal approach to equality is exceptionally not followed. The first exception concerns the protection of pregnant workers. The CJEU has offered these workers protection that goes far beyond the outcome of undisturbed market competition. It will often make good business sense for an employer not to hire or to no longer employ pregnant women, but equality rights oblige him to do so anyhow. The second exception concerns the case of the handicapped worker. In this case the CJEU has been willing to take into account the special needs of handicapped people in a strict version of the proportionality test. That is not in conformity with the court's approach in other cases.

The promotion of social rights to the level of fundamental rights in the European Union is undeniably of importance to the protection of employees in Europe. This impact may be most consequential on the political level. The fact that a certain social right is a fundamental right, may be a convincing argument for decision makers not to tinker with the level of protection of this right too frivolously. The visible impact of this development on the actual prevention of social dumping in member states or on the correction to the outcome of labour market competition for vulnerable individuals, however, has been quite modest so far.

LE DROIT DU TRAVAIL, LA RESTAURATION DE L'AUTONOMIE DE LA VOLONTÉ INDIVIDUELLE ET LA MONTÉE DE LA SOFT LAW

Fleur LARONZE*

« *Droit organisant une concurrence équitable entre entreprises, donc complémentaire, et non comme d'esprit différent du Droit de la concurrence* »[1], voilà la définition du droit du travail proposée par Gérard Lyon-Caen.

Le droit du travail, partie d'un droit de la concurrence sociale. Le droit du travail peut être envisagé comme partie d'un droit de la concurrence sociale qui inspire toutes les stratégies entrepreneuriales. Les entreprises recherchent l'inapplication de la norme sociale, ou à tout le moins le contournement de la norme sociale la plus contraignante afin de choisir la norme sociale la moins contraignante.

L'employeur peut donc élaborer des moyens lui permettant de ne pas appliquer la norme sociale. Le dumping social, « *dérive de la concurrence législative* »[2], permet à une entreprise de fausser la concurrence en échappant à ses obligations sociales, notamment celles prévues par la convention collective. Mais, le non respect des normes sociales entraîne mécaniquement une atteinte à la libre concurrence. Les mécanismes de contournement du droit du travail qui ont pour objectif l'amélioration de la compétitivité de l'entreprise s'avèrent alors ineffectifs puisque, si les sanctions propres au droit du travail ne sont pas dissuasives, celles

* Université de Strasbourg, France.

1 G. Lyon-Caen, « L'infiltration du Droit du travail par le Droit de la concurrence », *Dr. ouvr.* 1992, p. 313.

2 M. le professeur Muir Watt évoque, dans le prolongement du processus de dumping social à grande échelle, « *la problématique de la « spirale vers le bas », qui affecte indéniablement aujourd'hui le marché du travail au plan global* » et souligne le fait qu'elle « *est liée à la délocalisation par les firmes multinationales de leurs activités industrielles vers des pays à faible coût social, à la faveur d'une stratégie purement financière* » (« Les normes sociales et le marché global du travail : comment sortir de la spirale vers le bas ? », in *Le droit du travail à l'épreuve de la globalisation*, sous la direction de A. Lyon-Caen et Q. Urban, Dalloz, coll. Thèmes et commentaires, 2008, p. 9).

du droit de la concurrence le sont davantage[3]. Le choix de ne pas appliquer une norme sociale atteint alors rapidement ses limites compte tenu des sanctions susceptibles d'être imposées au titre de la rupture de l'égalité entre les entreprises devant la concurrence.

Néanmoins, les pratiques de dumping social apparaissent de plus en plus insidieuses et pourraient conduire, sur le fondement de la reconnaissance de leur légitimité[4], à la naissance d'un « *nouveau droit du travail* (...) [qui] *serait un droit de la concurrence fondée sur la réduction du coût de la main-d'œuvre* »[5]. Ce nouveau droit du travail favoriserait l'émergence de normes sociales plus souples, de prescriptions moins contraignantes afin de faciliter la libre concurrence entre les entreprises. Cependant, ce nouveau droit du travail ne pourrait pas garantir la dignité du travailleur.

Le droit du travail, source du droit de la dignité du travailleur. La conception du droit du travail en tant que droit protecteur des intérêts des salariés suppose de s'intéresser plus largement aux instruments du droit du travail qui ont fait évoluer les droits fondamentaux des travailleurs. Les instruments du droit du travail sont nombreux et peuvent être analysés par leurs sources : les sources collectives (négociées et non négociées) et les sources individuelles, telles que l'autonomie de la volonté individuelle, le contrat de travail étant l'acte exprimant

---

3 Mme Driguez évoque le cas de la seule intégration du droit social comme facteur de concurrence (L. Driguez, *Droit social et droit de la concurrence*, Bruylant, préface L. Idot, 2006, p. 418 et s.). Ainsi, « *le droit de la concurrence, en sanctionnant les pratiques de contournement du droit du travail, afin de restaurer une concurrence saine et efficace, garantit simultanément l'effectivité du droit du travail* » (L. Driguez, *Droit social et droit de la concurrence*, op. cit., n° 282, p. 419). C'est essentiellement le droit de la concurrence déloyale qui permet de sanctionner les distorsions de concurrence résultant de la violation des normes sociales (L. Driguez, *op. cit.*, n° 284 et s., p. 423 et s.). Par ailleurs, Mme Driguez distingue le contournement du droit du travail et son détournement, ce dernier correspondant à un mauvais usage de la liberté du travail et du droit du travail (L. Driguez, *op. cit.*, n° 293 et s., p. 441). C'est alors sous l'angle de l'obligation de non-concurrence et du droit de grève notamment, que le détournement du droit du travail est appréhendé. L'exercice de la liberté du travail et celui du droit de grève peuvent conduire à la mise en œuvre de pratiques restrictives de concurrence, appréciées diversement selon les situations par le juge national et le juge européen.

4 Certains Etats qui tentent de se prévaloir de leur atout majeur, à savoir une main-d'œuvre peu couteuse et un faible taux d'imposition, s'inscrivent dans la logique de concurrence des normes conduisant à un nivellement des normes sociales par le bas. Le droit de l'Union européenne ne s'y oppose que lorsque les libertés économiques sont entravées. En effet, il « *ne sanctionne ni la concurrence fiscale non dommageable entre les Etats ni l'édiction de taux d'imposition attractifs pouvant entraîner les délocalisations* » (B. Gabor, « Restructurations et interactions entre politiques sociales et fiscales nationales, Une réponse européenne au dumping social ? », *Ride* 2008, p. 247, spéc. p. 263). Cependant, « *au regard de l'interaction entre politique fiscale et politique sociale, si les Etats sont libres de définir leur politique fiscale, ils ne peuvent restreindre la liberté d'établissement (ni les autres libertés de circulation) du fait d'un conflit avec la politique sociale d'un autre Etat* » (B. Gabor, loc. cit., spéc. p. 262).

5 G. Lyon-Caen, « L'infiltration du Droit du travail par le Droit de la concurrence », loc. cit., spéc. p. 319.

cette autonomie. Mais une autre source s'affirme, sur le plan individuel, comme l'égal de l'autonomie de la volonté : la soft law.

Autonomie de volonté individuelle *versus* soft law. L'autonomie de la volonté individuelle est la source de la formation du contrat, la relation contractuelle peut prévoir l'exécution des obligations à la charge des deux parties ou encore la rupture de la relation contractuelle initiale puisque ce que l'autonomie de la volonté individuelle crée, seule l'autonomie de la volonté individuelle peut le détruire.

En droit du travail, l'autonomie de la volonté individuelle est largement encadrée en raison du déséquilibre de la relation de travail. Le salarié ne peut exercer sa liberté de contracter comme il l'entend. C'est la raison pour laquelle le contrat de travail est toujours envisagé comme une source subsidiaire, la loi ou encore la convention collective étant privilégiée.

De nombreux mécanismes permettent aujourd'hui de restaurer l'autonomie de la volonté individuelle en prétendant que le consentement du salarié peut être exprimé librement – accord de rupture d'un commun accord ; rupture conventionnelle ; la possibilité de travail le dimanche avec l'accord du salarié ; le forfait annuel en jours exigeant l'accord individuel du salarié). La restauration de l'autonomie de la volonté individuelle ainsi décrite s'accompagne d'un mouvement d'individualisation de la relation de travail.

L'individualisation de la relation de travail consiste à placer le salarié dans une position isolée face à l'employeur ; la communauté de travail se délite ; le contrat de travail auquel la convention collective renvoie, est instrumentalisé par les entreprises.

La soft law s'inscrit dans le prolongement de l'évolution actuelle du droit du travail. Ce concept peut être traduit par droit flou (sans précision), droit doux (sans obligation) ou droit mou (sans sanction), selon une distinction posée par le professeur Thibierge[6], ou encore droit vert, jeune[7]. Le droit souple constitue une forme de droit dans la mesure où « *sans précision ne signifie pas pour autant indéterminable ; sans obligation ne veut pas nécessairement dire non respecté ; et sans sanction ne s'assimile pas à sans effets* »[8].

Pour autant, les dispositions relevant de la *soft law* sont caractérisées par l'absence de sanctions efficaces et par une valeur juridique discutable.

---

6 C. Thibierge, « Le droit souple, Réflexion sur les textures du droit », *RTDciv.* 2003, p. 599, spéc. p. 611.

7 M. Mekki, « Propos introductifs sur le droit souple », in *Le droit souple*, Journées nationales Association H. Capitant, Tome XIII, Dalloz, coll. Thèmes et commentaires, 2009, p. 1.

8 C. Thibierge, « Le droit souple, Réflexion sur les textures du droit », loc. cit., spéc. p. 611.

L'objet de la norme individuelle : la protection de la dignité des travailleurs. Cependant, nonobstant toutes les critiques qui peuvent être formulées à l'encontre du code de conduite en tant qu'outil de la soft law, la dignité des travailleurs n'est elle pas naturellement l'objet de cet acte qui, à la différence du contrat de travail, a pour fonction d'imposer des principes éthiques permettant d'assurer à tous leur droit à la dignité ? L'éthique permet d'assurer le respect de valeurs comme celles promues par les textes relatifs aux droits de l'homme. Le code de conduite peut-il constituer un outil valable et efficace afin de protéger la dignité des travailleurs ?

La réponse à cette question dépend de la force juridique des codes de conduite ainsi que de leur contenu. Or, la force juridique des codes de conduite ainsi que leur contenu doivent être envisagés à la lumière de l'articulation des normes contractuelles et de la soft law. Les premières relèvent du droit du travail, du droit étatique du travail, les secondes résultent de l'autonomie normative privée. La garantie d'un véritable droit à la dignité repose sur des normes susceptibles de sanctionner son non respect. Or, il n'est pas certain qu'un code de conduite puisse garantir, à la manière du contrat de travail en tant que norme privée réglementée par le droit étatique, des droits opposables et protégés aux salariés.

L'articulation des normes contractuelles et de la soft law suppose de prime abord, une mise en question et, dans un second temps, une réflexion orientée.

La restauration de l'autonomie de la volonté individuelle évolue-t-elle en même temps que la montée de la soft law ? La soft law freine-t-elle ce mouvement ou au contraire le renforce-t-elle ?

Trois évolutions sont possibles : une évolution parallèle des sources où les systèmes privés en cause sont indépendants ; une évolution en vases communicants ou alternative, la restauration d'un système s'opposant à la montée de l'autre système et inversement ; enfin, une évolution simultanée définie par le renforcement d'un système par l'autre de telle sorte qu'ils apparaissent connectés l'un à l'autre.

La source de la norme individuelle : l'articulation de l'autonomie de la volonté individuelle et de la soft law. L'autonomie de la volonté individuelle et la soft law évoluent en parallèle mais ces sources individuelles interagissent de telle sorte qu'il n'est pas possible de les envisager indépendamment l'une de l'autre. Les interactions qui caractérisent leurs relations révèlent l'ambivalence des mouvements qui affectent le droit du travail.

Ainsi, la contractualisation du droit du travail dont l'élaboration repose de plus en plus sur la logique du commun accord, sur la logique négociée et non imposée, peut être analysée sous l'angle plus large de la privatisation du droit du travail qui laisse une grande place aux normes privées et qui réduit d'autant l'espace réservée à la loi, à la norme étatique. Mais, la contractualisation du droit du travail peut aussi s'émanciper sous la forme plus large de contractualisation de la société au sens donné par le professeur Alain Supiot, c'est à dire une forme d'hybridation des sources, mi étatique, mi privée[9].

Selon l'ordre juridique et l'acteur sous l'angle duquel on se place, les trois mouvements peuvent être caractérisés. Le conflit entre la norme contractuelle et la norme de soft law résulte de l'évolution parallèle de ces sources et de leur influence réciproque. Mais, la jurisprudence aura tendance à freiner la montée de la soft law en restaurant l'autonomie de la volonté individuelle. Cependant, les acteurs privés cherchent toujours à « vider » le contrat de travail afin de « substantialiser » le code de conduite, exemple topique d'instrument de soft law.

Dès lors, le conflit une fois réalisé (I) est résolu (II) de telle sorte que, soit l'une des sources se substitue à l'autre, soit l'une des sources est transcendée par l'autre.

I. LA RÉALISATION DU CONFLIT ENTRE L'AUTONOMIE DE LA VOLONTÉ INDIVIDUELLE ET LA SOFT LAW

La réalisation du conflit entre l'autonomie de la volonté individuelle et la soft law repose sur des conditions favorisant l'émergence du conflit (A). La reconnaissance de ce conflit, une fois apparu, produit des effets qu'il sera utile d'analyser (B).

A. LES CONDITIONS D'ÉMERGENCE DU CONFLIT

Le conflit entre l'autonomie de la volonté individuelle et la soft law dépend de la configuration des normes. L'existence du conflit est conditionnée d'une part, à l'articulation entre l'autonomie de la volonté collective et l'autonomie de la volonté individuelle (1) et d'autre part, à l'articulation entre la dimension individuelle et la dimension internationale (2).

1. L'existence du conflit conditionnée à l'articulation entre l'autonomie de la volonté collective et l'autonomie de la volonté individuelle

Le conflit entre la norme contractuelle et la norme de soft law dépend du rapport de ces normes avec la convention collective.

La convention collective voit sa finalité évoluée en même temps que celle du droit du travail. Ainsi, la convention collective prévoit des dispositions protectrices des intérêts des salariés, lorsqu'elle est animée par le principe de faveur. Mais, comme le droit du travail, la convention collective est ambivalente.

---

[9] A. Supiot, *Homo juridicus, Essai sur la fonction anthropologique du Droit*, Seuil, coll. La couleur des idées, 2005, p. 172 et s.

Elle peut constituer un instrument au profit des intérêts de l'employeur, lorsque les règles qu'elle prévoit sont dérogatoires à la loi. La convention collective est donc un mécanisme réversible, pour reprendre l'adjectif qualifiant le droit du travail selon Gérard Lyon-Caen[10]. Désormais, la convention collective est une technique d'organisation de l'entreprise, au détriment de la finalité protectrice qui la définissait. La convention collective ne s'adresse pas seulement aux salariés mais aussi à l'entreprise. Par exemple, la convention collective d'entreprise qui contient des dispositions sur le recours aux heures supplémentaires s'inscrit dans la politique poursuivie par l'entreprise qui définit elle-même son contingent[11] et le taux de majoration des heures effectuées au-delà de la durée légale[12].

En outre, le contrat de travail apparaît de plus en plus souvent comme une norme relai de la convention collective. Ainsi, la loi et la jurisprudence posent l'exigence d'une articulation entre les dispositions du contrat de travail et les dispositions de la convention collective en matière de période d'essai ou de forfait annuel en jours. Dès lors, le conflit entre la norme contractuelle et la soft law s'inscrit dans ce contexte. L'articulation entre l'autonomie de la volonté individuelle et l'autonomie de la volonté collective intensifie ce conflit qui emprunte encore un nouveau visage dans la perspective internationale.

2. *L'existence du conflit conditionnée à l'articulation entre la dimension individuelle et la dimension internationale*

La volonté de ne pas appliquer la convention collective conduit à instrumentaliser les autres normes, plus particulièrement, le contrat de travail. Mais, deux mouvements corrélatifs peuvent être mis en lumière : la décontractualisation du contrat de travail et la prévalence des techniques normatives internationales avec la mondialisation. Ces deux mouvements révèlent l'influence réciproque entre le contrat de travail et le code de conduite, instrument de la soft law.

D'abord, le contrat de travail est le support privilégié pour définir les éléments essentiels de la relation de travail. Mais depuis la fin du XXème siècle, la jurisprudence admet une décontractualisation des éléments essentiels du contrat. Cela signifie que certains de ces éléments ne sont plus des éléments contractuels par nature, comme le lieu de travail[13]. En réalité, le mouvement de décontractualisation affecte à la fois le contenu du contrat de travail qui n'est plus pour la majorité de ses stipulations, contractuel (contractuel par nature) et le contenant du contrat de travail qui n'est plus le support, l'acte

---

[10] G. Lyon-Caen, « Les fondements historiques et rationnels du droit du travail », *Dr. ouvr.* 1951, p. 1 ; du même auteur, *Le droit du travail. Une technique réversible*, Dalloz, coll. Connaissance du droit, 1995 ; « Permanence et renouvellement du Droit du travail dans une économie globalisée », *Dr. ouvr.* 2004, p. 49.

[11] C. trav., art. L. 3121-11.

[12] C. trav., art. L. 3121-22.

[13] Cass. soc., 3 juin 2003, *RJS* 8-9/2003, n° 980 ; *D.* 2004, Jurisp., p. 89 ; *JCP* G. 2003, 10 165, note M. Vericel ; *Dr. soc.* 2003, p. 884, obs. J. Savatier.

juridique privilégié pour accueillir les stipulations relatives aux caractéristiques essentielles de la relation de travail. Autrement dit, ce qui est dans le contrat de travail n'est plus contractuel – la décontractualisation est ici le symbole de la désubstantialisation des éléments contractuels du contrat de travail – et le contrat de travail se vide de ses stipulations qui sont désormais définies par d'autres sources – la décontractualisation correspond à un déracinement des stipulations contractuelles. Ce double mouvement conduit le juge à utiliser le droit de la modification du contrat de travail comme une bombe à fragmentation qui déconstruit pas à pas les différentes branches du droit du travail. Ainsi, la Cour de cassation, en reconnaissant la valeur simplement informative du lieu de travail, a pu admettre la possibilité pour l'employeur de procéder au changement du lieu de travail de plus de dix salariés pour un motif économique, sans que la procédure de licenciement pour motif économique ne soit respectée, puisque ce changement de lieu de travail ne constituait pas une modification du contrat de travail[14].

Ensuite, si le contrat de travail se vide de son contenu, d'autres normes apparaissent beaucoup plus opportunes pour accueillir les stipulations relatives aux caractéristiques essentielles de la relation de travail. Il s'agit, notamment, du code de conduite. A l'échelle internationale, les codes de conduite ont vu le jour alors qu'aucune législation nationale ne semblait pouvoir appréhender les questions auxquelles les entreprises multinationales sont confrontées. Plus la perspective du droit est mondiale, universelle et générale, plus la norme appliquée à l'individu relève d'une approche locale, régionale, particulière. La mondialisation renforce l'approche individuelle, comme certains sociologues l'ont démontré[15].

Le code de conduite est un document qui énonce la politique ou les principes que les entreprises s'engagent à suivre. Ces principes peuvent garantir la dignité des personnes dans l'entreprise en prévoyant un ensemble de bonnes conduites ou de bonnes pratiques. Mais, le code de conduite a, de prime abord, pour finalité de moraliser la vie des affaires, les entreprises cherchant à tirer un avantage comparatif de leur situation transnationale. Il prévoira des mesures individuelles et non des mesures collectives, ni des droits collectifs. En effet, le but d'un code de conduite est de démontrer l'impuissance des accords collectifs et au delà des syndicats et décourager ainsi les salariés de se syndiquer.

L'influence réciproque du contrat de travail et du code de conduite se manifeste donc par la capacité du code de conduite à prévoir des normes individuelles et par la souplesse du contrat de travail qui a une valeur informative pour la grande partie de ses dispositions.

---

14 Cass. soc. 21 janvier 2004, *Sem. soc. Lamy* 2 février 2004 n° 1154, note G. Lyon-Caen.

15 A.-J. Arnaud, *Entre modernité et mondialisation, Leçons d'histoire de la philosophie du droit et de l'Etat*, LGDJ, coll. Droit et société, 2e éd., 2004.

Le contrat de travail influence le contenu du code de conduite, le code de conduite influence l'instrument contractuel en tant que contenant, support juridique.

Par conséquent, le conflit entre le code de conduite et le contrat de travail peut surgir, lorsque ces deux actes font figurer des dispositions de même objet, mais aussi, en l'absence de dispositions de même objet, lorsque le code de conduite prévoit des dispositions qui ressortent normalement du contrat de travail, des dispositions sur les éléments contractuels par nature.

Intéressons nous aux effets de la reconnaissance du conflit.

B. LES EFFETS DE LA RECONNAISSANCE DU CONFLIT

Les effets de la reconnaissance du conflit sont de deux ordres : un effet automatique, qu'il est possible de qualifier de pavlovien (1), aujourd'hui constaté, et un effet secondaire (2), en réalité pervers et plus prospectif.

1. Un effet pavlovien

Le conflit entre l'autonomie de la volonté individuelle et la soft law résulte de la recherche de la norme sociale la moins contraignante dans la perspective d'une compétitivité durcie par la crise. La dimension internationale et le caractère volontaire de la norme de soft law mais aussi la souplesse de sa forme attirent incontestablement les entreprises.

Pourtant, le code de conduite n'a pas par nature vocation à accueillir des dispositions sociales. Si un code de conduite prévoit des dispositions qui relèvent normalement du contrat de travail, c'est pour ne pas être soumis aux règles du droit du travail. L'employeur qui prévoit donc l'insertion de mesures individuelles autrement dit de stipulations contractuelles, dans un code de conduite tente de contourner le droit de la modification du contrat de travail. L'objectif est de ne pas avoir à recueillir l'accord du salarié, en cas de changement des dispositions prévues dans le code de conduite.

Ainsi, dans une affaire ayant donné lieu à un arrêt publié de la Cour de cassation[16], la société Deloitte Conseil avait inséré dans la charte associative applicable aux actionnaires de l'entreprise, des dispositions sur la rémunération et prévoyant une obligation de non concurrence, en sus d'une clause compromissoire, ce qui a donné lieu à un contentieux sur la compétence du juge prud'homal.

Par conséquent, la montée de la soft law entraîne le recul de l'autonomie de la volonté individuelle, à la manière de vases communicants.

[16] Cass. soc., 30 novembre 2011, *Rev. Lamy Dr. Aff.* 2012, n° 68, p. 48.

2. *Un effet secondaire*

L'effet secondaire de la reconnaissance du conflit entre l'autonomie de la volonté individuelle et la soft law affecte la source contractuelle elle-même. Le contrat de travail disparaîtra. Le parallélisme des formes ne joue pas, le contrat de travail ne va pas accueillir les normes de la soft law. Si le code de conduite est envisagé comme le support des normes contractuelles, le contrat de travail ne sera à nouveau qu'une norme relai, fonction qui lui est déjà dévolue à l'égard de la convention collective. Cela signifie que lorsque la norme contractuelle est en dehors du contrat de travail, le contrat de travail n'a plus une valeur *ad validitatem*, mais *ad probationem*. Cette évolution du contrat de travail résulterait en définitive non seulement du conflit avec le code de conduite mais aussi de l'influence du droit américain.

Les premiers codes de conduite sont apparus dans les entreprises américaines dans les années 1930 et visaient initialement les activités publicitaires. Ils ont évolué pour prévoir des dispositions sur les pratiques de corruption et la gestion du personnel[17]. De plus, aux Etats-Unis, le contrat individuel de travail ne sert que de preuve. Le contrat collectif de travail contient des mesures individuelles. Il correspond à une projection au niveau collectif de la norme individuelle de telle sorte que le contrat collectif de travail lie tous les salariés individuellement[18].

Par conséquent, la montée de la soft law conduit irrémédiablement à la disparition de l'autonomie de la volonté individuelle. Cependant, les mécanismes de résolution du conflit entre l'autonomie de la volonté individuelle et la soft law peuvent faire obstacle à cette évolution.

II. LA RÉSOLUTION DU CONFLIT ENTRE L'AUTONOMIE DE LA VOLONTÉ INDIVIDUELLE ET LA SOFT LAW

La résolution du conflit entre l'autonomie de la volonté individuelle et la soft law peut être opérée par plusieurs mécanismes orientés par la finalité de la régulation ou par celle de l'anticipation. Les mécanismes de régulation permettent de déterminer la norme applicable en cas de conflit (A). Ils restaurent l'équilibre entre les normes, entre les intérêts particuliers défendus par les normes. Les mécanismes d'anticipation, en revanche, ont pour ambition d'éviter la survenance de la situation de conflit (B). Ils peuvent être d'origine normative ou institutionnelle. Il peut donc s'agir de normes ou de processus impliquant les acteurs du droit.

---

[17] T. Brugvin, « Les codes de conduite : un instrument à double tranchant », *Economie et Humanisme*, déc. 2001 – janv. 2002, n° 359, p. 77.

[18] *J.I. Case Co. v. NLRB*, 321 U.S. 332 (1944).

A. LA RÉGULATION DU CONFLIT

La régulation du conflit peut résulter de l'application de règles de conflit (1) ou de la requalification des normes en conflit par le juge (2).

1. *La régulation du conflit par l'application de règles de conflit*

Plusieurs règles de conflit déterminent la norme applicable en cas de conflit de normes. Mais l'identification de la règle de conflit compétente suppose préalablement de rattacher les dispositions contraires à des catégories juridiques. Autrement dit, il est indispensable de procéder à une qualification juridique préalable.

Dans l'affaire précédemment citée[19], une disposition d'une charte associative prévoyait une clause compromissoire permettant aux actionnaires destinataires, de saisir un arbitre en cas de litige sur une des questions traitées par la charte. Mais, cette charte était aussi applicable aux salariés dès lors qu'ils avaient aussi le statut d'actionnaire, puisqu'elle prévoyait des dispositions sociales. Un conflit surgissait entre les dispositions sociales de la charte ainsi que la clause relative à la compétence de l'arbitre et le contrat de travail des salariés qui détermine la compétence exclusive du conseil de prud'hommes. Les juges ont alors procédé à la qualification des dispositions prévues par la charte associative. Au regard des salariés actionnaires destinataires de la charte, ces dispositions pouvaient être qualifiées d'avenant au contrat de travail. En effet, certaines dispositions de la charte portaient sur la rémunération qui est un élément contractuel par nature[20], sur une obligation de non concurrence qui est soumise aux conditions de validité de la jurisprudence sociale[21] et sur une obligation de non débauchage autrement dénommée obligation de non démarchage qui est assimilée à une obligation de non concurrence.[22] La charte associative constituant pour les stipulations concernées un avenant au contrat de travail, le conseil de prud'hommes est compétent pour trancher le litige porté par les salariés devant lui et relatif à la clause de non concurrence, à la clause de non débauchage et au préavis de six mois. Par conséquent, la clause compromissoire insérée dans la charte est inopposable aux salariés.

Dans cette affaire, le conflit entre la charte associative, norme de soft law et les dispositions de nature contractuelle de la charte, relevant de l'autonomie de la volonté individuelle est le résultat d'une double complexité. Non seulement la charte associative prévoyait des dispositions de nature différente, certaines relevant de la soft law, d'autres de l'autonomie de la volonté individuelle, mais

19 Cass. soc., 30 novembre 2011, préc.

20 Cass. soc., 20 octobre 1998, *D.* 1998, p. 525 ; *RJS* 1998, n° 1448 ; *JCP* E. 1998, 1909 ; *Dr. soc.* 1998, p. 878 ; *D.* 1999, p. 525.

21 Cass. soc., 10 juillet 2002, *Bull. civ.* V., n° 239 ; *Sem. soc. Lamy* n° 1094, p. 6, note F. Favennec-Hery.

22 Cass. soc., 27 octobre 2009, n° 08-41.501, *Bull. civ.* V., n° 232.

elle était applicable à des destinataires différents, des actionnaires et aux salariés. La charte était donc pour cette raison d'une nature duale, cristallisant le conflit entre le mécanisme privé de l'arbitrage et les règles étatiques de compétence juridictionnelle.

Le juge a dû, dans cette affaire, qualifier la charte associative pour déterminer la règle de conflit applicable. En l'espèce, la règle de droit du travail d'ordre public sur la compétence du conseil de prud'hommes a mis fin au conflit en faisant prévaloir la norme étatique sur la clause compromissoire. Mais le juge peut aussi requalifier les normes en conflit afin de le faire disparaître.

2. *La requalification des normes en conflit par le juge*

Le juge peut requalifier les normes en conflit de telle sorte que le conflit se dissout dans l'opération de requalification. La finalité de l'action de juge n'est pas la même que celle précédemment évoquée. Il n'applique pas les règles de conflit qu'il doit préalablement identifier. En requalifiant les normes en conflit, le juge altère véritablement la nature privée et autonome de certaines sources afin de faire « plier » le conflit.

Ainsi, le conflit entre le règlement intérieur et le code de conduite de même objet peut être résolu par la qualification du code de conduite, d'adjonction au règlement intérieur. Le contenu d'un code ou d'une charte éthique peut être celui du règlement intérieur[23]. Le code de conduite est donc soumis aux règles applicables aux règlements intérieurs[24] à condition de constituer une adjonction à ce dernier et non une simple modalité d'application[25]. Le juge peut qualifier le code de conduite d'adjonction au règlement intérieur selon les dispositions qu'il prévoit, ou encore d'engagement unilatéral s'il définit des obligations à la charge de l'employeur. Mais si le code de conduite reconnaît des obligations à la charge du salarié, le juge envisagera la valeur contractuelle du code de conduite et pourra le qualifier d'avenant au contrat de travail. Le juge procède, par cette requalification du code de conduite, à une fusion des normes. L'opération de qualification ne

[23] Circ. DGT n° 2008/22 du 19 novembre 2008 relative aux chartes éthiques, dispositifs d'alerte professionnelle et au règlement intérieur, *Sem. soc. Lamy* 6 janvier 2009, n° 1381, p. 2 ; *RTDCiv.* 2009, p. 77, obs. P. Deumier.

[24] TGI Nanterre, 19 octobre 2007, *JCP* S. 2008, 1071, note A. Teissier ; P. Waquet, « Règlement intérieur, charte d'éthique et système d'alerte », *Sem. soc. Lamy* 12 novembre 2007, n° 1328, p. 8. Il est donc nécessaire de respecter la procédure conduisant à vérifier la légalité externe de la norme – C. trav., art. L. 1321-4 – qui repose sur l'avis des représentants du personnel et sa communication à l'inspecteur du travail et la procédure de contrôle de la légalité interne de la norme au regard des articles L. 1321-1, L. 1321-2 et L. 1321-3 du Code du travail et de la loi informatique et libertés du 6 janvier 1978. Dans l'affaire donnant lieu au jugement du Tribunal de grande instance de Nanterre de 2007, un dispositif d'alerte professionnelle avait été mis en place, ce qui justifie la mise en œuvre de la loi informatique et libertés.

[25] Cass. soc., 28 mai 2008, n° 07-15.744, *Bull. civ.* V., n° 120 ; *Sem. soc. Lamy* 1er septembre 2008, n° 1364, p. 13, note A. Teissier ; *Rev. Lamy Dr. aff.* 2008, n° 32, p. 68, note I. Desbarats ; *JCP* S. 2008, 1506, note A. Barege et B. Bossu.

permet pas de déterminer la norme applicable mais de faire disparaître le conflit. Cette fusion des normes que le juge réalise peut résulter d'une intervention des acteurs privés eux-mêmes qui anticipe l'émergence du conflit.

B. L'ANTICIPATION DU CONFLIT

L'anticipation peut être assurée par la fusion des normes individuelles au profit d'une des normes en conflit. Il s'agit de la fusion absorption (1). Mais il est aussi possible d'anticiper le conflit par la fusion des normes individuelles au profit d'une troisième norme, ce qui correspond à la fusion conception ou fusion intégration (2).

1. L'anticipation du conflit par la « fusion-absorption » des normes individuelles

Les acteurs privés peuvent choisir l'instrument qui renferme leur volonté et anticiper le conflit entre les normes. Pour cela, les acteurs privés doivent définir le système de valeurs qu'ils adoptent. Les textes sociaux fondamentaux peuvent leur servir de référence, de telle sorte que la dignité des travailleurs soit recherchée par la norme qu'ils adoptent. Mais leur système de valeurs peut être tout autre et s'appuyer sur des valeurs économiques détournées de toutes considérations sociales. Le juge, dans cette situation, sera placé dans une position délicate, tentant de respecter la volonté des personnes privées et d'imposer le respect des normes étatiques. Le moyen trouvé par le juge de concilier l'exigence du respect des règles étatiques et celle de la volonté des personnes privées consistera à privilégier la norme privée qui déclenche l'application de règles protectrices d'origine étatique, telle que le contrat de travail.

Le code de conduite peut être absorbé dans toutes ses dispositions par le contrat de travail. Le contrat de travail peut contenir des dispositions contractuelles par nature, déterminantes de la volonté des parties, mais aussi des dispositions plus souples, plus générales portant sur la conduite des parties. L'éthique et la prévention des conflits d'intérêts peuvent être prévues sans que la nature contractuelle des dispositions que le contrat définit n'en soit altérée. Le contrat de travail peut contenir des dispositions de nature différente. Il emporte avec lui un régime juridique plus solide et plus protecteur aux salariés que le code de conduite. D'où le choix par les personnes privées du contrat de travail comme norme absorbante, le code de conduite étant la norme absorbée. Mais, un autre mécanisme d'anticipation du conflit peut être mobilisé.

2. *L'anticipation du conflit par la « fusion-intégration » des normes individuelles*

Les acteurs privés disposent d'un autre mécanisme d'anticipation du conflit entre la soft law et l'autonomie de la volonté individuelle. Ce mécanisme consiste à fusionner les normes individuelles afin d'en faire naître une troisième. Fusion conception, fusion normative, fusion productive, fusion intégration... autant d'appellations susceptibles d'être données à ce mécanisme qui peut aboutir à la conception d'une nouvelle norme, loin d'être une « chimère juridique ». Cette norme aurait vocation à créer, par exemple, un statut adapté à la dualité de certaines situations.

Ainsi, la situation du salarié actionnaire est une situation hybride qui suppose l'intervention du droit des sociétés et du droit du travail. Mais ces disciplines n'appréhendent pas cette situation de manière satisfaisante. Une norme hybride ne rencontrerait pas l'obstacle du cloisonnement des branches du droit. De la même façon, la question du cumul entre le mandat social et le contrat de travail trouvera naturellement sa place au sein d'une norme hybride. En outre, la « concurrence sociale » pourrait faire l'objet de normes hybrides en appréhendant les conséquences des normes économiques sur les normes sociales, et inversement.

Les normes hybrides à la fois contractuelles et souples par nature, permettraient de créer une convergence interne des intérêts du salarié et de l'actionnaire et ce, afin de dégager un statut véritablement protecteur pour le salarié. Ces normes hybrides peuvent assurer la prise en considération des intérêts sociaux dans la mise en œuvre des règles de la concurrence. Elles seraient le fruit d'une concertation des acteurs privés et des acteurs étatiques à la manière des plateformes multi-parties prenantes développées dans le cadre de la responsabilité sociale des entreprises. Ces normes ne seraient pas uniquement hybrides par leur objet mais aussi par leurs sources. Elles seraient plus adaptées face à l'application isolée de la soft law et du droit du travail. Ces normes restaureraient la cohérence et la sécurité juridique dans le cadre des situations hybrides.

En conclusion, la défense du droit à la dignité des travailleurs dont la reconnaissance avec les lois AUROUX était l'expression de la fondamentalisation du droit du travail, est aujourd'hui remise en cause par les instruments mobilisés par l'employeur afin de détourner le droit du travail de sa finalité première – assurer la protection des intérêts des salariés. Consécration du pouvoir de l'employeur, technique d'organisation de l'entreprise ou mécanisme de régulation de la concurrence, le droit du travail exerce des fonctions ambivalentes qui peuvent aussi bien satisfaire le salarié, l'employeur, l'entreprise ou le marché. Mais, le droit du travail est aussi le seul droit tourné vers l'avenir, condamné à évoluer, à être réformé pour être toujours plus en adéquation avec la réalité sociale. Le droit du travail prend en compte les enjeux actuels afin de proposer les moyens permettant d'atteindre certaines fins : le code de conduite peut être ce moyen, dès lors qu'il est utilisé dans le cadre d'une logique hybride. Dans ces conditions seulement, il peut restaurer la dignité des travailleurs. Il ne reste plus qu'à définir les limites à ne pas franchir et les objectifs à atteindre.

MUTATING OR DISSOLVING LABOUR LAW? THE FUNDAMENTAL RIGHT TO DIGNITY OF WORKING PEOPLE QUESTIONED (ONCE AGAIN)

Barbara KRESAL*

I. THE RIGHT TO DIGNITY AND HUMAN RIGHTS – WHY IS IT SO DIFFICULT TO TAKE THEM SERIOUSLY IN LABOUR RELATIONS?

I will start with an obvious truth that *'labour is not a commodity'*. Why is it constantly repeated if it is so obvious? If it is so obvious, why do so many people not see and accept it and why does the reality of labour relations all over the world not reflect it? Some would say that this famous statement from the ILO Constitution is repeated so often because we would like to believe it, but – in fact – labour *is* a commodity. I do not share this view. *Labour is often (still/again) treated as if it were a commodity.* However, that does not turn it into a commodity! If someone is treated as a slave, is denied being a human being – does it mean that he or she is really not a human being? If persons are treated as something they are not, this does not turn them into that; it just means that we have a wrong perception and a wrong presentation, that a mistake has been made (consciously or unconsciously?, voluntarily or involuntarily?, because of lack of knowledge and competence to understand?, because of greed and lack of humanity?). Labour should not be treated as a commodity, because it is not one!

We have to keep in mind that workers, offering their labour, are human beings. Our work cannot be separated from our personality, our identity as human beings: we work as human beings (that refers to work of all kinds, regardless of what we do) and therefore, we should all have the opportunity to work and live in conditions which respect human dignity.

* University of Ljubljana, Slovenia.

It is a complex task to define human dignity. The essence of human dignity is equality. *There is no human dignity if people are not treated equally.* On this pillar of equality, a whole set of human rights is built (covering different aspects of human existence and activities, some being more concrete and others more general), aimed at guaranteeing people freedom and security in order to be able to live and pursue their activities, develop their personal and professional life according to their needs and interests and capacities, also taking into account equal rights of other persons, while at the same time enabling people to fulfil their duties towards society and other members of society. There is no freedom without security and there is no security if people do not enjoy freedom; however, there is no freedom and security without equality. Human rights are not only about individual rights. Human beings are individuals and at the same time members of society. Human rights have an individual as well as a collective aspect.

I would also like to point out that *there could be no human rights' society and human dignity if fundamental social rights as human rights were not fully respected as well.* The different types of human rights – social, economic, civil, political, cultural – are *indivisible* and interdependent. In short, they should, in principle, all have the same legal nature, legally binding value, the same enforceability. Of course, there are differences between different human rights, some need more and some need less state interventions, some are more complex than others, etcetera, of course we have to be careful to take into account different perspectives of human rights, their relative nature, their dynamic progressive substance, as well as their 'western societal concept' and their limits. To some extent, however, these limits and special characteristics refer to all types of human rights, not just to social human rights, and they cannot be used as arguments against the increasingly widely accepted doctrine according to which *fundamental social rights are human rights and should be treated and respected as such, at the same level as other human rights.* Social rights are not just additional option, 'collateral benefits', or conditional, whenever a society can afford them; fundamental social rights are essential for the development of every human society. Fundamental social rights actually reflect and derive from the substantive, material approach to equality and human rights. They are necessary for the concretisation of the principle of equality in its material, substantive meaning. And equality is at the heart of human rights, it is the essence of human dignity.[1]

Why such a long exposé on human rights and human dignity? In my view, *the aim of labour law is the actual realisation/concretisation of human rights, i.e. human*

[1] On equality, human rights and labour law, on fundamental social rights, the principle of the indivisibility of human rights see also Dorssemont 2011, p. 217–235; De Schutter 2010, p. 561; Davies 2009, p. 38–54; Herrera 2009; Hepple 2001, p. 5–18, Castel 2003; Supiot 2010a; de Burca/de Witte (eds.) 2005; Pellonpää 1993; Moreau 2009, p. 509–534; ILO 1999, ILO 2011; Rosanvallon 2011; Freeman 2011; Aliprantis 2009; Sheppard 2012, p. 1–19.

dignity, for the majority of people who earn their living by working for someone else. Labour law has the potential to bring human rights (declared in a very abstract and general manner and acknowledged by constitutions and many international treaties) into people's everyday lives. It is true that, historically, labour law did not emerge and develop as a result of the human rights paradigm. Labour law is older than modern human rights law. From the historical point of view, labour law was more a reaction to an excessive exploitation of workers, a reaction to extremely inhumane conditions of work. It can be seen as a means of preserving social peace, as an instrument to resolve conflicts between capital and labour, as a set of rights giving a minimum (necessary) protection to workers because of their subordinate and weaker, dependent position in relation to the employer.[2] Labour law can be regarded as a consequence of an economic progress ('collateral benefit') or as an instrument to achieve social progress.

After a century of intensive development of the human rights paradigm, especially after World War II, and taking into account the most important international treaties on human rights it is necessary to approach labour law from *the human rights perspective.* It is also necessary to evaluate the aims and goals of labour law, its effects and functions, all from the human rights perspective.

Unfortunately, the constitutions and international, including European, treaties on human rights are not taken seriously enough. The fundamental right to human dignity and the beautiful powerful "building" of human rights constructed on this pillar are misused at the declarative level all too frequently, whereas at the same time human rights are all too often overlooked in people's everyday lives, also within the framework of labour relations. It is our duty as (labour) lawyers to remind society and to keep repeating that constitutions and international treaties on human rights are legally binding documents. Therefore, human rights, including fundamental social rights, have to be taken seriously.

It is inadequate and misleading to consider workers as costs and workers' rights, i.e. labour law, as an obstacle to higher productivity, higher competitiveness. There is nothing wrong with competition, but this competition should not result in working and living conditions which do not respect human rights and the fundamental right to human dignity. Therefore, as Professor Rigaux has

2 Historically, the starting point was the rule of freedom of contract which applied without restrictions to employment relationships as well as other contracts. *Formal* freedom and equality of the contracting parties in practice meant that the employer had the power to determine conditions of employment. Gradually, more and more legal rules setting minimum rights of the employees limited the employer's absolute freedom. (see also Bajič 1936, p. 20–23; Kresal 1998, p. 17–19).

emphasised, free social competition has to be regulated and limited by labour law standards, labour law is a correction to free social competition.[3]

Labour law is one of the results of society's progress. Taking into account the human rights perspective, labour law has to promote quality jobs and non-discriminatory practices of employers, prevent precariousness of labour and working poverty, it has to guarantee decent work for all, i.e. working conditions and labour rights which respect human dignity and put human rights into practice. Putting human rights into practice is a reflection of society's social and economic progress and it gives the working people a fair share in the total output.

Economic, social as well as environmental progress have to go hand in hand. The goal should be a quality of living and working conditions as high as possible. Therefore, labour law should not be perceived as an obstacle to economic progress. Instead, *developed labour law and a high level of workers' rights should be considered as overall goals and also as assets* which, in the long term, add to the general level of well-being of people, their capacities, motivation, innovation and consequently also to the quality of work, higher productivity and competitiveness.[4]

If one takes this as a starting point, there is something awfully wrong with the doing business index of the World Bank, the employment protection legislation (EPL) index of the IMF and similar indexes in two ways: what they measure and how they do this.[5] I will not elaborate further on the methodology of 'how it is measured'; I will only focus on the question of 'what is measured'. These indexes are not acceptable from the human rights perspective as regards what they measure, because they treat labour as a commodity and workers as costs rather than human beings. Due to such misleading and inacceptable starting point which does not correspond to the prescribed human rights perspective, a country's score is worse if its labour law guarantees more rights and more protection to workers (in this case labour law is labelled as 'rigid'), whereas its score is better if there is less protection for workers, even if the minimum ILO and other international labour standards are not respected. There is something very wrong with the recent EU socio-economic policy and 'the Troika's' neo-liberal demands in relation to social welfare and labour law reforms as well. It is all about perspective and the question what the role of labour law is and should be. *From*

3 Rigaux 2004, p. 73–98.

4 There are many studies which show the positive effect of developed labour legislation, for example Auer/Berg/Coulibaly 2005; Auer/Cazes 2003, Kresal 2012, p. 246–249; Cazes/Verick/Hussami 2011; European Commission 2007, ILO 2012 and many others.

5 Kresal Šoltes 2012, p. 183–206; Supiot 2010b, p. 157; Deakin/Lele/Siems 2007, p.155; Bronstein 2009, p. 26–27 and others. An alternative could be, for example, a 'decent work index' (see Standing 2002, p. 441–454).

the human rights perspective, labour law is not rigid if it gives workers a high level of protection, if it is well-developed. In relation to that, I have to emphasise that if we take the legally binding international treaties and constitutions seriously instead of just considering them as declarative statements with no content and no legal effect, the human rights perspective is the prescribed, obligatory perspective. It is all about the question of what society we want to live in. More equality means a better life for everybody, as Professor Daubler has emphasised. Equality is the essence of human dignity. Inequalities generate tensions, conflicts, wars.[6] I strongly agree with Professor Rigaux who stresses that we need an adequate social counterpower at the appropriate level that could balance the current predominance of the neo-liberal model.

The neo-liberal model is not consistent with the human rights perspective and should be rejected as such. It does not treat working people as human beings with human rights; instead, it considers them as a cost and a commodity, which is not consistent with human dignity. Sustainable economic, social and environmental progress corresponds to the prescribed human rights pillars of our societies. So, developed labour and social law should be the goal, i.e. decent working and living conditions for all. It is necessary to protect and promote developed labour law against the neo-liberal attack which has, once again, become particularly strong during the recent crisis, although it is not something new.

II. CURRENT CHALLENGES OF LABOUR LAW IN THE LIGHT OF THE RIGHT TO HUMAN DIGNITY

Especially since the 1980s we have witnessed constant pressure from the neo-liberal paradigm and we have seen many different methods of squeezing out as much labour law protection (and other aspects of the social state principle) from our societies as possible.

In the field of labour relations, this trend can be summarised as follows:

- Constant pressure to lower the level of labour law protection.
- Growing segmentation/dualism on the labour market, which is the result of the promotion of different 'flexible' forms of employment.
- The narrowing scope of labour law protection: more and more people are working outside the scope of labour law protection, as self-employed persons

6 The statement from the ILO Constitution "(u)niversal and lasting peace can be established only if it is based upon social justice" is a more than relevant answer to today's threats of the persistent and strengthening neo-liberal paradigm as well, which causes more and more inequalities and social injustice.

and in similar legal forms, although they are in a situation that requires (labour law) protection.
- The pressure of unemployment.
- Uncertain relationship between labour law and social security.

All that leads to more precarious working and living conditions, more inequalities, more dependency and insecurity of people, i.e. it all results in a higher risk of not being able to live and work according to human dignity standards.[7]

The demands for lowering labour law protection have been and still are explicit. However, it is sometimes difficult to lower the general level of labour law protection for all employees (by way of legislative reforms, by way of concluding new, less favourable collective agreements), since there is a potential of strong opposition from numerous people, who are workers, voters and consumers at the same time.

Therefore, apart from the explicit formal lowering of labour law protection, an indirect, silent, *de facto* dissolution of labour law has been and still is going on, for example, by non-observance of formally binding workers' rights in practice. Enforceable workers' rights provided for by legislation or collective agreements are not respected in practice. Due to different reasons, many workers do not claim their rights before courts (lack of knowledge, fear, costs, ineffective sanctions, etcetera) and labour inspection does not prevent numerous breaches of workers' rights. It is the actual, enforced level of labour law protection which is relevant. In many countries, the difference between law in theory and law in practice in terms of labour law is really incredible. *The level of non-observance of labour law in practice and the ineffectiveness of labour inspection actually mean silent lowering, sometimes even abolition of certain workers' rights.*

In addition, another neo-liberal trend has been going on, especially since the 1980s – the expansion of different 'flexible', 'atypical' forms of employment. If it was not possible (or if it was more difficult) to lower the general level of labour law protection for all workers, it was easier to promote (by claiming that they raise employment opportunities and have a positive effect on employment)[8] fixed-term, part-time, agency work and other flexible forms of employment contracts. A lot of people work within flexible forms of employment, which are linked to, *de iure* and especially *de facto,* less employment protection and fewer rights. These

[7] Kresal 2012, p. 246–247.

[8] There are many critical studies which emphasise that more flexible labour legislation does not have any positive effect on employment, on the contrary. Weaker labour regulation does not reduce informal employment and raise formal employment. Developed labour legislation can even prevent higher unemployment and reduce other negative social effects of the crisis. (see, for example, Bronstein 2009, p. 11–16; Supiot 2010b, p. 151–162; Freeman 2010, p. 163–183; Kucera/Roncolato 2008, p. 341; ILO 2012 and many others).

workers have, for instance, weaker opportunities to participate in promotion, less professional training, usually lower wages and different bonuses, less effective enforcement of their rights in practice, due to their greater dependency, more insecurity.[9] Flexible employment often means a less favourable situation within the social security system as well.[10] In some countries *certain flexible forms of employment which were meant to be an exception are being increasingly used in practice*, they are no longer 'atypical' and exceptional.

Another way of *gradual indirect, silent (not easy to see) dissolution of labour law is the trend of narrowing the scope of labour law'*, the trend of externalisation, contractualisation. A growing number of people work outside the scope of labour law protection, as self-employed people, under different civil law contracts, ...[11] By defining the contract of employment and the employment relationship, the scope of application of labour law is determined as well. If the definition of employment relationship or its interpretation in practice (by labour inspection, by labour courts) is too narrow, *labour law does not apply to situations where people are in need of such protection*. This could lead to *de facto* dissolution of labour law. It is important that the determination of the existence of an employment relationship is guided by facts and not by the name given to it by the parties (the principle of the primacy of facts). Special attention should be given to ILO Recommendation No. 198 concerning the employment relationship from 2006. There are many dilemmas regarding this issue. Sometimes it is difficult to draw a clear line between labour and civil law contracts. There are the so-called *disguised employment relationships* where a person works for another person without having formally concluded a contract of employment although all characteristics of an employment relationship exist, and there are contractual relationships where the situation is *objectively unclear*, since characteristics of that relationship are mixed. There is also a category of so-called *quasi-employees*. Should a special category of economically dependent contractors be recognised in (labour?) legislation and what minimum (labour?) protection should be applied to these persons?[12]

This trend of promotion and expansion of different flexible forms of employment, atypical employment contracts, as well as self-employment and other legal forms of performing work outside the scope of labour law, with less or even no labour

---

9 The so-called segmentation and dualism on the labour market creates a distinction between standard and non-standard workers (insiders and outsiders) and causes inequalities as regards the level of labour law protection. Flexible employment means *de facto* a more precarious situation, less favourable labour and social conditions (Kresal 2012, p. 245–262).

10 Strban 2006, p. 331–354.

11 On the scope of labour law, definition of employment relationship and other forms of work Bronstein 2009, p. 23; Freedland 2007, p. 3–22; Tičar 2008, p. 329–342; Kresal 1999, p. 65–91 and many others.

12 Ojeda Avilés 2009, p. 47–67; Senčur Peček 2012, p. 223–244; Končar 2008, p. 38; Kresal 2012, p. 255.

law protection at all, presents *a strong indirect pressure* on the so-called regular workers and the general level of their rights. There is also the problem of *apparent conflict of interests* between different groups of working people with different employment or contractual status; instead of acting as a more or less homogeneous group of people who earn their living by working in a dependent relationship and who have similar interests, i.e. as a strong social counterforce against the interests of the employers, the working people are dispersed and divided into different groups with different (apparently conflicting) interests.

Consequently, there are problems with the representation of interests within trade unions and within the collective bargaining process as well. On the one hand, flexible workers and contractors outside an employment relationship are not organised and their interests are not always represented in trade union actions and the collective bargaining process. On the other hand, if trade unions predominantly represent regular workers and their interests, trade unions can lose members as well as their legitimacy, relevance and social power.

Another problem that labour law and the decent work concept are faced with is the growing and persistent unemployment. If work is the prerequisite for acquiring a set of labour (and indirectly also social) rights empowering people with security and freedom to live and work in conditions of human dignity,[13] then how is it possible that so many people do not have equal access to this important source of human dignity? *The true meaning of the right to work and of the concept of full employment should be reviewed.* In the current system, the (relatively high) percentage of unemployment is used as a lever to put pressure on those who are employed. Activation policies and social welfare reforms, reducing social benefits and, consequently, lowering income security for those who are not working, can make this pressure even stronger.[14] Under the pressure of unemployment, people are willing to work under worse working conditions, for lower pay, with less or even without any labour law protection, just to get a job and earn some money, regardless of whether the job offers decent working conditions or not.

Finally, one of the challenges of labour law is its relation to the social security system. How should the 'burden' be divided? What should be the responsibility of the individual employer and what should be collectively guaranteed through the social security system? This question is especially relevant nowadays when so many people do not fall within the scope of labour law protection, either because they do not work under a contract of employment or because they do not work at all. Should human dignity be based on the decent work concept (i.e. being

[13] This should be the aim of labour (and social) law, although it is unfortunately less and less realised in today's practice due to the predominant neo-liberal paradigm.

[14] See Leskošek 2012, p. 103–112. On activation policies see also Van Aerschot 2011.

a worker with decent working conditions and an adequate level of labour law protection), or should we broaden the basis to the so-called *'social citizenship'*?[15] In my view, these concepts are not alternatives: they are rather complementary and interdependent aspects of the same human rights approach.

III. CONCLUSION: THE WAY FORWARD – MUTATING OR DISSOLVING LABOUR LAW?

Since the crisis, the demands for a 'more flexible' labour market and for lowering workers' rights have been growing stronger again, the main argument being the need to raise competitiveness of the economy also by cutting labour costs. According to this neo-liberal doctrine, labour is a commodity and labour costs/labour law is seen as an obstacle to higher competitiveness and economic growth.

The human rights perspective of labour law is being overlooked and the fundamental right of working people to human dignity is threatened.

Such a neo-liberal model has to be rejected because *it is not consistent with the human rights perspective* and because it is *economically unsuccessful* (going from one crisis into another),[16] *socially ineffective* (it has not lowered or erased poverty, it produces more inequalities, higher unemployment, etcetera)[17] and is also *environmentally non-sustainable.*

It is necessary to *widen the scope of labour law protection* and to make the *enforcement of workers' rights more effective.* Labour legislation should efficiently cover *all* those who are in need of such protection, including in certain cases also the self-employed, economically dependent persons/workers and other who work in a dependent relationship. An adequate and comparable level of labour law protection should be guaranteed to all forms of work. *Labour law must not be dissolved; it has to be strengthened and adjusted to the current challenges.*

In order to be able to fulfil its functions and aims, labour law has to develop further, also *at the international level.* It is not possible to develop labour law only

15 One of the methods of establishing social citizenship is the introduction of the universal basic income, basic (citizen's) income, universal living wage, etcetera, i.e. the right of every person as a human being to a certain minimum income necessary to lead a decent life. There are many theoretical variations on this idea, some of them even follow the neo-liberal concept, but the predominant concepts of the universal basic income are in line with the human rights perspective (see, for example, Standing 2011). On challenges of social protection in general see also Guillemard 2008. See also Castel 2009, p. 87–118.

16 ILO 2010; Stiglitz 2009, p. 1–13; Freeman 2010, p. 163–183; ILO 2012.

17 Leschke/Jepsen 2012, p. 289–312; Vaughan-Whitehead 2012; Laulom/Mazuyer/Escande Varniol 2012; Kaufman 2004, 630–631.

within one country and only at the national level. Within the globalised world such an approach supports the neo-liberal concept and pushes countries towards irrational competition by way of social dumping. 'Law shopping' is taking place.[18] As explained by Professor Rigaux, countries, too, are becoming commodities. This has to be stopped. The question is: who might be the relevant actors at the international as well as national and local level. What is the role of the ILO? What is the role of the social partners? What is the role of various social movements? A strong social counterpower is urgently needed. And where will the EU stand: will it support the destroying neo-liberal paradigm or will it respect and care for the precious, but fragile labour and social rights?

REFERENCES

Aliprantis, N. (ed.) (2009), *Les droits sociaux dans les instruments européens et transnationaux: Défis à l'échelle mondiale*, Bruyant, Brussels.

Auer, P., Berg, J., Coulibaly, I. (2005), Is stable workforce good for productivity? *International labour Review*, Vol. 144, No., 3, p. 319–343.

Auer, P., Cazes, S. (2003), *Employment stability in an age of flexibility – evidence from industrialized countries*, ILO, Geneva.

Bajič, S. (1936) *Delovno pravo* [*'Labour Law'*], Ljubljana.

Castel, R. (2003), *L'insecurité sociale*, Seuil, Paris.

Castel, R. (2009), *La montée des incertitudes: Travail, protections, statut de l'individu*, Seuil, Paris.

Cazes, S., Verick, S., Al Hussami, F. (2011), *Diverging trends in unemployment in the United States and Europe: Evidence from Okun's law and the global financial crisis*, ILO, Geneva, 2011 (www.ilo.org/wcmsp5/groups/public/---ed_emp/---emp_elm/---analysis/documents/publication/wcms_170782.pdf).

Davies, A. C. L. (2009), *Perspectives on Labour Law*, Cambridge University Press, Cambridge.

De Burca, De Witte (eds.) (2005), *Social Rights in Europe*, OUP, Oxford.

De Schutter, O. (2010), *International Human Rights Law*, Cambridge University Press, Cambridge.

Deakin, S., Lele, P., Siems, M. (2007), The evolution of labour law: Calibrating and comparing regulatory regimes, *International Labour Review*, Vol. 146, No. 3–4, p. 133–162.

Dorssemont, F. (2011), How the European Court of Human Rights Gave us Energy to Cope with Laval and Viking, In: Moreau (ed.), *Before and After the Economic Crisis: What Implications for the 'European Social Model'?*, Edward Elgar, Cheltenham, p. 217–235.

European Commission (2007): *Flexibility and competitiveness: Labour market flexibility, innovation and organisational performance (Flex-Com)*, Final report, Luxembourg

[18] Supiot 2010, p. 155–157; see also Bronstein 2009, p. 25 and others.

(http://bookshop.europa.eu/eubookshop/FileCache/PUBPDF/KINA21950ENS/KINA21950ENS:002.pdf

Freedland, M. (2007), Application of labour and employment law beyond the contract of employment, *International Labour Review*, Vol. 146, No. 1–2, p. 3–22.

Freeman, M. (2011), *Human Rights – An Interdisciplinary Approach*, Polity, Cambridge.

Freeman, R. B. (2010), It's financialization!, *International Labour Review*, Vol. 149, No. 2, p. 163–183.

Guillemard, A.-M. (2008), *Où va la protection sociale?*, Presses Universitaires de France, Paris.

Hepple, B. (2001), Equality and empowerment for decent work, *International Labour Review*, Vol. 140, No. 1, p. 5–18.

Herrera, C. M. (2009), *Les droits sociaux*, Presses Universitaires de France, Paris.

ILO (2012), *Better Jobs for a Better Economy*, World of Work Report, Geneva.

ILO (2011), *Equality at Work*, ILC, 100th Session, Report I (B), Geneva.

ILO (2010), *From one crisis to the next?*, World of Work Report 2010, Geneva.

ILO (1999), *Decent Work*, Report of the Director-General to the 87th Session of the ILC, Geneva.

Kaufman, B. E. (2004), *The global evolution of industrial relations*, ILO, Geneva.

Končar, P. (2008), Komentar k 4. in 11. členu Zakona o delovnih razmerjih [*'Commentary to Articles 4 and 11 of the Employment Relationships Act*], In: Bečan, I. et al., *ZDR s komentarjem*, Ljubljana.

Kresal, B. (2012), Primerljivost delovnopravnega varstva v različnih oblikah zaposlitve [*'Comparable Labour Law Protection within Different Forms of Employment'*], *Delavci in delodajalci*, Vol. 12, No. 2–3, p. 245–262.

Kresal, B. (1999), Pogodbeno delo: med civilnopravno in delovnopravno ureditvijo [*'Contractual Work: Between the Civil and Labour Law'*], *Podjetje in delo*, Vol. 25, No. 1, p. 64–93.

Kresal, F. (1998), *Zgodovina socialne in gospodarske politike v Sloveniji od liberalizma do druge svetovne vojne* [*'History of Social and Economic Policy in Slovenia from Liberalism to World War II'*], Ljubljana.

Kresal Šoltes, K. (2012), Spornost EPL in drugih indeksov fleksibilnosti zaposlovanja – prezrti delovnopravni vidiki [*'Discussible EPL and other Indices of Flexibility of Employment – Neglected Labour Law Aspects'*], *Delavci in delodajalci*, Vol. 12, No. 2–3, p. 183–206.

Kucera, D., Roncolato, L. (2008), Informal employment: Two contested policy issues, *International labour Review*, Vol. 147, No. 4, p. 322–348.

Laulom, S., Mazuyer, E., Escande Varniol, C., Vielle, P. (eds.) (2012), *Quel droit social dans une Europe en crise?*, Larcier.

Leschke, J., Jepsen, M. (2012), Introduction: Crisis, policy responses and widening inequalities in the EU, *International Labour Review*, Vol. 151, No. 4, p. 289–312.

Leskošek, V. (2012), Vpliv socialne države na (ne)odvisnost delavcev od tržnih pogojev zaposlovanja, Časopis za kritiko znanosti, let. 39, št. 247, p. 103–112.

Moreau, M.-A. (2009), Les droits de l'Homme au travail en 2008: au-delà de la logique des drotis de l'homme et des droits sociaux fondamentaux, In: Boy, Racine, Siiriainen (eds.), Droits economiques et drotis de l'homme, Larcier, p. 509–534.

Ojeda Avilés, A. (2009), The 'externalization' of labour law, *International Labour Review*, Vol. 148, No. 1–2, p. 47–67.

Pellonpää (1993), Economic, social and cultural rights; In. Macdonald et al. (ed.), *The European System for the Protection of Human Rights*, Nijhoff.

Rigaux, M. (2004), Le droit du travail, la concurrence sociale et les restructurations: quelques observations d'ordre théorique destinées à proposer une hypothèse de travail; In: Sachs-Durand, C. (ed.), La place des salariés dans les restructurations en Europe Communautaire, Presses universitaires de Strasbourg, Strasbourg.

Rosanvallon, P. (2011), *La société des égaux*, Seuil, Paris.

Senčur Peček, D. (2012), Delavci - zunanji izvajalci? [*'Workers - Outsourced?'*], *Delavci in delodajalci*, Vol. 12, No. 2–3, p. 223–244.

Standing, G. (2011), *The Precariat - The New Dangerous Class*, Bloomsbury, New York.

Standing, G. (2002), From People's Security Surveys to a Decent Work Index, *International Labour Review*, Vol. 141, No. 4, p. 441–454.

Strban, G. (2006), Fleksibilnost v sistemih socialne varnosti [*'Flexibility in Social Security Systems'*], *Delavci in delodajalci*, Vol. 6, No. 2–3, p. 331–354.

Sheppard, C. (2012), Mapping anti-discrimination law onto inequality at work: Expanding the meaning of equality in international labour law, *International Labour Review*, Vol. 151, No. 1–2, p. 1–19.

Stiglitz, J. (2009), The global crisis, social protection and jobs, *International Labour Review*, Vol. 148, No. 1–2, p. 1–13.

Supiot, A. (2010a), *L'esprit de Philadelphie: La justice sociale face au marché total*, Seuil, Paris.

Supiot, A. (2010b), A legal perspective on the economic crisis of 2008, *International Labour Review*, Vol. 149, No. 2, p. 151–162.

Tičar, L. (2008), Temeljna vprašanja kroga oseb delovnopravnega varstva [*'Basic Issues Concerning Personal Scope of Labour Law Protection'*], *Delavci in delodajalci*, Vol. 8, No. 2–3, p. 329–342.

Van Aerschot, P. (2011), *Activation Policies and the Protection of Individual Rights*, Ashgate.

Vaughan-Whitehead, D. (ed.) (2012), *Work inequalities in the crisis - evidence from Europe*, ILO, Geneva.

HUMAN DIGNITY AND DECENT WORK AS ULTIMATE OBJECTIVES OF LABOUR LAW

Towards 'basic social law' with a labour law component?

Kelly Reyniers*

I. HUMAN DIGNITY

A. A DYNAMIC CONCEPT WITH ETHICAL AND PHILOSOPHICAL ROOTS

The right of every person to live in dignity and to be treated in a decent way is no longer under debate *as such*.[1] Because it is so inherently connected to the essence of human being, the right to human dignity is almost taken for granted. It is therefore approached as a *universal* concept. However, it is very difficult to describe human dignity and to pinpoint what the term covers exactly. Primarily, human dignity does indeed seem to relate to (the right to) life and in particular to (the right to) survival of man. In that sense, it posits amongst others an adequate income – from work or other means[2] – that allows the person to provide for himself and his family. This also includes proper housing; protection of bodily integrity; access to health care; education and training. However, does human dignity not go beyond that? Education and training, for instance, can be considered as a mere means of finding a job (more easily) and thus of generating an income. However, education and training serve other purposes as well: self-development, emancipation, even recreation and relaxation. Are those not aspects of human dignity as well? Defining the essentials of a dignified life is therefore extremely

* University of Antwerp, Belgium.

1 Obviously, this does not alter the fact that unfortunately actual realisation of this often leaves much to be desired.

2 The first things that come to mind are systems of social security or social welfare.

delicate.[3] At any rate, human dignity (in a general sense) seems to refer to the protection and realisation of the *physical* as well as the *mental integrity* of human beings.

The difficulty regarding the delineation of the concept of human dignity is due, first of all, to the *vagueness* that is typical of the concept and its *ethical and philosophical roots*.[4] Furthermore, it concerns a *dynamic* concept in the sense that the *concretisation* depends on time, place and culture. In a way, this finding also holds true for the concept of 'decent work', which is analysed below.

B. ... BUT ALSO A LEGAL CONCEPT

Through the explicit or implicit acknowledgement of human dignity in various legal sources on an international, regional (e.g. European) and national level, the concept was enshrined in the legal order as well,[5] as a rule with the status of *fundamental right*. This is not surprising: most of the definitions of 'fundamental rights' or 'human rights' invariably refer to *the promotion and protection of human dignity* as the essential characteristic and purpose of fundamental rights/human rights. The right to human dignity can therefore be considered as *an overall fundamental right* that spans and binds all other fundamental rights.[6] Indeed, it transcends the classic division between 'political and civil rights' on the one hand and 'socio-economic rights' on the other hand. Both categories concern purpose-bound rights, which aim at achieving human dignity. Nevertheless, this does not

---

3 This is obvious when, for instance, more controversial topics of discussion such as asylum policy, prostitution, abortion, euthanasia and such are dealt with on the basis of the right to human dignity.

4 For a (brief) overview, see a.o. B. Van Rompu, *La dignité de la personne humaine dans les relations de travail*, doctoral dissertation Université de Lille II, ANRT, 2006, 17 et seq; O. de Tissot, "Pour une analyse juridique du concept de « dignité » du salarié", *Dr.Soc.* 1995, 973; J. Fierens, "La dignité humaine comme concept juridique", *JTT* 2002, 577–578.

5 An elaborate analysis of human dignity as a legal concept does not fit in with the objective of this paper. Please see specialised literature for this:
- for a general analysis, e.g. J. Fierens, "La dignité humaine comme concept juridique", *JTT* 2002, 577–578;
- regarding the Belgian legal system in particular, a.o. W. Pas and J. Van Nieuwenhove, "Het recht een menswaardig leven te leiden: een vergelijking van de grondwetsbepalingen in België en Duitsland", *Jaarboek Mensenrechten* 1994, 113–138; F. Kurz, "L'application du principe du respect de la dignité humaine: un défi pour les les jurisdictions du travail", *JTT* 2002, 273–278; M. Palumbo, "La dignité de la personne humaine en droit social ou la relativité d'un concept absolu", *Soc.Kron.* 2003, 1–14; D. Cuypers, "Universaliteit, territorialiteit en individualisering van de menselijke waardigheid in het sociaal recht" in S. Dewulf and D. Pacquée (eds.), *60 jaar Universele Verklaring van de Rechten van de Mens (1948–2008)*, Antwerp, Intersentia, 2008, 179–212.

6 G. Maes, *De afdwingbaarheid van sociale grondrechten*, Antwerp, Intersentia, 2003, no. 810, p.410–411; M. Rigaux, *Tussen burgerschap en sociale concurrentie. Over arbeid in zijn verhouding tot kapitaal doorheen het recht*, Antwerp, Intersentia, 2004, 107, No. 120.

alter the fact that in a number of legal sources[7] the right to human dignity is closely linked to socio-economic fundamental rights. This is probably due to the fact that the realisation of the right to human dignity is all too often considered as a way of guaranteeing the right to an adequate standard of living. As already stated above, in my view this only concerns one aspect.

The right to human dignity is *explicitly* acknowledged in several *international and European legal sources*. For instance:

- Part II, sub a Declaration concerning the aims and purposes of the ILO (Declaration of Philadelphia) (1944): "*all human beings*, irrespective of race, creed or sex, have the right to pursue both their material well-being and their spiritual development in conditions of freedom and *dignity*, of economic security and equal opportunity".
- Preamble of the Charter of the United Nations (1945): We the peoples of the United Nations determined (...) to reaffirm faith in fundamental human rights, in the *dignity and worth of the human person*, in the equal rights of men and women and of nations large and small (...)".
- Preamble of the Universal Declaration of Human Rights (1948): "Whereas recognition of the inherent *dignity* and of the equal and inalienable rights *of all members of the human family* is the foundation of freedom, justice and peace in the world (...)";
  Article 1: "*All human beings* are born free and equal in *dignity* and rights";
  Article 22: "*Everyone, as a member of society*, has the right to social security and is entitled to realisation, through national effort and international co-operation and in accordance with the organisation and resources of each State, of the economic, social and cultural rights indispensable for his *dignity* and the free development of his personality.
- Preamble of the International Covenant on Civil and Political Rights and of the International Covenant on Economic, Social and Cultural Rights (1966): "Considering that, in accordance with the principles proclaimed in the Charter of the United Nations, recognition of the *inherent dignity* and of the equal and inalienable rights *of all members of the human family* is the foundation of freedom, justice and peace in the world".
- Article 1 Charter of the fundamental rights of the European Union (2000 revised in 2007): "*Human dignity* is inviolable. It must be respected and protected."

[7] This is the case, for instance, in the Belgian Constitution. The right of every person to live in dignity was incorporated in Article 23 of the Constitution which proclaims a number of socio-economic fundamental rights, even though it was suggested during the parliamentary preparation of this article to insert the right to human dignity at the top of title II of the Constitution ("De Belgen en hun rechten") precisely because it constitutes the essence of all fundamental rights.

Various *national constitutions* also *explicitly* refer to this, for example:

- Art.23, para. 1 Belgian constitution: "Ieder heeft het recht een menswaardig leven te leiden" (Everyone has the right to live in dignity)
- Art.1 German constitution: "Die Würde des Menschen ist unantastbar. Sie zu achten und zu schutzen ist Verpflichtung aller staatlichen Gewalt" (The dignity of man is inviolable. To respect and protect it is the duty of all state authority.)

It should be noted that in some legal sources human dignity is explicitly linked to the *specific capacity of* a *person* (e.g. employee) *and/or context* (e.g. labour relations/ employment). See for instance:

- Part I, Article 26 Revised European Social Charter (1996): "*All workers* have the right to *dignity at work*".

Apart from the numerous conventions on human rights and constitutional texts (but also other regulations) which explicitly proclaim human dignity, it should be pointed out that sometimes case law acknowledges human dignity as a *general principle of law*. This is the case, for instance, in France where the *Conseil constitutionnel* judged in 1994 that guaranteeing human dignity is a constitutional principle that should be protected against "*toute forme d'asservissement et de dégradation*".[8]

The legal scope of the right to human dignity will have to be examined for every legal source separately. Because of the vagueness of the concept, mentioned above, it is often argued that the right to human dignity is too obscure and unspecific to be able to derive enforceable rights from it. In a lot of legal sources human dignity has no autonomous meaning: it has to be considered in conjunction with other fundamental rights. However, in combination with a fundamental right that is directly enforceable (such as the right to equal treatment and the right to privacy) it can generate legal consequences too and it becomes indirectly enforceable. Furthermore, the right to human dignity can function as an objective for the government when it shapes its policy regarding other fundamental rights. Similarly, human dignity can also be used as a standard of interpretation when it comes to the substantiation of open norms. However, this does not alter the fact that in several legal sources the recognition of (the right to) human dignity is rather a political statement, with a.o. an educational value.

---

8 Cons.const. 27 July 1994. See a.o. O. de Tissot, "Pour une analyse juridique du concept de « dignité » du salarié", *Dr.Soc.* 1995, 973 et seq.; B. Van-Rompu, *La dignité de la personne humaine dans les relations de travail*, doctoral dissertation Université de Lille II, ANRT, 2006, 632p.

II. DECENT WORK: A FACTOR OF HUMAN DIGNITY

A. AN OBVIOUS NEXUS BETWEEN DECENT WORK AND HUMAN DIGNITY

On the one hand, it is apparent from various legal sources that work/labour is considered as a means to achieve a dignified life. See for instance:

- Part II, Article 4.1 Revised European Social Charter: With a view to ensuring the effective exercise of the right to a fair remuneration, the Parties undertake: (1) to recognise the right of workers to a remuneration such as will give them and their families *a decent standard of living*
- Part III, Article 7 International Covenant on Economic, Social and Cultural Rights: "remuneration which provides all workers, as a minimum, with: (...) (ii) a *decent living* for themselves and their families in accordance with the provisions of the present Covenant

The fact that work/labour is considered as a means to achieve human dignity does not only follow from the *economic meaning* of work/labour (i.e. a means to support oneself). Indeed, work is also the fundamental activity that allows people to *develop themselves personally and socially.*[9] In a way, people take their identity from their work, which also gives meaning to life.

On the other hand, these social functions are only part of labour insofar as this involves work of an acceptable quality, *decent* work.

B. DECENT WORK: CONCEPT

1. *In general: ensuring the employee's fundamental rights in the best possible way*

Although the concept of decent work– just like the concept of human dignity – is difficult to delineate, in my opinion it seems – within a professional context – to refer to the type of employment that ensures the employee's fundamental rights in the best possible way. This presumes the fact that the work must meet certain *demands of quality* on the following levels:

9 This is bidirectional. On the one hand, the individual is "socialised" by his work. On the other, (paid) work is a kind of commitment to the community, in the sense that the individual contributes to the social and economic progress of society through his professional activities.

1) *terms of employment* (for instance reasonable working hours, fair pay, ...)
2) *working conditions* (for instance a safe and healthy work environment, ...)
3) *content of the work* (for instance nature of the tasks to be carried out, ...)
4) and *labour relations* (for instance the social climate within the enterprise, including equal treatment and non-discrimination; possibility to feed into the decision-making process, ...)

2. *Specifically: a means of identifying the ILO's major priorities*

At the end of the 20th century the concept of 'decent work (travail décent, trabajo decente)' was also introduced by the International Labour Organization (ILO) as a way of translating the fundamental goal of the Organization – 'its mandate' – to the 21st century. From then on, the Organization's activities and policy were built around 'pillars of decent work' that form the Decent Work Agenda (DWA).[10] Through this new and integral approach the ILO intended to and still does intend to offer a firm response to the excrescences of globalisation (a.o. increased social competition, exploitation and exclusion) and to consolidate its social dimension.

Here too, decent work is distinctly considered as a means to live in dignity: "*For many, it* (decent work) *is the primary route out of poverty. For many more, it is about realizing personal aspirations in their daily existence and about solidarity with others. And everywhere and for everybody, decent work is about securing human dignity*".[11]

The recent ILO Declaration on Social Justice for a Fair Globalisation (2008), which formalised the Decent Work Agenda, does not contain a definition of the concept of decent work. Consequently, one has to revert to the various ILO reports of the Director-General for a description. In these instruments decent work was described as *productive labour* being carried out "*in conditions of freedom, equity, security and human dignity*".[12] Decent work is both a personal individual objective and a development target for states.[13] Here too, the description of decent work remains quite vague. This is not surprising since decent work is a dynamic and evolving concept. What it means exactly and which standards should be applied therefore varies considerably from society to society. In that sense, former ILO

---

[10] The previous 39 programmes were reduced to one programme that is based on the four strategic goals. For each pillar, a series of 'International Focus' programmes of high priority were planned. See: ILO, *Activities of the ILO, 1998–99,* report 1A of the Director-General, Geneva, 2000; G. Rodgers, E. Lee, L. Swepstone and J. Van Daele, *The ILO and the quest for social justice, 1919–2009,* ILO, Geneva, 2009, 225.

[11] ILO, *Reducing the decent work deficit – a global challenge*, report 1A of the Director – General, 89th session IAC, Geneva, 2001, 6.

[12] ILO, *Decent Work*, Report ILC, 87th session 1999, 6, www.ilo.org. Not only was this description repeated in other reports, it was also used on the website, in brochures etcetera to denote the ILO mandate.

[13] ILO, *Reducing the decent work deficit – a global challenge*, Report 1A ILC 89th session, 2001, 4, www.ilo.org.

Director-General J. Somavia[14] declared the following: "*The notion Decent Work comes from the way people themselves define it; why work is important to an individual, what are peoples expectations from work*". That is also why the DWA– of which human dignity is both the basis and a part of the objective – uses a '*people centred approach*'.

As mentioned before, the ILO's activities are focused on *four strategic objectives* that form the pillars of the Decent Work Agenda. These objectives are equal in value and not subject to hierarchy. They are "*inseparable, interrelated and mutually supportive*".[15] Gender equality and non-discrimination are two topics that run through all four pillars.[16]

The first pillar of the DWA refers to the *fundamental principles and rights at work*. The phrasing used is certainly rather striking: "*respecting, promoting and realizing the fundamental principles and rights at work*",[17] a phrasing which links up with the Declaration on the Fundamental Principles and Rights at Work (1998), in which the 'core labour standards[18]' were established. In the discussions about and concrete development of the 'rights at work' pillar in the ILO reports on decent work too repeated references are made to these core labour standards. This is rather confusing because at the same time numerous general ILO texts show that there is a wish to interpret this pillar broadly so as to include other labour standards than core labour standards in 'rights at work'. According to J.M. Servais,[19] however, the other international labour standards should be considered as a way of achieving the four objectives. The Declaration on Social Justice for a Fair Globalisation emphasises – as do other ILO instruments – that violation of the principles and rights should not result in any kind of competitive advantage to the states.

Employment and income opportunities for women and men, the second pillar, deals with the promotion of a socio-economic and institutional framework that

---

14 J. Somavia, "The ILO Decent Work Agenda as the aspiration of people: the insertion of values and ethics in the global economy" in D. Peccoud, *Philosophical and spiritual perspectives on Decent Work*, Geneva, IILS, 2004, 5–7.

15 Part I, B Declaration on Social Justice for a Fair Globalisation. It goes without saying that the pursuit for a high level of employment, for instance, should be coupled with the realisation of qualitative work.

16 Part I, B Declaration on Social Justice for a Fair Globalisation.

17 Part I, A, iv Declaration on Social Justice for a Fair Globalisation.

18 The 'core labour standards' comprise: (i) the freedom to set up trade unions and the actual recognition of the right to collective bargaining, (ii) the abolition of all forms of hard labour or forced labour, (iii) the actual abolition of child labour and (iv) the elimination of discrimination in employment and occupation.

19 "*(...) the other norms, a majority, are only means of achieving them all*" (J.M. Servais, "A new Declaration at the ILO: what for?", *European Labour Law Journal* 2010, issue1, 286 and 297.)

maximises employment. This concerns work under proper conditions and in decent circumstances, always within a local frame of reference.[20]

The third pillar, *social protection*, aims at increasing the quality of (formal) social security systems on the one hand, always in accordance with the financial possibilities of the member state. Other forms of social protection are developed and supported as well. Microfinance systems or micro insurances that are very effective in the informal economy are perfect illustrations of this.[21] On the other hand, the pillar also consists of aspects of employment protection such as health and safety at the workplace, working conditions and liveable wages.

Finally, *the social dialogue and tripartism* pillar aims at reinforcing social consultation and tripartism. It concerns the method by which the realisation of the aforementioned pillars can be promoted, which once again demonstrates the interdependence of the four pillars.

It goes without saying that the aforesaid demands of quality of work also take shape in these pillars.

The strength of the ILO decent work concept is undoubtedly to be found in the broad reception of this concept by various stakeholders. On the one hand, the ILO has succeeded in giving decent work a prominent place on the international and regional agenda, and on the other, in warming society and the shop floor to the Agenda for Decent Work. However, we must also consider the fact that this broad reception could contain a danger of decent work becoming a container concept with an eroded meaning.

C. SOME REMARKS FROM A (BELGIAN) LEGAL POINT OF VIEW

Firstly it should be noted that in law making and case law the term 'decent work' is not (yet) used. Even in the doctrine relatively little attention is paid to this concept. So we cannot but conclude that, at present, 'decent work' is not an operational legal concept in Belgium.[22]

20 Part I, A, i Declaration on Social Justice for a Fair Globalisation.

21 J. Somavia, "The ILO Decent Work Agenda as the aspiration of people: the insertion of values and ethics in the global economy" in D. Peccoud, *Philosophical and spiritual perspectives on Decent Work*, Geneva, IILS, 2004, 8; ILO, *Decent Work. Some strategic challenges ahead*, report Director-General, 97th session ILC, 2008, 19.

22 A. Supiot ("Conclusion: Esquisse d'un accord-cadre relatif a l'extension de la protection sociale", *Semaine sociale Lamy* 2006, n°1272, édition spéciale, 91) comes to the same conclusion: *"Le concept de travail décent n'est pas (...) une catégorie juridique opératoire, mais plutôt un guide que l'OIT s'est donné depuis 1990 pour orienter son action"*.

In the ILO reports of the Director-General as well as in the 2008 Declaration on Social Justice for a Fair Globalization the concept of decent work is not so much worded in terms of a (new) individual right, but rather in terms of a (political) goal of the ILO's activities. Of course, this does not alter the fact that law has an important role to play in the realisation of decent work (also see point III).

If decent work were to be worded in terms of an individual 'right to decent work', this would be very similar to the fundamental right to live in dignity (applied to employment relations). Therefore, from a Belgian legal point of view and given the fact that the right to live in dignity is enshrined in the Belgian legal system, one could ask if incorporating a right to decent work in the legislation would have added value.

In 1994 'the right to live in dignity' was incorporated in the Belgian Constitution. Although in the context of the inclusion of socio-economic rights in the Constitution, a bill[23] was put forward to add a 'right to decent work', the Constitutioner opted for a more general wording and proclaimed the right of every person to live in dignity.[24] This right is further realised through other fundamental rights[25] which in turn are elaborated in legislation.[26] Beside the pillar 'rights at work' the other DWA pillars too can be directly related to the fundamental rights mentioned in Article 23, last paragraph of the Belgian Constitution with a view to realising the overall fundamental right to live in dignity. More specifically, this involves the right to work (the employment pillar), the right to social security and health protection, the right to fair working conditions and fair remuneration (the social protection pillar) and the right to information, consultation and collective bargaining (the social dialogue pillar). As far as Belgium is concerned, one can argue that the fundamental rights do appear to cover the various legal aspects of decent work. What is more, incorporating a new 'right to decent work' in the legislation might cause problems of interpretation regarding the relation of this right vis-à-vis the other fundamental rights.

III. LABOUR LAW AS (NECESSARY) INSTRUMENT TO ENFORCE AND ACHIEVE DECENT WORK

The poor working conditions created by the industrial revolution cultured the development of a new branch of law at the end of 19th and beginning of the 20th century. Until that time, labour relations were controlled by the freedom of work

[23] *Parliamentary Documents* Chamber of Representatives, B.Z. (Special Session) 1991-'92, No. 218/1. The proposal refers to a "right of decent work /*un travail convenable*)".

[24] Article 23, first paragraph Belgian Constitution.

[25] Article 23, last paragraph Belgian Constitution.

[26] Article 23, second paragraph Belgian Constitution.

and to carry on a business, contractual freedom and the freedom to arrange one's own affairs. The rules of civil law were fully applicable. As a result, labour law was a necessary correction to the free labour market and (unfair) social competition. This correction consisted, amongst others, of limiting contractual freedom of economically unequal parties – employee and employer – (e.g. by standardisation of wages and terms of employment) and the introduction of a system of employee representation bodies.[27] Although the regulator did not explicitly invoke fundamental rights when he made protective rules in terms of labour law, M. Rigaux[28] rightly argues that the genesis of labour law could be considered as a realisation of fundamental rights "*avant la lettre*". Realisation of employees' dignity (first of women and children, then of adult men as well) was a central part of this. Legal literature correctly remarks that labour law in a social welfare state aims *at the promotion and protection of the employee's dignity.*[29] Through the rules of labour law decent work can be concretised and refined and, if necessary, enforced in court. However, this also means that the various factors that promote the *direct disintegration*[30] or the (silent, dormant) *dissolution*[31] of labour law (potentially) threaten human dignity in labour relations.[32]

IV. TOWARDS BASIC SOCIAL LAW WITH A LABOUR LAW COMPONENT?

A. THE ISSUE

One should wonder whether the aforementioned objective of labour law – which is the promotion and protection of the employee's dignity and the implementation/concretisation of fundamental rights – is of such a nature that (at least certain aspects of) *labour protection should be extended to everyone who performs labour.* The outlines of its personnel scope are therefore, in my opinion, one of the

27 Also see M. Rigaux, *Labour law or social competition law? On labour in its relation with capital through aw: Francqui Chair Lectures*, Antwerp, Intersentia, 2009, p.15 a.f.

28 M. Rigaux, *Labour law or social competition law? On labour in its relation with capital through law: Francqui Chair Lectures*, Antwerp, Intersentia, 2009, p.125–126.

29 In Dutch legal literature, see a.o. M. Stroobant, "De arbeidsovereenkomstenwet van 10 maart 1900 en het recht op arbeid" in M. Stroobant and O. Vanachter (eds.), *Honderd jaar arbeidsovereenkomstenwet,* Antwerp, Intersentia, 2001, 35; M. Rigaux, *Tussen burgerschap en sociale concurrentie. Over arbeid in zijn verhouding tot kapitaal doorheen het recht*, Antwerp, Intersentia, 2004, 233; M. Van Putten, *Het arbeidsrecht en de onderneming*, Antwerp, Intersentia, 2009, 146–154; F. Hendrickx, "Arbeidsrecht voor de spiegel", *TSR* 2010, issue1, 35–37; W. Vandeputte, *Ontslagrecht en de arbeidsmarkt. Naar een modernisering van het Belgische ontslagrecht* in *Begasoz Reeks*, Bruges, die Keure, 2012, p. 396 a.f.

30 For instance by the direct abolition of protective regulation.

31 For instance by the individualisation and contractualisation of labour law (for instance the system of opening clauses), by replacing hard law with more soft law instruments, etcetera.

32 See other contributions in this book as well.

important challenges of labour law in the light of the fundamental right to live in dignity.

Anyone who reflects upon the feasibility and advisability of "basic social law with a labour law component[33]" is inevitably confronted with a number of fundamental questions and issues (both from a legal and a policy point of view):

- To which type of workers/labour performances should labour protection be extended?
- Which aspects of labour protection should be granted?
- To what extent do fundamental rights, international labour standards and/or EU regulations make a similar social protection desirable or even obligatory?
- Which model should be used? Is a concentrically organised labour law possible, with a hard core that is applicable to all workers?
- Can 'subordination' be rejected as determining criterion for the acknowledgement of labour protection? Could work/labour be considered as the first application criterion for labour law?
- and others.

A number of these questions and issues are briefly clarified below.

B. LABOUR LAW… "FOR EVERYONE WHO PERFORMS LABOUR"

If labour protection were to be extended to "*everyone who performs labour*" the question arises as to exactly who would be covered by that phrase. Literature primarily seems to mention the "self-employed", who form a heterogeneous[34] group on their own. Generally, it concerns persons who work for a client in return for remuneration without them being under the client's authority.

Full protection under labour law of self-employed workers was traditionally not considered necessary. On the one hand this is demonstrated by the fact that in principle national labour law does not apply to self-employed persons, and on the other, by the fact that in a lot of countries there are hardly[35] any similar rules to protect the person of the self-employed worker. In international labour law – one

33 The term 'social law' is used as a generic term for labour law and social security law. It should be noted that, in principle, labour law is only applicable to employees. A separate social security scheme, however, was developed for self-employed workers in Belgium in the sixties of the previous century.

34 A typology of the "self-employed" could be established using, amongst others, the following criteria of differentiation: working for one or more clients, working with or without staff, the nature of the activity/service.

35 In Belgium for example there are only a few Laws that also affect the person of the self-employed worker, for example a law concerning the opening hours in commerce, trade and services. But that kind of laws are quite limited.

of the foundations of national labour law – this also seems to be more or less the case. Because of its origins the ILO has paid most attention to the needs of wage workers in formal enterprises.[36] That is why ILO Conventions are only applicable to self-employed persons to a limited extent.[37]

It seems that self-employed workers must derive their protection from their legal "freedom to work". The fact that self-employed persons are in control of their labour and are able to work under the conditions and in the circumstances determined by themselves is apparently considered to be an *adequate* protection mechanism. However, since the self-employed worker is economically dependent on his principal/client this 'freedom' is often nothing more than an apparent freedom. Considering the reality of false self-employment, the growing group of people that are in the grey area between the properly (formally acknowledged) self-employed workers/undertakers and employees the question arises once again whether a social protection (or a stronger one) is needed for this type of workers.

Unlike Belgium, a number of countries such as for instance Italy,[38] acknowledge a third professional status, apart from employees and self-employed persons: "economically dependent labour". It is an intermediary category of service providers who are not bound by a formal employment contract but who are still very much like employees because of their (economic) dependence on the client. As a result of that dependence, they are eligible to special social protection.[39] Within the ILO as well, a discussion was held concerning the provision of social protection to the so-called "contract labour", which is considered to be a third category by legal literature and which covers people whose professional status cannot be accurately described as being employees nor self-employed workers. The initiatives regarding contract labour in 2006 resulted in Recommendation no.198 concerning the employment relationship.

Finally, one could consider whether the extension of labour protection should remain limited to everyone who performs labour in order to make a living (so-called professional labour). Should volunteers, for instance, not be able to claim adequate social protection as well?[40]

---

36 ILO, *Decent Work*, Report ILC, 87th session 1999, 6,

37 Regarding the applicability of international labour standards to self-employed workers, see a.o. J.M. Servais, *Droits en synergie sur le travail. Eléments de droit international et comparé du travail*, Brussels, Bruylant, 1997, 155–157; J.M. Servais, "L'OIT et le travail décent. La difficile médiation entre croissance, création d'emploi et protection des travailleurs", *Revue de droit comparé du travail et de la sécurité sociale* 2011, issue1, 73–74.

38 The so-called "Para subordinazione".

39 See for intance A. Perulli, *Economically dependent / quasi-subordinate (parasubordinate) employment: legal, social and economic aspects*, report for DG Employment and Social Affairs, Brussels, 2003, 119 p.

40 In Belgium, the question as to whether or not certain labour laws with a broad scope (such as the Labour Act of 16 March 1971, the Well-Being Act of 4 August 1996) are already applicable

C. FUNDAMENTAL RIGHTS AND INTERNATIONAL LABOUR STANDARDS AS INCENTIVES TO CHANGE OR EXTEND THE PERSONNEL SCOPE OF LABOUR LAW

Since labour law – as shown above – is the concretisation of various fundamental rights (a.o. the right to live in dignity, the right to work and to free choice of employment, the right to just conditions of work etcetera), the question arises as to whether those very same fundamental rights could not inspire or even oblige the regulator to extend labour protection to other categories of workers as well. To the extent that the fundamental rights in question are legally enforceable and have a broad personnel scope,[41] this does seem to be the case. Apart from the socio-economic fundamental rights, the principle of equal treatment could play a part in this as well. If different categories of workers turn out to be working in similar circumstances in practice (for instance both in a vulnerable position due to economic dependence), one could argue that they are entitled to similar, adequate social protection.

The broad scope of the ILO Decent Work Agenda too could be an incentive to (re)evaluate and, if necessary, change or extend the legal protection of certain categories of workers. Indeed, in a report by the Director-General, the following can be found: "*The ILO Constitution calls for the improvement of the conditions of labour, whether organized or not, and wherever work might occur, whether in the formal or informal economy, whether at home, in the community or in the voluntary sector*".[42] That very same report on decent work also mentions "*a concern for all workers*" and "*all those who work have rights at work*". By this broad formulation the universal need of decent work is acknowledged with good reason and this irrespective of a person's occupational status, the context in which the work is carried out (formally, informally...). However, this does not alter the fact that – as pointed out above – the applicability of international labour standards to self-employed workers is limited.

D. "LABOUR" AS THE FIRST APPLICATION CRITERION FOR LABOUR LAW

The granting of a particular form of social protection is currently linked to the category of workers to which one belongs. As a rule, in the private sector these are

to volunteers, is currently under debate. See for instance K. Reyniers, *(Verboden) Arbeid*, Antwerp, Intersentia, 2012, p. 256 et seq.

41 In Belgium, the right to just conditions of work is traditionally only related to employees, whereas the right to work and the right to free choice of employment are related to the occupational activity, of both employees and self-employed workers.

42 ILO, *Decent Work*, Report ILC, 87th session 1999, www.ilo.org.

the categories of employee or self-employed person.[43] Labour law is primarily[44] applicable to employees. As a result, (legal) subordination might be considered as the key to the door of labour law. In practice, however, the application of exactly this criterion is cause for debate. The distinction between employee and self-employed person is not always clear in the current professional context. At times, it is even a very artificial distinction. Consequently, it is questionable whether subordination is still an adequate criterion in terms of social protection. If a concentrically organised labour law with a hard core that is applicable to all workers would be opted for, subordination would no longer be the decisive criterion. It could be replaced by the *performance of labour in an organizational context*. If so, the concretisation of the term "labour"[45] would require certain policy choices. Taking into account the right to human dignity and decent work, a broad interpretation of the term labour would be desirable in terms of the application of a hard core of protective labour rules (the first level, as it were).[46] At this level, labour should not be limited to the so-called "professional labour" (this is labour performed with the intention of generating an income in order to provide for oneself). It should also include activities of trainees and apprentices … and even of volunteers maybe. Depending on the needs that are typical of a certain type of labour, additional rules can then be established. For labour that is performed in return for remuneration, for instance, special protection of the income will have to be provided for.

V. CONCLUSION

Anyone who reflects upon the origin, evolution and future of labour law, cannot but reflect on its personnel scope too. With a view to realise "decent work for all", conventional reasoning about labour law "as a law for the protection of employees" shall have to be discarded. The social protection of other categories of workers should be given a great deal of thought too during the reflection about modernised labour law for the 21st century.

43 As mentioned earlier, a number of countries acknowledge a third professional status: "economically dependent labour".

44 As mentioned earlier, certain labour laws in Belgium are not only applicable to employees but also to a category of people who are put on an equal footing with employees. It concerns persons who perform labour under the authority of another person but without an employment contract (for instance people who are employed with an apprenticeship contract).

45 For an analysis of the concept of labour in a number of core laws of Belgian Labour Law, see K. Reyniers, *(Verboden) Arbeid*, Antwerp, Intersentia, 2012, p. 204–269.

46 In my opinion, rules concerning health, safety and well-being should definitely be part of this hard core.

LABOUR LAW OR SOCIAL COMPETITION LAW: SOME CONCLUDING CRITICAL REMARKS

Amanda Latinne*

During a two-day symposium on 22 and 23 November 2012, speakers from different national and institutional backgrounds reflected on the mutation of labour law, a process intensified by the ongoing liberalisation of the world market, the computerisation and the economic integration of Europe. Governments increasingly stress the individual responsibility and flexibility of workers, which drastically changes the concepts of work and working time. Market freedoms receive preferential treatment over social rights and collective bargaining is restricted to the sector or company level, thereby strongly limiting its emancipatory power.[1]

Rather than summarising the contributions of the authors, this conclusion attempts to open up the debate by placing the concepts of labour law and competition within their historical framework. Labour law, which evolves in dialogue with the surrounding society, mirrors the relationship between capital and labour. In times of global crisis, it can be inspirational to consider that the contemporary dominant free market paradigm, with its central idea of competition, is a relatively recent phenomenon in human history. Next, some strategies and key players of free market competition are highlighted.

---

* University of Antwerp, Belgium.

1 I.e. C. Barnard, S. Deakin, B. Hepple, G. Morris (eds.), *The Future of Labour Law: Liber Amicorum Sir Bob Hepple QC*, Oxford, Hart Publishing, 2004; M. Biagi, R. Blanpain, M. Weiss, *Changing Industrial Relations and Modernisation of Labour: Liber Amicorum in Honour of Professor Marco Biagi*, The Hague, Kluwer Law International, 2003; J. Craig and M. Lynk (eds.), *Globalization and the Future of labour Law*, Cambridge, Cambridge University Press, 2007; M. Moreau, *Normes sociales, droit du travail et mondialisation*, Paris, Dalloz, 2006; A. Nayer, A. Cieslar and B. Smeesters, *Le droit à l'épanouissement de l'être humain au travail : métamorphoses du droit social*, Brussel, Bruylant, 2007; J. Pelissier, A. Supiot, A. Jeammaud, *Droit du travail*, Paris, Dalloz, 2006; M. Rigaux, *Droit du travail ou droit de la concurrence sociale ? Essai sur un droit de la dignité de l'Homme au travail (ré)mis en cause*, Brussel, Bruylant, 2009; A. Supiot, *Critique du droit du travail*, Paris, Quadrige/PUF, 2007; A. Supiot, P. Meadows, *Beyond Employment: Changes in Work and the Future of Labour law in Europe*, Oxford, Oxford University Press, 2001.

Then, corrections through corporate responsibility and co-operative business alternatives are discussed. Finally, I seek to re-inspire labour law through the strengthening of social rights on a global basis and by making a call for a countervailing power of consumers, local companies, workers, trade unionists and academics.

EXIT SOLIDARITY, ENTER LABOUR AS A COMMODITY

Our medieval ancestors organised their craft economy through a strictly regulated system of professional guilds that banned competition and favoured solidarity with their professional fellows as well as with the surrounding society.[2] Masters worked alongside their apprentices. After the learning period, apprentices could become masters themselves and start up their own workplace. Masters were not allowed to employ apprentices in two or more different shops. The resulting economic fabric, characterised by several small "businesses", sustained transparent face-to-face commercial relations.[3]

This balanced system was completely unarmed against the changes that followed from the rise of commodity trade.[4] Merchants moved the most important branches of industry to the countryside or received privileges to set up large workshops in the cities, thereby strongly undermining the traditional guild economy.[5] Meanwhile, trade advocates increasingly depicted the guild system as a protectionist system of rules and regulations, and steadily stressed the idea of *Liberté*.[6] The resulting French Revolution of 1789, with its motto of *Liberté, Egalité, Fraternité*, was the triumph of capitalist industry, not of liberty or equality in general. The concept of liberty of the Eighteenth Century was absolute, free from moral inhibitions or transcendent rules.[7] *Fraternité*, the old solidarity value, ended up last in line. Dissenting corporatists, protesting against the abolishment of guilds, explicitly stated they witnessed the birth of an individualistic society

2 It was common practice for guilds to provide services of general interest, and it was forbidden to use publicity to entice clients into leaving their traditional suppliers; J. Benet, *Le capitalisme libéral et le droit au travail, I, La doctrine*, Neuchâtel, Editions de la Baconnière, 1947, 98.

3 J. Benet, *Le capitalisme libéral et le droit au travail, I, La doctrine*, Neuchâtel, Editions de la Baconnière, 1947, 98.

4 J. Fornäs, *A Companion to Marx's Economy Critique*, London, Routledge, 2013, 147–149.

5 F. Braudel, *Civilization and Capitalism, 15th-18th Century: The Wheels of Commerce*, Berkeley, University of California Press, 1982, 315–318.

6 G. Bossenga, "Protecting Merchants: Guilds and Commercial Capitalism in Eighteenth-Century France", *French Historical Studies* 1988, (693) 693; E. Tarle, *L'Industrie dans les campagnes en France à la fin de l'Ancien Régime*, Paris, 1910, 53; L. Vardi, The Abolition of the Guilds during the French Revolution, *French Historical Studies* 1988, (704) 707.

7 J. Benet, *Le capitalisme libéral et le droit au travail, I, La doctrine*, Neuchâtel, Editions de la Baconnière, 1947, 206–212.

in which money became the key factor for controlling production and exchange.[8] The boundless interpretation of the concept of liberty even led to a prohibition of interest groups,[9] leaving thousands of marginalised workers at the mercy of capital owners.

It is not surprising that this focus on liberty was reflected in an ongoing liberalisation of trade, starting with the 1786 Eden-Rayneval Treaty and culminating in the 1860 Treaty on the free exchange between France and England.[10] In the world view of Adam Smith and other advocates of free trade, the economic order was the balance of uninhibited antagonistic individual interests, a balance that resulted from the working of natural laws. These natural laws had no need for external modifications or corrections. Notwithstanding the pure theoretical presumption that free trade can multiply wealth when well-dosed, it obviously favours dominant countries as well as smaller countries that focus on trading activities. When free trade is imposed on weaker countries it is lethal for their industries, which results in the impoverishment of a large number of people.[11] The mere existence of the 1860 Treaty on the free exchange between France and England caused a downward pressure on the salaries of workers in France. All industrial sectors that could not withstand the competition of English firms, e.g. the textile sector, withered.[12] For Smith the suffering of workers, living below subsistence level, was inevitable: "*functioning merely as a kind of security valve for releasing the excess of population that the system had no purpose for*".[13] Following the emergence and growth of market dependence, labour was reduced to a (perishable) production factor, a commodity.[14]

---

8 With the d'Allarde Law of 1791 anyone who paid for a trade license (patente) could keep a shop, exercise a craft, a practice or a profession; Sibalis, "Corporatism after the Corporations: The Debate on Restoring the Guilds under Napoleon I and the Restauration", *French Historical Studies* 1988, (718) 722.

9 Loi Le Chapelier, 1791, forbidding all forms of collective interest groups.

10 Treaty that was copied by treaties with Belgium (1861), Italy (1863) and with the Netherlands and Spain in 1865S. Gherardi, "Le rêve d'une paix éternelle", *Le Monde* 26 May 1998, reprinted in *Le Monde* 4 December 2012, 18.

11 S. Gherardi, "Le rêve d'une paix éternelle", *Le Monde* 26 May 1998, reprinted in *Le Monde* 4 December 2012, 18.

12 J.-M. Vaslin, "En 1860, Napoléon II impose le libre-échange", *Le Monde* 4 December 2012, 18.

13 J. Benet, *Le capitalisme libéral et le droit au travail, I, La doctrine*, Neuchâtel, Editions de la Baconnière, 1947, 206–212.

14 R. Brenner, *The Economics of Global Turbulence. The Advanced Capitalist Economies from long Boom to Long Downturn, 1945–2005*, London, Verso, 2006 (reprint of text originally printed in the *New Left Review*, I, 229, May-June 1998).

UNDER PRESSURE

Under pressure of worker power, national labour law was created to compensate for the economic imbalance between the worker and the employer.[15] The substantive content of labour law evolved in relation to the surrounding society from safety regulations, over guaranteeing a certain basic income to collective issues.[16] Following the efforts of the International Labour Organization, ILO, national legal systems incorporated international labour standards, although mostly in advanced countries which already had strong labour traditions.[17]

The primacy of the market, however, remained unquestioned.[18] No ethical boundary prevented the further liberalisation of trade. Since extreme protectionist measures had led to two world wars, it seemed only logical that the United States, in their position of new world leader, would advocate free trade in the aftermath of the Second World War. Neo-liberalism replaced the 19th century *laissez faire,* which meant that governments were commissioned with an active promotion of competition. Initially, this led to economic growth on both sides of the Atlantic. With the collapse of the original Bretton Woods system in the seventies, the rapid pace of globalisation and the emergence of the neo-liberal Washington Consensus, the system of (international) labour law came under great pressure.[19] While labour law relies on a perception of a community as more than a market place,[20] market-oriented scholars suggested to reconceptualise labour law, starting from its potential advantages and disadvantages to the economy in general and to employers in particular. Free market fans thought it no longer appropriate to focus on the "protective" features of labour law in an efficient economy.[21]

---

15 H. Arthurs, "Labour Law After Labour" in G. Davidov and B. Langille (eds.), *The Idea of Labour Law,* Oxford, Oxford University Press, 2011, (13) 14; A. Sobczak, "Are Codes of Conduct in Global Supply Chains really voluntary? From Soft Law Regulation of Labour Relations to Consumer Law", *Business Ethics Quarterly* 2006, (167) 167; A. Supiot, *Beyond Employment: Changes in Work and the Future of Labour Law in Europe,* Oxford, Oxford University Press, 2001.

16 H. Arthurs, "Labour Law After Labour" in G. Davidov and B. Langille (eds.), *The Idea of Labour Law,* Oxford, Oxford University Press, 2011, (13) 14.

17 D.M. Trubek, "The Emergence of Transnational Labor Law", *The American Journal of International Law,* 2006, (725) 726.

18 As opposed to the primacy of justice, cherished by several utopian socialists, J. Benet, *Le capitalisme libéral et le droit au travail, I, La doctrine,* Neuchâtel, Editions de la Baconnière, 1947, 236.

19 D.M. Trubek, "The Emergence of Transnational Labor Law", *The American Journal of International Law,* 2006, (725) 726.

20 G. Mundlak, "The Limits of Labour Law in a Fungible Community" in J. Conaghan, R. Fischl and K. Klare, *Labour Law in an Era of Globalization: Transformative Practices and Possibilities,* Oxford, Oxford University Press, 2004, (279) 280.

21 G. Davidow and B. Langille, *Boundaries and Frontiers of Labour Law,* Oxford, Hart Publishing, 2006, 3–4 cited in B. Hepple and B. Veneziani, "Introduction" in B. Hepple and B. Veneziani (eds.), *The transformation of Labour Law in Europe,* Oxford, Hart Publishing, 2009, 14.

Increasingly, worldwide capitalism seemed the only possible future and all debates on the social consequences of breaking down trade barriers were silenced. The fall of the Berlin Wall efficiently erased communism as an alternative path.[22]

With the creation of the World Trade Organization, WTO, in 1994, several European countries, the U.S., Japan as well as non-governmental organisations and labour unions of developed countries supported a social clause. This social clause would make trade liberalisation conditional upon the observance of basic labour laws as expressed in core labour standards of the ILO. Freedom of association, the right to organise and to bargain collectively, anti-discrimination regulation as well as the abolishment of forced labour and the most acute forms of child labour would have to be respected.[23] Most developing countries and their labour movements, as well as mainstream trade economists, were opposed to the clause as they felt it was biased against the developing countries.[24] As a result, the members of the WTO only expressed their commitment to the observance of internationally recognised labour standards without making them legally enforceable.[25]

Debates on the enlargement of the European Community during the late seventies (in the run-up to the entry of Greece, Spain and Portugal) as well as during the nineties (with the planned enlargement of the Union to Eastern Europe) did not lead to enduring measurements against possible disruptive shifts.[26] Moreover, within Europe, the economic principles became the most fundamental values, a process that reached its peak with the debates concerning the freedom of services.[27]

---

22 C. Jian, "Tiananmen and The Fall of The Berlin Wall: China's Path Toward 1989 and Beyond" in J. Engel (red), *The Fall of The Berlin Wall: The Revolutionary Legacy of 1989*, Oxford, Oxford University Press, 2011, (96) 124.

23 H. Lim, " Social Issues and Challenges", 2011, http://actrav.itcilo.org/actrav-english/telearn/global/ilo/guide/hoelim.htm; M. Bernaciak, *Social Dumping: Political Catchphrase or Threat to Labour Standards*, ETUI Working paper 2012.06, Brussels, ETUI, 2012, 8.

24 M. Bernaciak, *Social Dumping: Political Catchphrase or Threat to Labour Standards*, ETUI Working paper 2012.06, Brussels, ETUI, 2012, 9; J. Bhagwati, "Trade Liberalisation and 'Fair trade' Demands: Addressing the Environmental and Labour Standards issues", *The World Economy* 1995, 745–759; V.A. Leary, "The WTO and the social clause: post-Singapore", *European Journal of International Law* 1997, 118–122.

25 M. Bernaciak, *Social Dumping: Political Catchphrase or Threat to Labour Standards*, ETUI Working paper 2012.06, Brussels, ETUI, 2012, 9.

26 M. Bernaciak, *Social Dumping: Political Catchphrase or Threat to Labour Standards*, ETUI Working paper 2012.06, Brussels, ETUI, 2012, 11–17; D. Vaughan-Whitehead, *EU Enlargement versus Social Europe: The Uncertain Future of the European Social Model*, Cheltenham, Edward Elgar, 2003, 325.

27 S. Giubboni, *Social Rights and Market Freedom in the European Constitution*, Cambridge, Cambridge University Press, 2006.

The ongoing globalisation that has been taking place since the nineties, has led to a worldwide concentration of business activities, which has resulted in the concentration of capital and the widening of the income gap between winners and losers of this first round. After this concentration, transnational companies started to delocalise their activities, thereby openly taking advantage of differences in practice and legislation in the social, environmental and fiscal field. National states race each other for foreign capital investments and labour law flexibilisation has proven to be a powerful instrument in this international "beauty contest".[28]

ME AND MY CAR

In a globalised economic world order, fragmented (national) labour law only offers weak protection. Flexibility instruments, developed on sector or company level, create a wide range of contracts that differ greatly from the standard employment contracts.[29] Moreover, the flexibility measurements have different effects on different categories of workers. Whereas at the high end of the hierarchy people decide autonomously on their working schedules, interim workers and part-timers have to adjust to a heteronomously imposed flexible planning. Later, this flexible organisation of labour becomes the new standard in several industrial sectors[30] and even throughout people's lives. Periods of employment alternate with periods of unemployment and people are made responsible for their own employability.[31]

Meanwhile, trade unions are losing the connection to multitudes of non-unionised, precarious workers in an increasingly individualised world. Considering the fact that national unions can only represent national interests, they are successfully played out against each other. Local branches of multinational companies try to outrace their sister companies in other regions or states by achieving the highest possible productivity while pressuring local politicians for tax favours and other advantages.[32]

---

[28] M. Bernaciak, *Social Dumping: Political Catchphrase or Threat to Labour Standards,* ETUI Working paper 2012.06, Brussels, ETUI, 2012, 21; D. Marteau, *Enjeux sociaux et concurrence internationale : du dumping social au mieux-disant,* Paris, Les éditions des journaux officiels, 2006, 8.

[29] J. Buelens and J. Pearson, *Standard Work: An Anachronism?* Cambridge, Intersentia Ltd., 2012.

[30] E.g. in the distribution sector.

[31] E. Martinez, "Le droit du travail et les modifications apportées au marché du travail" in M. Rigaux, J. Buelens and A. Latinne (eds.), *Labour Law or Social Competition Law,* Antwerp, Intersentia, 2014, 45–56.

[32] J. Schubert, "Instruments of Labour Law" in M. Rigaux, J. Buelens and A. Latinne (eds.), *Labour Law or Social Competition Law,* Antwerp, Intersentia, 2014, 21–32.

The automotive industry fine-tuned this strategy. Management would start by singling out one plant as a pilot bargaining arena for changes in working time and organisation. The agreement concluded in this pilot setting, enforced as a benchmark upon other plants all over the world, started a downward spiral for workers' rights.

In the late eighties, the GM Opel plant in Antwerp negotiated a revolutionary working time agreement that set the benchmark for other agreements in GM Europe plants in 1997–1998.[33] The pilot position of Opel Antwerp did not protect the loyal factory workers against later rounds of benchmarking that led to the closing of the plant in 2010. GM, however, had successfully traded temporary security of employment for increasingly flexible work organisation schemes that were from then onwards considered inevitable in order for western industries to survive.

In France, PSA and Renault shamelessly used national politicians who were ready to accept decentralisation of collective bargaining to offer the most favourable local labour regulations possible. However, even this could not outbid the Slovakian offer to PSA, which consisted of state subsidies of an amount equivalent to labour costs on the site for the first five financial years. The vast number of these grants (some of which have been invalidated by the EU) offer further testimony of the widespread competition between countries for foreign capital investments.[34]

Highly competitive environments promote a strong individualist attitude in workers who increasingly view each other as rivals for access to competences and skills and ultimately for access to and security of jobs. People with an employment contract are in competition with (fictively) self-employed[35] and several national governments have even created special intermediate categories of semi-independent workers. As a result more people are excluded from the full protection of labour law.[36] Chains of subcontracting further erode the scope of labour law.[37] When competition is considered the most efficient form of

33 B. Hancke, "European Works Councils and Industrial restructuring in the European motor Industry", *European journal of Industrial Relations* 2000, (35) 43–45.

34 The Hungarian government offered a 49.5 m euro grant to Audi and the Romanian state offered substantial grants to Nokia and Ford, V. Delteil and P. Dieuaide, "French multinational companies, new state regulations and changes in the employment relationship during the crisis: the exemplary case of the automobile sector", *Transfer: European Review of Labour and Research* 2012, (429) 437–442.

35 J. Buelens and M. Rigaux, *Droit du travail ou droit de la concurrence sociale ? Essai sur un droit de la dignité de l'Homme au travail (ré)mis en cause,* Brussels, Bruylant, 2009, 8.

36 See e.g. these semi-independents in Italy and Spain as well as in the Netherlands (ZZP), K. Reyniers, "Human Dignity and Decent Work as Ultimate Objectives of Labour Law" in M. Rigaux, J. Buelens and A. Latinne (eds.), *Labour Law or Social Competition Law,* Antwerp, Intersentia, 2014, 161–176.

37 J. Buelens, *Collectief overleg in (onder)aannemingsverhoudingen. (Prospectieve) analyse van concepten, procedures en structuren in rechtsvergelijkend en Europeesrechtelijk perspectief.* Bruges, die Keure, 2012.

organising, it leads to a widening income gap, which results in increased poverty, even in industrialised countries.[38]

It is obvious that the increasingly open economies do not lead to a significant progress regarding the rights of workers; on the contrary, it is not even clear whether the most outrageous forms of exploitation are decreasing.[39] Globalisation is a term which covers several loads and which masks the frantic race for the exploitation of new commercial opportunities. This race has caused a greater pressure for short-term profitability and competition, leading many companies to disregard cultural diversity or environmental risks. Companies are attracted to developing countries where huge work forces are combined with undemocratic political structures. They refuse to address the issue of exploitation of the least protected workers, including children. In effect, globalisation has led to the widespread destruction of industrial jobs in western economies and it directly or indirectly supports dictatorial regimes, which enforce labour docility.[40]

SYMPATHY FOR THE CORPORATIONS

All speakers participating in the symposium regret the degradation from labour law into social competition law. They have suggested several possible paths to overcome this evolution. It was also generally accepted that the conflict between social values and economic values is a false one. Companies should not pursue economic advantages only. On the contrary, a rehabilitation of environmental and social values and an equal distribution of wealth would increase the quality of life. Shareholders' values should be made subordinate to stakeholders' interests. Codes of conduct as well as social labels, adopted by companies that recognise their social responsibility, could support labour law goals.[41]

For Europe, the historic antecedents of the social responsibility of companies can be traced back to the social doctrine of the Church, starting in the nineteenth century. At the end of the twentieth century, the French legislator incorporated social responsibility in the notion of "*citoyenneté d'entreprise*". The International Labour Organization as well as the European Commission adopted the concept, defining it as the social responsibility of the enterprise to incorporate social and

---

38 W. Däubler, "Labour Law and Competition" in M. Rigaux, J. Buelens and A. Latinne (eds.), *Labour Law or Social Competition Law*, Antwerp, Intersentia, 2014, 57–66.

39 C. Granger and J-M Siroen, "La clause social dans les traits commerciaux" in I. Daugareilh (ed), *Mondialisation, Travail et droits fondamentaux,* Brussels, Bruylant, 2005, 181–212.

40 Y. Pesqueux, "What is Globalization? The Paradoxes of the Economic and Political Substance of Markets", *South Asian Journal of Business and Management Cases* 2013, 2 (I), 1–15.

41 R. De Quenaudon, "Droit du travail ou droit dde la concurrence sociale?" in M. Rigaux, J. Buelens and A. Latinne (eds.), *Labour Law or Social Competition Law*, Antwerp, Intersentia, 2014, 15–20.

environmental preoccupations voluntarily in their commercial activities, thus contributing to the realisation of the Lisbon strategy and the European strategy of sustainable development.[42]

All initiatives concerning social responsibility try to formulate a solution for the fact that globalised enterprises do not have a global jurisdictional personality.[43] Critical consumers act as an accelerator. Whereas, in the past, Western consumers have been realising maximum buying power through the globalised economy, they are now becoming aware of the contradiction in their position. Cheap imported products lead to the extinction of huge parts of the manufacturing industry in Europe and the US, causing consumers to lose their buying power through the loss of their jobs.

However, the problems with these social responsibility instruments are manifold. Firstly, as soft law instruments they are free in form and content. Consequently, only a small number of corporate codes of conduct or social labels refer to current international labour standards that could raise their legitimacy.[44] In addition, there is some understandable unease about the social labelling being left in the hands of the big players themselves. Although one can easily imagine that producers and traders would translate the ISO Quality norms[45] to social norms, recent food scandals have proved exactly what these systems are worth when left in the hands of profit seeking individuals and companies. Moreover, it seems illogical to presume that transnational companies, after specifically seeking out countries with weak national legal systems and laws for the protection of people and the environment, would at the same time be genuinely interested in imposing these social norms upon themselves.[46]

---

42 I. Daugareilh, "La responsabilité sociale des entreprises transnationales et les droits fondamentaux de l'homme au travail: le contre-exemple des accords internationaux" in I. Daugareilh (ed), *Mondialisation, travail et droits fondamentaux,* Brussels, Bruylant, 2005, (349) 350 -353.

43 G. Murray and G. Trudeau, "Une régulation sociale de l'entreprise?", *Relations industrielles/ Industrial relations,* 2004, 3; C. Gendron, A. Lapointe and M.-F. Turcotte, "Responsabilité social et régulation de l'entreprise mondialisée", *Relations industrielles/Industrial Relations,* 2004, 73 as cited in I. Daugareilh, "La responsabilité sociale des entreprises transnationales et les droits fondamentaux de l'homme au travail: le contre-exemple des accords internationaux" in I. Daugareilh (ed.), *Mondialisation, travail et droits fondamentaux,* Brussels, Bruylant, 2005, (349) 352.

44 A. Sobczak, "Are Codes of Conduct in Global Supply Chains really Voluntary? From Soft Law Regulation of Labour Relations to Consumer Law", *Business Ethics Quarterly* 2006, 167–184.

45 ISO Quality system that was created to guarantee quality through traceability.

46 T. Collingsworth, "Bringing the Rule of Law to the Global Economy – Using ATS to Hold MNCs Accountable for Human Rights Violations", http://198.170.85.29/Terry-Collinsworth-commentary.pdf cited in J. Nolan and L. Taylor, "Corporate Responsibility for Economic, Social and Cultural Rights: Rights in Search of a Remedy?", *Journal of Business Ethics* 2009, (433) 443.

It is even more problematic that these instruments, created to please consumers, seem to imply that consumers' interests outweigh workers' interests. These codes and labels presuppose responsible and pro-active behaviour of consumers and citizens. Conflicts of interest are imminent. Consumers could stress certain issues e.g. child labour, and react indifferently to other forms of disrespect to social values. Consumers' interests could also easily come in conflict with workers' interests when considering environmental issues versus employment issues or when opposing the workers 'right to strike versus the consumers' interest in receiving continuous service.[47]

On the other hand, however, when consumers' and workers' interests are similar, a more effective countervailing power could be achieved. In Germany, companies as well as trade unions and consumer organisations can legally sue a company that does not commit itself to binding collective agreements, a possibility that should be considered more often[48] and that could be used as a model for corporate responsibility issues. It could even be possible for local companies, in alliance with unions and consumers, to ask their governments for protection against unfair competition by companies that do not take their social and environmental responsibility.

COME TOGETHER

Several speakers support social economy and the revival of, or renewed interest in, co-operative organisations. Co-operative initiatives, however, need co-operative people and neo-liberal thoughts went hand in hand with a sociological process of ongoing individualisation and social competition. A market society concentrates on individual needs that can be relieved with goods and services and thus denies the social nature of humanity.[49] Even in former communist countries, there is often resistance against collectivisation efforts because this brings about bad memories.[50]

Although co-operatives can be a genuine expression of people realising their right to work through collective self-employment, it cannot be denied that even successful organisations show some disturbing signs of adaptation to the

47 A. Sobczak, "Are Codes of Conduct in Global Supply Chains really Voluntary? From Soft Law Regulation of Labour Relations to Consumer Law", *Business Ethics Quarterly* 2006, 167–184.

48 W. Däubler, "Labour Law and Competition" in M. Rigaux, J. Buelens and A. Latinne (eds.), *Labour Law or Social Competition Law*, Antwerp, Intersentia, 2014, 57–66.

49 P. Kirby, "Theorising Globalization's Social Impact: Proposing the Concept of Vulnerability", *Review of International Political Economy* 2006, (632) 648–649; K. Polanyi, *The Livelihood of Man*, New York, 1977, 29.

50 B. Kresal, "Mutating or Dissolving Labour Law?" in M. Rigaux, J. Buelens and A. Latinne (eds.), *Labour Law or Social Competition Law*, Antwerp, Intersentia, 2014, 149–160.

competitive motto of transnational organisations. Mondragon, for example, is a transnational enterprise with 83.569 employees and a sales total of 14.832 million euro in 2011.[51] It originated as an industrial co-operative in the nineteen fifties in the Basque region of Spain but developed into an international conglomerate of co-operatives and traditional (joint venture) enterprises. It is an interesting object for research on alternatives to the traditional capitalist economy.[52] However, the inspiring conciliation of labour and capital covers some disturbing contradictions between image and reality.

These contradictions are partly due to the initial founding co-operatives duplicating the hierarchical division of labour of their capitalist surroundings. Their products mirrored the post-war American way of life, their ambition that of the upcoming Fordist middle-class and their business strategies, promoted by their own co-operative bank, the *Caja Laboral*, followed the economic growth model of the West. This growth model, embedded in the trend of Europeanisation and globalisation, opened them up to the world. Though initially started as Basque co-operatives producing for their Spanish *Hinterland*, they developed into a transnational corporation with 281 enterprises of which only 111 are co-operative companies.[53] The fierce competition they encountered in their traditional sector of household appliances seduced them to takeovers, joint ventures and buy-outs. As a result, their original purpose was lost.

The economic competition led to investments in low-wage countries and ongoing flexibility demands in the Spanish co-operatives. Worker-owners increasingly agree with lower wages, work in other co-operatives or switch jobs. A considerable amount of people works in the co-operatives without being real worker-owners, thus forming a flexible buffer for the economic difficulties. In the absence of trade union delegations and collective bargaining, subsequent changes in co-operative law facilitated this labour flexibility.[54]

Fiscal advantages and a very flexible labour policy are important factors of Mondragon's resilience to the global economic crisis. Notwithstanding all changes, they managed to uphold a utopian democratic image. Governments

---

51 Www.mondragon-corporation.com/CAS/Magnitudes-Economicas/Cifras-mas-reseñables.aspx.

52 It has been studied by numerous scholars of which Cheney, Clamp, Freundlich, Greenwood, Hacker, Kasmir, Lindenfeld, Rotschild-Whitt, Whyte & Whyte, Wiener & Oakeshott are the most renowned.

53 Www.mondragon-corporation.com/CAS/Magnitudes-Economicas/Cifras-mas-reseñables.aspx.

54 The official position of the Mondragon Group is that every worker is free to join a trade union but that an organised union delegation has no place in the co-operatives as the workers are owners themselves.

should be aware of the dangers of global competition for the integrity of social economy initiatives.

NOW THAT WE HAVE FOUND OUT, WHAT ARE WE GOING TO DO?

Clearly, labour law is in need of a reformulation on a global level. European and ILO norms can be referential beacons to guide us to a system that brings social competition to a tolerable level.[55] However, in the future, as in the past, the crucial element in both the creation and transformation of labour law will be the power of capital and the countervailing power of organised labour, consumers and active citizens.[56] In view of the omnipresence of liberal economic worldviews, this requires the genesis of an effective social countervailing power. A countervailing power that seeks to reconcile labour and economic development, labour and social development as well as labour and environment, can entrust (labour) law with the elaboration of rules for guaranteeing the balance that is vital to a sustainable global future.[57] This balance requires a more thorough focus on basic social rights as an equal counterpart of the fundamental European economic freedoms.[58]

There is still a lot of work to be done. The fact that there is a variety of opinions, even on the side of advocates of labour law, complicates matters. A strong current of authoritative scholars still favours a wider use of soft law instruments over e.g. (trade) sanctions although they stress the importance of WTO-ILO collaboration.[59] Others suggest a trade-off between respect for social norms and eligibility for external funding or even between a generalisation of basic social rights and free access to certain markets.[60]

Up until now, effective business lobbying in combination with a divided countermovement of labour law advocates has succeeded in obstructing effective

---

55 M. Rigaux, *Droit du travail ou droit de la concurrence sociale ? Essai sur un droit de la dignité de l'Homme au travail (ré)mis en cause,* Brussels, Bruylant, 2009, 175.

56 B. Hepple and B. Veneziani, "Introduction" in B. Hepple and B. Veneziani (eds.), *The transformation of Labour Law in Europe,* Oxford, Hart Publishing, 2009, 28–29.

57 R. de Quenaudon, "Droit du travail ou droit dde la concurrence sociale?" in M. Rigaux, J. Buelens and A. Latinne (eds.), *Labour Law or Social Competition Law,* Antwerp, Intersentia, 2014, 15–20.

58 G. Orlandini and F. Dorssemont, "Market Rules and the Right to Strike: a Different Approach" in M. Rigaux, J. Buelens and A. Latinne (eds.), *Labour Law or Social Competition Law,* Antwerp, Intersentia, 2014, 67–106; T. Jaspers en W. Roozendaal, "Fundamental Social Rights: an Added Value to the Protection of Workers?" in M. Rigaux, J. Buelens and A. Latinne (eds.), *Labour Law or Social Competition Law,* Antwerp, Intersentia, 2014, 107–133.

59 E.g. Hepple; D.M. Trubek, "The Emergence of Transnational Labor Law", *The American Journal of International Law,* 2006, 725–733.

60 C. Granger and J.-M. Siroen, "La clause social dans les traits commerciaux" in I. Daugareilh (ed.), *Mondialisation, Travail et droits fondamentaux,* Brussels, Bruylant, 2005, 211.

progress. The 2004 "failure" of the United Nations Norms, which proposed an almost "ready to apply" system of legal rules based on international human rights, may be illustrative of the power of certain business groups, such as the International Chamber of Commerce and the International Organisation of Employers, as well as of the resistance of certain countries.[61]

After more than two decades of proliferation of codes of conduct and voluntary standards of behaviour, it seems time to move further onwards and use the heightened sensitivity of consumers and enlightened corporations to develop hard law. The corporate criminal responsibility debate and the legal corpus on anti-corruption provide useful models that combine national enforcement and international standards.[62] Additionally, the localisation strategy that proposes alternative economic models to globalisation can be of great value. By consciously favouring the local over the global, thus strengthening local economies "from the grassroots up", negative globalisation effects can be countered.[63]

Maybe the most important lesson to be learned is that we should "watch what happens" and that we should care, that we take our (academic) knowledge of what we see happening towards a broader forum, that we take the responsibility of being openly critical and that we go into constructive dialogue with people, politicians, trade unions and non-governmental organisations, NGOs. This is what true democratic freedom should stand for.

---

61 A. Voiculescu, "Human Rights and the New Corporate Accountability: Learning from Recent Developments in Corporate Criminal Liability", *Journal of Business Ethics, Supplement 2: Spheres of Influence/Spheres of Responsibility: Multinational Corporations and Human Rights* 2009, (419) 422.

62 J. Nolan and L. Taylor, "Corporate Responsibility for Economic, Social and Cultural Rights: Rights in Search of a Remedy?", *Journal of Business Ethics* 2009, (433) 434, 446; A. Voiculescu, "Human Rights and the New Corporate Accountability: Learning from Recent Developments in Corporate Criminal Liability", *Journal of Business Ethics, Supplement 2: Spheres of Influence/ Spheres of Responsibility: Multinational Corporations and Human Rights* 2009, (419) 421.

63 J. Cavanaugh et al., "The Case for Subsidiarity: Bias Away from the Global Toward the Local" in J. Cavanaugh et al. (eds.), *Alternatives to Economic Globalisation: A Better World is Possible,* San Francisco, Barrett-Koehler Publishers, 2002,105–120; C. Hines, "Time to Replace Globalisation with Localisation", *Global Environmental Politics* 2003, 3, 1–7.

Publications on Labour Law

With the series "Publications on Labour Law" the Research Unit Social Competition and Law pursues a triple objective: publicising high-quality academic legal research; profiling the unit's research (even) more adequately and making a (small) contribution to the preservation of a consistent type of labour law. For a considerable time now the members of the Antwerp Research Unit Social Competition and Law (previously called Social Law Unit) haven been taking part, quite prominently, in the scientific study of labour law by means of articles in scientific journals, monographs, research reports and obviously also by compilations of papers. With the launch of a publication series in its own name the research unit wants to continue and confirm this tradition of contemporary quality research. The series also aims at producing a stronger profile of the research unit, its research methodology and the fundamental values the unit adheres to in its law approach. The labour market adjusting function of labour law, its fundamental rights aspect and emanci- patory dimension as well as the analysis of legal phenomena from a compre- hensive legal perspective are all of them elements characterising the scientific initiatives of the research unit. By publishing serial research results in the field of labour law the research unit wants to help preserve consistent labour law protection. Attracting new researchers with new ideas is a key factor in this respect, just like the promotion of transnational study projects. The information and explanations presented in this publication series are intended to contribute scientific arguments to the legislative, jurisprudential and doctrinal debates. Prior to publication all the contributions in this series will be peer reviewed.

www.ingramcontent.com/pod-product-compliance
Ingram Content Group UK Ltd.
Pitfield, Milton Keynes, MK11 3LW, UK
UKHW051922100926
8556IPUK00021B/1331

9 781780 682